WEST of the WE
Perspectives on California State History
D1108991
one-time
online
access
code
included
ROGER H. HALL

Kendall Hunt
publishing company

Cover image © Roger H. Hall

Kendall Hunt
publishing company

www.kendallhunt.com
Send all inquiries to:
4050 Westmark Drive
Dubuque, IA 52004-1840

Revised Printing: 2018

Text Alone ISBN: 978-1-5249-5440-6
PAK ISBN: 978-1-5249-5438-3

Published in the United States of America

"When I am in California, I am not west, I am west of the west.
It is just California."

—Theodore Roosevelt, 1903

Dedication

This book is dedicated to

Robert Smetherman, Bernard Sternsher,

and Paul Henggeler.

Contents

Introduction

History is a myth that men agree to believe."

—Napoleon

I don't believe the truth will ever be known,
and I have a great contempt for history.

—George Mead

Historians, it is said, fall into one of three categories:
Those who lie, those who are mistaken, those who do not know.

—Anonymous

Look up opinions regarding history and you will encounter plenty of cynicism for the subject. What is it about history as a subject of academic study that breeds such animosity? As a professor, I hear the complaints from students: It is too dense but also incomplete. It is "fuzzy;" full with facts yet loaded of contradictions. Topics are too distant in time and space to be of meaning in the present.

It is true that the content of history can be very deep. And it does have inconsistencies, contradictions, and sometimes, conjecture. It is a reflection of people who write it and the society from which they come from. There are verifiable truths that may stand next to long-held false assumptions. There can be consensus, but there is no one agreed-upon history, at least not for the big topics. And, of course, not everything from the past has direct application to current situations.
As a life-long learner of the subject, I understand these complaints. There is poorly written history just as there are biased or less informed or uninspired teachers. The subject is so very broad that simply deciding what to teach can be a challenge. As I regularly tell students, many of the topics that are covered in one or two classes sessions could easily be given an entire semester of study. And because it is such a vast topic, it would be unreasonable to think that all its many subjects would appeal to any one person. The diversity of history is both its grace and its burden. Still, there is much to be gained from its study.

"The most effective way to destroy people is to deny
and obliterate their own understanding of their history."

—George Orwell

"History is important. If you don't know history it is as if you were born yesterday. And if you were born yesterday, anybody up there in a position of power can tell you anything, and you have no way of checking up on it."

—Howard Zinn

"The further backward you can look, the further forward you are likely to see."

—Winston S. Churchill

One thing historians can provide is a refocus of a subject. One book, one film, or one exhibit can change the public conversation on a part of the past. Historical reputations can rise or fall, and long-ignored or simply unknown topics may be brought into the academic or greater public realm. And, so, the consensus answers for history change over time. The more you learn about a topic, it not only becomes more complex, you realize how much you don't know about it. At the same time, one can realize how invaluable the past can be to the present. It provides context to the current state of things and offers a richness and appreciation that can spark an interest in preservation of ideas and objects which might otherwise be missing. Or, in the oft-repeated quote by George Santayana: "*Those who cannot remember the past are condemned to repeat it.*"

Here is what I hope this book, this deliberately narrowed text of the California past offers: First, it is an attempt to respond to the common student complaints—well, at least some of them. Foremost, it is hoped this book and its format will spark an interest in the subject. Just as writers will strive to "find their voice," dedicated educators will identify and enhance methods to engage their students in the course material. This book is intended to assist in this task. *West of the West* is not a comprehensive textbook. It looks selectively at certain events in the state's history from which the student can further explore some of the broader trends and themes raised by these topics. The usefulness of the information in this book will be more fully realized after it is augmented by additional presentations by the instructor and through external reading and research by the student.

The goal of this text is to provide information that can create an understanding of the overall "portrait" of California. Some subjects and facts included here do not generally appear in standard textbooks. I believe many of these are necessary, however, to gain a more complete view of the state. There is a detailed statistical comparison between California over time and the United States as a whole. One will see there is a considerable amount of information related to the land, geography, and environment of California. Several selections from other writers are included, some by academic historians and some not. Detailed "snapshots" of controversial events will challenge students to see multiple sides of an argument and to defend and criticize a particular point of view. Many sections include a short series of review "learning outcome" points for students to consider and, perhaps, be prepared to answer. Some of these are framed for class discussion, and some are for research and essay writing. A major goal is to help students in their development of critical thinking skills by becoming better thinkers and writers.

At the end of the book there are many assignments including a capstone essay assignment based on themes that appear in studying California history. By following one of these recurring lines of study, it is anticipated that students will better appreciate the inter-connectedness of events. It should also be apparent that the past is not as "far-back" as it may appear at first glance, as one recognizes in the state's history many of the same issues and conditions in the present. If the reader finds this book to be engaging, if it sparks an interest in learning more on a topic, or piques a desire to travel to visit and experience some of the places described here, then I would consider the effort to create this 4th edition of this book to have been worthwhile. Any and all errors and shortcomings are solely the responsibility of the author.

The Origins of the California name

Introduction

How California got its name is not entirely certain. While it does seem clear that the Spanish applied the term to a region much larger than the present-day state, early European maps offered no explanation as to the origin of the word itself. It has been suggested that the name was derived from the Spanish Catalan words calor ("warm" or "hot") and horno ("oven"). One may also consider the 18th century explanation that the term had an indigenous Mexican origin, coming from the phrase, kali forno ("high hill or mountain.") The Spanish califa is derived from the Latin calipha. That was taken from the Arabic khalīf. Perhaps fittingly, the most agreed-upon version is a fictional story that includes a large mistake in geography and some spectacular myths.

In the early 16th century, Spanish explorers, who traveled north on the Pacific coast and encountered water on both sides of the Baja Peninsula, concluded they had discovered an island. In 1535, attracted by reports of large beds of pearls, Hernan Cortes landed on the "island," claimed it for Spain, and called it Santa Cruz. The town he established about one hundred miles from the land's southern tip would later become La Paz.

By 1541, Spanish officials were referring to it as "Isla de California." Tales circulated at the time that this distant land contained great wealth and strange beings. One popular story came from the Spanish novelist Garcia Ordonez de Montalvo. He wrote five volumes that centered on the Crusades and the conflict between Christians and Muslims. In the final saga, published in 1510, the hero adventurer traveled to an island called *California* where there were vast quantities of pearls and the only metal was gold. The land was populated entirely by women, and ruled by a beautiful black Amazon queen, *Calafia*. In Spanish language, her name is the feminine form of *Calif,* a woman ruler of a Muslim kingdom. The extraordinary women of California flew about on massive griffins—creatures that were half-lion and half-eagle. They guarded the shores while unsuspecting sailors were lured to them to mate and proliferate.

Given these fantastic mythological origins, it would seem appropriate that California has long been viewed as a "land apart," uniquely different in many ways from other places. California has a history of being exceptional. It is defined as a place of great wealth, opportunity, and natural beauty. One can argue to what degree this image has been fostered by local pride and state boosterism. As Theodore Roosevelt said in Ventura during his 1903 tour of the state: "*I had known from hearsay and from books of the wonderful fertility, the wonderful beauty of this semi-tropical climate and soil, but I had not realized all that it was until I saw it myself . . . a veritable little earthly paradise*."

In 1542, Spain's knowledge of the region was improved following the exploration of Juan Rodriguez Cabrillo who sailed from Navidad, Mexico up the Pacific coast to as far north as Point Conception in present day Santa Barbara County. Yet, Cabrillo's voyage was considered a failure by Spain. No easy riches or cities of gold were discovered—no flying griffins either, for that matter. The land appeared rugged and inhospitable. So too were the natives and one encounter with a band of island Chumash left Cabrillo mortally wounded. But from Cabrillo's first-hand accounts and mapping of the coastline there came the knowledge that the "island" was actually a peninsula and the term California was given to it. After 1769, there emerged the concept of an Alta (upper) California and a Baja (lower) California. Alta California today consists of the state of California.

A Timeline of the California Past

Introduction

This chronology of events covering the long period before and throughout the state's history is intended to have multiple purposes. It offers readers a quick reference to significant people and events in state history. Each of the more then 250 entries can be used as the starting point to do more extensive research on individual topics. Some entries are reoccurring topics, such as U.S. Census data which offers the state population every ten years, beginning in 1850. Taken as a whole, the timeline suggests certain themes and trends in California's history, from its rapid growth, to its dealing with competing interests for the use of its lands.

20,000 BC to 12,000 BC — Nomadic hunters from northeast Asia follow herds of caribou, bison, and mammoth across the Bering Straits on a landmass that is exposed for 10,000 years and gradually migrate throughout California and the Americas. At the time of Spanish settlement in the 1770s, there are over 300 distinct tribes and more—than 75 language groups within the region known as California.

13,000 BC — Earliest evidence of human existence in California is learned in 1999 through radiocarbon dating of a femur from a human, known as "Arlington Springs Woman," discovered by Phil Orr in 1959 on Santa Rosa Island. This is one of the earliest finds in all of North America.

9,000 BC — Human remains of a young female are found at the La Brea tar pits, the only prehistoric human remains found at the site. The skull and partial skeleton is preserved in the Page Museum located on the tar pit grounds in Los Angeles.

8,000 BC — Chumash tribal settlements are established on the central California coast.

2,000 BC — Large coastal villages have developed with smaller populations in the interior regions and on the Channel Islands. Archeological evidence suggests both alliances and warfare between tribes.

458 — Chinese explorer Hui Shan sails the Pacific and it appears he either landed on, or at least saw, the California coast as his journals describe visiting a coast with tall trees that had a red wood.

1510 — Garcia Ordonez de Montalvo publishes a romantic novel in Spain in which the name California is first used to describe what Montalvo describes as an island west of the Indies "very close to the side of the Terrestrial Paradise."

1535 — Hernan Cortes follows up an expedition to the southern tip of Baja California with one of his own in which he claims the land for Spain and founds a small colony on what is later La Paz. The colony fails after a few years.

1539 — Francisco de Ulloa rounds the southern tip of Baja and explores up its western coast.

1540 — Hernando de Alarcon sails up the Gulf of California and reaches the mouth of the Colorado River. These explorers are the first Europeans to reach California land.

1542 — Juan Rodriguez Cabrillo, sailing for Spain, explores the California coast. He is the first European to land in what is now San Diego Bay and Santa Barbara. Cabrillo (who did not survive the expedition after being injured in a fight with Chumash natives who live San Miguel island, one of the Channel Islands) was charged with the task of finding gold, rich native cities, and a northwest water passage. None of these goals are accomplished and the Spanish government considers the voyage to be a failure.

1545 — Earliest known epidemic in California as the consequence of European-introduced disease. In this case, it is typhus and it results in the death of hundreds of thousands of natives.

1579 — Sir Francis Drake, sailing for England, lands near San Francisco Bay to make repairs to his ships. He has contact with indigenous natives who live in the area; nevertheless, he claims the land for England, naming it New Albion. For several reasons, not the least of which is its great distance from Europe, Great Britain never attempts to colonize the area.

1602 — Sebastian Vizcaino, sailing for Spain, explores the California coast, retracing much of Cabrillo's voyage, though he went farther north, reaching Monterey Bay. Vizcaino was prolific in naming places, including Monterey. He also renamed many of the places others had first visited. Because of him Santa Cruz became La Paz, San Miguel became San Diego, and Desert Island became Coronado Island.

1602 — Father Antonio de la Ascension presides over the first recorded mass in California, celebrating the feast day in San Diego.

1606 — Spain discontinues its explorations of California, believing it has little value. For the next 160 years Europeans have little contact with the region.

1697 — Mission at Loreto, in Baja California, on the western coast of the Sea of Cortez, is established by Jesuit missionaries. It was the first capital of California. Loreto is the first of twenty-three missions to be founded in Baja over the next seventy-two years.

1746 — Philip V, King of Spain, put to rest a misconception that had endured two centuries when he formally declares the "island of California" to be a peninsula.

1767 — Jesuits are expelled from all New Spain territories. Their missions in Baja California are turned over to Franciscans. Gaspar de Portola, appointed governor of California, is charged with carrying out the actions.

1769 — Gaspar de Portola, sailing for Spain, establishes settlements in San Diego, Monterey Bay, and San Francisco.

1769 — First Mission in (Alta) California is established by Spain. San Diego de Alcala is founded by a Franciscan monk, Junipero Serra. In 1775, area natives attack the mission, killing Father Luis Jayme and two others, and burn the wooden buildings. The next year, the mission buildings are rebuilt with tile roofs and thick stucco walls. Over fifty-four years, a total of twenty-one missions are built, mostly near the coastal region, between San Diego to Sonoma, 650 miles to the north, along a trail known as El Camino Real.

1769 — First Presidio in California, a Spanish military outpost, is founded in San Diego. Other presidios will be established in Monterey (1770), San Francisco (1776), and Santa Barbara (1783) to protect Spain's fledgling mission colonies from European competitors in the region and to put down any Indian uprisings. The Monterey presidio also serves as the capital for the provincial governors appointed in Mexico City.

1769 — La Brea Tar Pits discovered by the expedition of Gaspar de Portola. La Brea, Spanish for "tar" is said to be the first indication of oil in western America. Located in what is now Hancock Park in Los Angeles, more than one million fossil bones dating 10,000 to 40,000 years old have been recovered and are housed at the Page Museum next to the site.

1770 — Native population in California is an estimated 300,000 people, with more Indians per square mile (1.5) than anywhere else in pre-colonial North America. They are primarily hunters and gatherers and did not farm or raise livestock to survive.

1776 — Mission Dolores, the sixth of the twenty-one Spanish missions, is founded near the settlement of Yerba Buena, later renamed San Francisco. Today, the mission church is the oldest intact building in the city and it designated by the state as "*Registered Landmark Number 1.*" The mission's first mass is celebrated five days before the signing of the Declaration of Independence in Philadelphia.

1777 — First Pueblo in California, a Spanish civilian town, is founded by a dozen families at San Jose de Guadalupe by settlers from the Monterey and San Francisco presidios. This farming community provided agricultural products to the presidios. Today, San Jose, as it is now called, is the largest city in northern California with a 2006 population of 929,936.

1781 — Los Angeles is founded through the effort of Spain's governor of California, Felip de Neve. It is the second Spanish pueblo in California. Forty-four people, eleven men, eleven women, and twenty-two children from eleven families, along with four Spanish soldiers who escorted the party, come from Mexico and settle next to what will be named the Los Angeles River. The families represent a mix of European, African, and Native American heritages. More than half of them are either black or mulatto. Today, Los Angeles is the second largest city in the United States (after New York City), with a 2006 population of 3,849,378 people living within its 498 square miles. Los Angeles is one of 88 cities found within Los Angeles County, one of the largest and the most populous counties in the United States, at 4,084 square miles and 9,878,554 people (2007). More than one-fourth of the state's population lives in Los Angeles County.

1784 — Father Junipero Serra dies at age seventy and is buried at Mission San Carlos Borromeo in Monterey, having founded nine missions in fifteen years. In 1987, Pope John Paul II beatified Father Serra, the second of three steps necessary to achieve sainthood.

1810 — Mexico's war for independence begins with Miguel Hidalgo y Costilla, a parish priest from the small town of Guanajuato in central Mexico, inciting a small band of followers to attempt to break nearly three centuries of Spanish rule. The following year Hildago is captured and executed but others take up his cause and fighting continues for the next decade.

1812 — Fort Ross, ninety miles north of San Francisco, is established by Russian fur traders, near the present day town of Jenner. Its name comes from the root word for Russia also pronounced *Rossiya.* It is the most southern of the Russian colonies in North America. While its presence was opposed and resented by Spain, their hold on California was too weak to expel the heavily-armed fort (32 cannons) and for thirty years the Russian settlers engaged in the lucrative hunting and trading of seal and sea otter pelts.

1821 — Mexico wins independence from Spain and California comes under Mexican rule. Many Spanish holdings are converted into vast land grants of ranches and farms. California is made a territory of Mexico with an appointed governor.

1824 — Mission Indians at Santa Ines rise up against floggings being administered by Spanish authorities. In the course of fighting, two natives were killed. Upon receiving this news, many natives at Mission La Purisima revolt. They take control of the mission for almost a month. Sixteen are killed (and seven others executed) as the revolt is suppressed.

1826 — Mission Indians at San Francisco Solano revolt, angry at the physical mistreatment administered by Father Jose Altimira. After looting and burning buildings and supplies, they force Altimira to flee to Mission San Rafael and eventually back to Spain.

1826 — Jedediah Strong Smith and a group of trappers are the first Americans to cross overland into California, crossing the Mojave Desert and entering through San Bernardino Valley in the southern region. Smith made a second trip to California the following year. On both trips, Smith and his group were briefly detained by Mexican officials concerned at the prospect that other Americans would make their way into California.

1833 — Yosemite Valley is seen and explored for the first time by a group of white American explorers, led by Joseph Walker. Walker's party is also the first to cross the Sierra Nevada in an east-to-west direction and, the following year, is the first to see the huge redwood trees that became known as *Sequoiadendron giganteum.*

1834 — Spanish mission system in California ends. Under Mexican rule, the government moves to "secularize" the missions, to remove the mission natives, and to take control of mission lands away from the Spanish Franciscan priests. More than six hundred rancho land grants are made to Mexican citizens. As a result, the Indian population gradually disappears, and the missions decay. By the 1850s, many are falling into ruins.

1839 — John Sutter arrives in the Sacramento Valley on August 13. One of only approximately 1,000 Europeans, he came to possess a Mexican land grant for nearly 50,000 acres, given to him in return for his becoming a citizen of Mexico. With the help of the local Maidu natives, Sutter constructed a fortified, adobe-walled settlement he named New Helvetia. Sutter's fort would become the primary destination for immigrants to California who arrived from overland trails. Sutter would also become world-famous for employing James Marshall who accidently discovered the nugget and flakes which ultimately sparked the Gold Rush.

1841 — Bidwell-Bartleson party is the first organized group of emigrants to cross the United States and settle in California, arriving in November after a seven-month trip. The group arrives on horseback and foot, having been forced to abandon their wagons prior to crossing the Sierra Nevada. Among the settlers are the future first mayor of San Jose and the founders of Stockton and Chico. During the journey, half of the party decides to settle in Oregon instead, thus giving rise to the name "Oregon Trail" for the entire route.

1844 — Stephens-Townsend-Murphy party is the first overland emigrants to California to arrive by wagons, having successfully established a route across the Sierra Nevada at what is now known as Donner Pass. Elisha Stephens will be the first non-native to settle in what becomes Bakersfield.

1845 — Non-Indian population of California is an estimated 7,000 people.

1846 — Mexican War begins as the United States invades Mexico for control over Texas, which the United States claimed in 1845. Critics charge President James Polk, backed by southern slaveholders, with provoking the war in an effort to gain more land for the United States. The war ends when U. S. General Winfield Scott, with a force of 12,000, fight their way to Mexico City and, in September 1847, occupy the capital. Total United States deaths are 13,000, while Mexican losses are an estimated 25,000.

1846 — Donner Party, the most ill-fated group of settlers to come to California prior to the gold rush, begin their journey west. Through a combination of bad luck, poor decisions, and wildly inaccurate route information, 87 emigrants are trapped for months at Truckee (now Donner) Lake during the worst recorded winter in the Sierra Nevada Mountains. Suffering from famine, some members of the group resort to murder and cannibalism in a desperate effort to live. In total, 41 die before the last of the 46 survivors are rescued by four relief parties that came from Sutter's Fort.

1847 — First English-language school in California opens at Mission Santa Clara. It is founded by Olive Mann Isbell, who emigrated from Springfield, Illinois in 1846.

1848 — James Marshall, a carpenter working for John Sutter on the construction of a sawmill, unexpectedly finds some pieces of gold in six inches of water in the American River near Coloma. Marshall's discovery comes nine days before the signing of the Treaty of Guadalupe, formally ending the Mexican War and transferring California to the United States. Upon testing, the gold is found to be 96 percent pure. Word of Marshall's find gradually spreads, setting the stage for one of the most significant events in California history—the gold rush. Over the next five years, 300,000 people, from nearly all parts of the world, and 95 percent of them men, make their way to California's streams and mountains to try and "strike it rich." Although only a few ever do, the rush has numerous pivotal effects on California, many of which continue to resonate today.

1848 — Treaty of Guadalupe-Hidalgo is signed, formally concluding the Mexican War. California, along with New Mexico, Nevada, most of Arizona, and parts of Colorado, Utah, and Wyoming, come under control of the United States. Under the terms of the treaty, Mexico is paid $15 million for 525,000 square miles, or what had been 55 percent of its country.

1849 — California Constitutional Convention begins in September as forty-eight delegates gather in Monterey. Two months later, the new constitution is overwhelmingly ratified by white, male citizens of the United States, which, according to the terms of the constitution, is the only segment of the population allowed to vote.

1850 — California is admitted as the 31st state of the United States on September 9th, bypassing the preliminary territorial stage. In 1854, Sacramento is chosen as the permanent state capital. As the nation's sixteenth free state, California's entry is initially blocked by southern political leaders from the fifteen slave states. Their objections are overcome by the Compromise of 1850 which includes a newly strengthened Fugitive Slave Law.

1850 — Original twenty-seven counties of California, including San Luis Obispo and Santa Barbara counties, are approved by the state legislature. In 1907, Imperial becomes the fifty-eighth and most recently created county.

1850 — An Act for the Government and Protection of Indians is passed by the seven month old California state legislature. The law gives total legal authority of natives to justices of the peace, who are part of a white government that deeply despises the natives. Natives are barred from testifying in court, leaving them defenseless to all manner of crime. They can be forced into servitude that clearly is slavery. Indian children are a major segment of the enslaved labor. Major portions of the Act are repealed in 1872. By this time, there has been substantial and permanent disruption and destruction of many tribal societies.

1850 — Foreign Miners license tax is passed by the California state legislature to reduce competition for gold mining from Mexico, Chile, and Peru. The $20 per month fee results in two-thirds of those affected leaving California.

In 1852, another tax is created, aimed at discouraging Chinese miners. It is less successful in achieving its intended goal, but it provides one-fourth of the revenue in state budgets while it is in effect. The tax is declared unconstitutional in 1870.

1850 — **Census** records the state population of California as 92,597.

1851 — **Santa Clara, first college** in California opens. Built in 1777 as one of Spain's Franciscan missions; today, a private Catholic university, Santa Clara enrolls about 8,000 students.

1852 — **Immigration records** show that of the 11,794 Chinese living in California only seven are women. Twelve years earlier, the 1840 U.S. Census listed eight Chinese in the entire United States.

1853 — **California Academy of Natural Sciences** opens in San Francisco, the first society of its kind in the western United States. Known today as the California Academy of Sciences it one of the largest museums of natural history in the world.

1854 — **Largest piece of gold** ever discovered in California, a mass weighing 195 pounds, is found at Carson Hill in southwestern Calaveras County. Valued at the time at $43,530, it is the second largest gold nugget ever found in the world.

1854 — ***People v. Hall,*** California Supreme Court rules that all races other than Caucasian may not testify against a white person, effectively excluding every non-white in the state from the judicial system and its protections. The ruling is repealed in 1872.

1857 — **Agoston Haraszthy,** born in Hungary, travels widely across Europe and the United States, moves to California at the start of the gold rush. The first county sheriff of San Diego, he is better remembered for importing 100,000 wine-grape roots from Europe, introducing the zinfandel wine grape and establishing the twenty-five acre Buena Vista Winery in Sonoma, the first premium winery in California. For all of this, Haraszthy is known as the "father of modern viticulture" in California.

1860 — **Pony Express** begins operating, providing the first courier mail service between Sacramento, California and the St. Joseph, Missouri. A series of riders (who had to be under the age of 18 and weigh about 120 lbs.) change horses every fifteen miles at 165 way-stations along a 2,000-mile route between St. Joseph, Missouri, and Sacramento. A one-way trip takes roughly ten days in the summer. The fastest trip is seven days, delivering news of President Abraham Lincoln's first inauguration. Although a colorful adventure, even while charging $5 for ½ ounce letter, it proves unprofitable and is discontinued after eighteen months.

1860 — Census records the state population of California as 379,994. Nearly 40 percent are foreign-born, more than three times the national rate.

1861 — Civil War begins and California remains part of the Union. A total of 15,700 Californians join Union armies, though there are many Confederate sympathizers in the state due to the large number of southerners who have moved to the Los Angeles area. By far, the state's most significant contribution to the Union cause is millions of dollars of gold shipped east to help support the northern armies.

1861 — Fort Point is completed. Located at the mouth of the San Francisco Bay, is was intended to protect San Francisco from confederate attack, something which did not happen. Today, the historic fort is nearly directly under the Golden Gate Bridge.

1862 — The "Anti-Coolie" Act applies a $2.50 monthly tax to most adult Chinese workers in California in an attempt to discourage Chinese immigration to the state and lessen the competition for jobs for white laborers. The law also made any employer who hired Chinese workers responsible to ensure the special tax was paid. The Act was ruled unconstitutional in 1863.

1862 — Pacific Railway Act is signed by President Abraham Lincoln to support the construction of a 1775-mile transcontinental rail line between California and the eastern United States. The federal government provides the right of way, raw materials such as timber and rock, and vast squares of land, as incentives to two competing railroad companies, the Central Pacific of Sacramento, California, and the Union Pacific of Omaha, Nebraska. Scheduled for fourteen years, the unprecedented industrial project is completed in seven.

1863 — Groundbreaking ceremonies for the transcontinental rail line are held in Sacramento. Leland Stanford, president of the Central Pacific Railroad, turns the first shovel of dirt at the foot of K Street. For the next two years, the railroad is plagued with a myriad of challenges leaving the success of the project in doubt.

1863 — Stephen Johnson Field is selected by President Abraham Lincoln to be associate justice of the United States Supreme Court. A New York lawyer, Field came to California during the gold rush. His legal practice flourished, and in 1857 he was elected to the state's Supreme Court. He is the first Californian to sit on the U.S. Supreme Court. He serves until 1897.

1864 — Yosemite Valley, in recognition of its scenic and scientific value, in an act signed by President Abraham Lincoln, becomes the first land in the United States to be given federal protection to preserve it from development. This law is the basis for a national park system, governed by the National Park Service, created in 1916.

1865 — Central Pacific Railroad hire Chinese workers at the suggestion of Charles Crocker, who, as head of construction, is chronically short of white laborers willing to perform the grueling work. More than 12,000 Chinese men, the vast majority from the southeastern region of Canton, are recruited by Crocker and successfully work on the western portion of the transcontinental railroad.

1869 — Transcontinental Railroad is completed as the Union Pacific from the east (Omaha, Nebraska) meets the Central Pacific from the west (Sacramento, California) at Promontory, Utah. Considered the nation's greatest industrial accomplishment of the nineteenth century, the transcontinental railroad provides the "missing link" between California and much of the rest of the country—an efficient and rapid transportation service. In September, the first westbound train arrives in San Francisco.

1870 — Balboa Park is created in San Diego. Named after the Spanish explorer Vasco Nunez de Balboa, the 1,440-acre expanse is the first urban park west of the Mississippi. Today one of its best-known attractions is its world-famous zoo.

1870 — Census records the state population of California as 560,247.

1870 — Anti-Chinese legislation continues to be passed in California in an ongoing effort to discourage the presence of the Chinese in the state; **Cubic Air Ordinance**, requires 500 cubic feet per inhabitant; **Pole Law** bans the use of carrying baskets on poles, a common Chinese practice.

1870 — San Francisco becomes the tenth largest city in the United States with a population of 149,500.

1870 — Southern California population remains low with 5,700 people in Los Angeles and 2,300 in San Diego.

1871 — Chinese Massacre occurs in October in Los Angeles when 500 men attack the estimated 200 Chinese living in the city, killing 20.

1872 — Modoc War begins as 200 Modoc Natives leave the Klamath reservation in Oregon and attempt to move to land near Tule Lake in northern California. In 1873 the tribe is defeated by the U.S. military and survivors are sent to the Indian Territory in the Midwest. It is the last Indian war in California.

1873 — Levi Strauss designs durable denim pants with rivet buttons that become popular with workers. The pants known as "blue jeans" help Levi Strauss & Company of San Francisco become one of the largest clothing manufacturers in the world.

1875 — Page Law enacted; it is the first federally restrictive immigration law in the United States. It bars entry into the United States any Chinese, Japanese, or person from an "oriental" country who is a felon, or is suspected of planning to engage in prostitution or contract labor. In practice, it keeps out nearly all Asian women, the great majority of whom would have come to California.

1877 — "Mother of Modern Dance," Isadora Duncan, is born in San Francisco. She is a leader in teaching and choreographing forms of free dance that reject the conventional restraints of movement required in classical ballet.

1878 — American Speaking Telephone Company begins California's first commercial telephone service in San Francisco.

1879 — New California State Constitution forbids the employment of any Chinese person by a corporation or for any state, county, or municipal public work. In practice, the only legal occupation allowed to the Chinese in the state was self-employment.

1880 — U.S. Senator George Hearst becomes owner of the *San Francisco Examiner,* a small daily newspaper, as payment for a gambling debt. A few years later, having little interest in running a paper, Hearst agrees to let his son, William Randolph, a Harvard student at the time, take over the *Examiner,* and unwittingly starts one of the nation's great newspaper chains and media empires.

1880 — Mussel Slough Tragedy occurs near Hanford in the San Joaquin Valley, the result of a legal dispute over land titles between settlers and agents for the Central Pacific Railroad. On May 11, a confrontation between the two sides becomes violent and seven men (two U.S. Marshalls and five ranchers) are killed in a shoot-out. Despite the fact that five settlers are convicted of wrongdoing, the killings re-enforce a popular anti-railroad opinion that the Central Pacific is run by callous and greedy men.

1880 — Census records the state population of California as 864,694.

1882 — Chinese Exclusion Act is enacted by the United States Congress. The law bars all Chinese immigration to the United States and is the culmination of decades of racism and resentment against the Chinese in California. At the time, the state has over 22,000 Chinese residents, many with family members still in China. Originally coming as gold miners and railroad workers, many had worked their way into other businesses. As the state fell into a severe economic depression during the 1870s, anti-Chinese sentiment rose to new heights. The Act is renewed in 1902. It is not repealed until 1943.

1884 — ***Ramona*** by Helen Hunt Jackson is published. Dismayed by the pitiful conditions and extreme prejudice endured by the California Indians, Jackson is inspired by *Uncle Tom's Cabin,* a powerful antislavery story written by her friend Harriet Beecher Stowe thirty years earlier. Jackson writes a romantic tragedy of a mixed-blood senorita and her Indian husband who suffer repeatedly at the hands of prejudiced whites and racist government policies. The novel, the first set in Southern California, sells more than 600,000 copies in sixty years and has never been out of print.

1884 — **"The Big Four,"** Leland Stanford, Collis P Huntington, Charles Crocker, and Mark Hopkins, the directors of the Central Pacific Railroad who helped build the transcontinental rail line, are the wealthiest and among the most politically powerful people in California. To a degree unmatched anywhere in the United States, they control a monopoly on public transportation in the state and the far west. Through their holdings, they also own a total of 11,588,000 acres of land, or 11 percent of California making them, by far, the state's largest private landowners. Because of their abusive use of their power to enrich themselves, they are also likely to be the four most resented and hated men in the state.

1888 — **Lick Observatory** opens, funded by a $700,000 bequest from James Lick of San Francisco (who is buried under the site of the telescope). Located on the top of the 4,200 foot Mt. Hamilton east of San Jose, it is the world's first mountain-top astronomical observatory. At the time its 36-inch refracting telescope is the world's largest. Today, it is operated by the University of California.

1888 — **Scott's Exclusion Act** expands on the Chinse Exclusion Act of 1882 by preventing the return to the United States of any Chinese person who leaves the country.

1890 — **Sequoia and Yosemite National Park** are established just weeks apart. They become the second and third national parks created in the United State, after Yellowstone. Within Sequoia is the General Grant National Park, created by Congress to protect the grove of giant sequoias, including the General Grant Tree, the second largest tree in the world. Yosemite, known for its sheer granite cliffs and some of the world's tallest waterfalls is, today, the country's most heavily visited park, attracting four million people annually.

1890 — **Tournament of Roses Parade** is held for the first time on New Year's Day in front of 2,000 spectators. The idea for the parade comes from the Valley

Hunt Club of Pasadena, a private social club, to promote Southern California's beauty and mild winter climate.

1890 — Census records the state population of California as 1,213,398.

1891 — Leland Stanford Junior University is established near Palo Alto by Leland Stanford. Coeducational and non-denominational, unusual for its time, today, Stanford is one of the leading education and research universities in the United States.

1892 — Sierra Club is founded in San Francisco by the conservationist John Muir and 181 others to protect and enhance the natural environment in California and across the nation. Muir serves as its first president until his death in 1914. Today it is one of the largest organizations of its kind in the United States with 3 million members in 2018.

1895 — Pacific Electric Railway begins operating in Los Angeles, the region's first inter-urban mass transit system. Founded by Edward Henry Huntington, the "Red Car" rail line eventually totals more than 1,000 miles and is the largest rail system in the world.

1895 — San Andreas Fault is discovered by Andrew Lawson, a geologist at UC Berkeley. He named it after the lake in San Mateo County through which the fault passes.

1896 — Offshore Oil Drilling begins with the construction of a well from a wooden pier near Summerland in Santa Barbara County. By 1902, there are 412 wells extracting oil from under the Pacific Ocean along the California coast.

1898 — Joseph McKenna is selected by President William McKinley to be associate justice of the United States Supreme Court. Born in Pennsylvania, McKenna moves as a youth with his family to California in 1855. He becomes a lawyer at age twenty-two and works his way up the Republican party ladder. He is the second Californian to sit on the U.S. Supreme Court and replaces Stephen Field who was the first. McKenna serves twenty-seven years until 1925 when he resigns due to declining health.

1899 — Oil is discovered along the Kern River, starting production that continues today. Through 2003, 1.8 billion barrels of oil have been extracted through 36,000 wells, making Kern the largest oil producing region in California.

1900 — Census records the state population of California as 1,485,053.

1901 — *The Octopus: A Story of California* by Frank Norris is published. The realistic novel describes the brutal struggle between San Joaquin wheat farmers and the Southern Pacific Railroad monopoly. The novel was inspired by, and climaxes with, the real-life Mussel Slough shootings of 1880 near Hanford in which five farmers and two U.S. Marshalls were killed in a fight over the railroad's attempt to evict the farmers.

1902 — Tally's Electric Theatre opens in Los Angeles, the first permanent movie theater designed expressly for showing films.

1902 — Reclamation Act is enacted by the federal government. The measure is the cornerstone in the government's plan to promote and assist family farming in the arid West by building dams and canals to supply low-cost irrigation water. Under the original legislation, an individual who owned 160 acres was eligible to receive federally subsidized water. That acreage would be increased over time. In California, the Bureau of Reclamation interpreted the act to allow subsidized water for 160 acres for each member of a family.

1903 — Commonwealth Club of California founded in San Francisco as a non-profit, non-partisan education organization to promote awareness and interest in public affairs.

1903 — African American population of Los Angeles doubles as the Southern Pacific Railroad brings in 2,000 black laborers to break a strike by Mexican American construction workers.

1903 — ***The Call of the Wild*** by Jack London, born in San Francisco and raised in Oakland, is published. The novella about a pet dog, Buck, who is forced to use his survival instincts as a sled dog in the Yukon, expresses London's interest in individualism and Darwin's laws of nature.

1903 — **Initiative, Referendum, and Recall,** progressive political reforms spurred on by Dr. John Haynes, are adopted by Los Angeles voters into a new city charter, making it the first city in the world to adopt such measures.

1905 — Motor Vehicle Registration on a statewide basis began as the secretary of state was authorized to issue registration and licenses. By the end of the year, 17,015 vehicles had been registered by owners who paid the $2 fee.

1906 — San Francisco Earthquake occurs as 296 miles of the San Andreas Fault violently rupture at 5:12 am, April 18. The quake is an estimated 7.8 magnitude and is regarded as one of the worst natural disasters in United States history. As a result of the quake and days of uncontrollable fires that follow it, four-fifths of the city is destroyed, an estimated 3,000 people are killed, and three-quarters of the 410,000 pre-quake population are left homeless.

1907 — Hetch Hetchy Valley controversy erupts as San Francisco officials, in the wake of the devastating 1906 earthquake and fire, decide the city can secure a reliable supply of water and electricity by damming the Tuolumne River in the Hetch Hetchy area of the recently created Yosemite National Park. In a first for the United States, a significant campaign emerges, led by John Muir and the Sierra Club, to preserve and protect what they argue is a right of people to experience the country's natural grandeur. In 1913, Congress passes the Raker Act, granting San Francisco the right to dam and flood Hetch Hetchy. In 1923 construction of the O'Shaughnessy Dam is completed. Today, electricity produced at the dam, and water from the reservoir, serves 2.4 million people in San Francisco, San Mateo, and Alameda Counties. There are also several organized environmental groups dedicated to the removal of the dam and the restoration of the valley to its natural condition.

1908 — *The Heart of a Race Tout,* the first theatrical film shot on location in Los Angeles, California, is made by the William Selig Company, which, the following year, builds the first film studio in Los Angeles.

1909 — Rebuilding San Francisco moves at a rapid pace. Three years after the earthquake and fire destroys 28,000 buildings, 20,000 new buildings have been completed to take their place.

1910 — *In Old California,* a dramatization of a Spanish woman during the time of Spain's control of the region, is the first theatrical film made in Hollywood, California. It is directed by D.W. Griffith, who was attracted to the beautiful landscape of the area.

1910 — Angel Island, the "*Ellis Island of the West,*" opens as a point of entry to the United States for many immigrants. Located in San Francisco Bay, it processes the entry of people from different parts of the world, though the majority were from Asian nations. It also serves as a temporary prison for hundreds of Chinese immigrants as part of the enforcement of the Chinese Exclusionary Act. Whereas the actual Ellis Island terminal in New York harbor rejected three percent of its immigrants, at Angel Island 18 percent of immigrants were turned away. Approximately one million immigrants came through Angel Island before it closed in 1940.

1910 — Lakeview Gusher, the largest oil spill in United States history, begins near Taft when an oil strike went out of control. Oil flowed for seventeen months before it was contained. By that time, 378 million gallons of oil had run out onto the surrounding land.

1910 — Fresno Junior College opens, the first junior (later community) college in California.

1910 — Census records the state population of California as 2,377,549.

1910 — Los Angeles Times building is destroyed by a dynamite bomb planted by union activists who are involved in a dispute with the newspaper. Twenty employees of the paper are killed in the explosion.

1911 — Ishi, the last surviving member of the Yahi tribe, and considered the last Native American in California to live most of his life apart from European American culture, walks into Oroville in northern California. First called "wild man" by the whites, Ishi (this name, meaning "man" in his language, is given to him by the first anthropologist to see him) becomes a popular sensation. He is moved to the Museum of Anthropology at the University of California, San Francisco, where he lives and is studied by anthropologists until his death in his mid-forties, from tuberculosis, in 1916.

1911 — Women's Suffrage is enacted in California, the sixth state to grant women voting rights, following a special general election on a state senate constitutional amendment.

1912 — *Mission Play,* written by John Steven McGroarty, veteran reporter for the *Los Angeles Times,* is first performed near Mission San Gabriel outside of Los Angeles. The epic production with a cast of three hundred, underwritten by boosters of Los Angeles, tells a highly romanticized story of the rise and fall of the Spanish missions in California. It becomes one of the most famous theatrical productions of the period and a theatrical institution in Los Angeles, with 2.5 million people seeing it by 1929.

1912 — Japanese Americans own 12,726 acres of farmland in California.

1913 — California Alien Land Law enacted; it prohibits non-citizens from owning property in the state. In 1922, the U. S. Supreme Court rules in *Ozawa v. United States* that Japanese immigrants are not eligible for American citizenship because they are neither white nor of African descent.

1913 — Water from the Owens Valley River is first transferred to Southern California by a newly completed aqueduct. At 233 miles, the Los Angeles Aqueduct is the second-longest in the world. It provides water crucial for the continued development of Los Angeles.

1913 — Lincoln Highway is completed. The nation's first trans-continental highway, the western terminus for the 3,389 mile road is Lincoln Park in San Francisco.

1915 — Panama Pacific International Exposition in San Francisco, to many people, symbolized the city's revival from the 1906 earthquake. More than 19 million people visited the exposition during its nine-month run to see its eleven exhibition palaces, gardens and courts, $10 million in exhibits, and nightly light show. The same year, a Panama-California Exposition is held in San Diego and attracts two million visitors.

1920 — Census records the state population of California as 3,426,861.

1921 — Signal Hill oil field, near Long Beach, is discovered, the largest field ever found in Southern California. In 1923, Signal Hill is producing 244,000 barrels a day and California is the nation's leading oil producing state. That year, one-quarter of the world's entire oil production comes from California. By 1980, Signal Hill, later known as the Long Beach Field, has produced over 900 million barrels, one of the most productive fields per acre in the world.

1921 — Roscoe "Fatty" Arbuckle, a gifted screen comedian and one of the highest paid motion picture actor/directors, is charged with the rape and murder of Virginia Rappe at a party held at the Saint Francis Hotel in San Francisco. Although there was considerable evidence to exonerate Arbuckle, and a jury finds him innocent, his career is shattered, the result of intense and savagely negative media coverage.

1923 — Los Angeles Memorial Coliseum opens. It is not only the largest stadium in the state, seating 101,574, today it is perhaps the most celebrated, having hosted two Olympics and thousands of other athletic and entertainment events.

1923 — "Hollywoodland" sign is installed on Mt. Lee to advertise a new housing development. In 1949, the last four of the fifty-foot tall letters are removed, creating what is now an iconic sign of the region and its film industry.

1923 — Honda Point Disaster occurs as seven U.S. Navy destroyers run aground in a dense fog at night on the coast of Santa Barbara County. Twenty-three sailors die in the Navy's largest peacetime loss of ships, due to human error in navigation.

1924 — All Asians, including Chinese, Japanese, and Koreans, as well as Indians living in California are fully segregated by law, denied citizenship and naturalization, and prevented from marrying Caucasians or owning land.

1925 — Automobile registration in Los Angeles is one vehicle for every three persons, more than twice the national average.

1927 — *The Spirit of St. Louis,* a customized, 223 horsepower, M-1 monoplane, is built in San Diego by Ryan Airlines. The $10,000 plane is flown by Charles Lindbergh in the world's first solo trans-Atlantic flight and makes Lindbergh an international hero. The next year, the plane is donated to the Smithsonian; today, it is prominently displayed near the entrance to the National Air and Space Museum in Washington, D.C.

1927 — Academy of Motion Picture Art and Sciences is founded in Los Angeles. The honorary organization is best known for its annual Academy Awards program which honor acting and technical achievement in the motion picture industry.

1928 — **St. Francis Dam** collapses less than two weeks after it was completely filled for the first time. One the state's greatest man-made disasters, the 185-foot concrete dam gave way on the night of March 12, the result of poor geologic analysis and insufficient engineering. Twelve billion gallons of water drained out in 70 minutes, smashing through San Francisquito Canyon on the Santa Clara River to the Pacific Ocean, killing more than 450 people.

1930 — **Census** records the state population of California as 5,677,251.

1930 — **People of Mexican birth** make up 4.5% of California's population. This is a three-fold increase since 1915 with economic instability in Mexico due to its continuing Revolution seen as the primary cause for the growth.

1930 — **The population of Los Angeles grew** 114 percent during the 1920s, according to the U.S. Census, as the city gains more new residents than any city in the world during the decade. Its 1.2 million people is a twelve-fold increase from 1900.

1930 — **Automobile ownership** in California hits two million, or one car for every 2.8 people. This is more than double the national average.

1932 — **Great Depression** in California enters its third year with farm income less than half of what it has been in 1929, while the number of building permits issued is down 90 percent.

1932 — **Summer Olympics** are held in Los Angeles. Due to the global depression, no other city made a bid to stage the games, and only 1,408 athletes attend, compared to the 3,014 that took part in the 1928 Amsterdam games. Still the games are considered a success and become the first to make a profit, about one million dollars. Among the innovations of this Olympics is the building of an "athlete village" to house teams during the competition.

1933 — **San Francisco Ballet** is founded, the oldest professional ballet company in the United States.

1933 — **Long Beach earthquake** kills 115 people and results in the establishment of new stricter building codes.

1934 — **Alcatraz Island,** in San Francisco Bay and site of a former military fort, opens as a high security federal penitentiary. There are no confirmed successful escapes during its twenty-nine years in operation.

1934 — **More than 1.25 million** Californians, 20 percent of the state's population, are out of work and on public relief. In agriculture, there are 142 farm workers for every 100 jobs.

1934 — **General Strike** in San Francisco develops after a strike by longshoremen seeking to protect their unions culminates with fighting between unionists and police in which two strikers are killed.

1934 — End Poverty In California (EPIC), Upton Sinclair's radical proposal for ending the Great Depression once he is governor of California, attracts a record primary vote for the well-known socialist novelist. His loss in the general election is attributed to a multi-million dollar negative advertising campaign directed at him by a range of prominent business leaders.

1934 — Civilian Conservation Corps begins restoration of La Purisima Mission, making adobe bricks and roof tiles in much the way the originals were made. Major restoration was completed by 1941. Today, La Purisima is the most completely reconstructed of the California missions.

1935 — Central Valley Project construction begins to build a statewide system of water transfer and storage. Today, it manages twenty-two reservoirs with a combined storage of eleven million acre-feet to provide drinking water to two million people, and to irrigate more than three million acres of farmland in twenty-nine counties in the state.

1936 — Bay Bridge opens, connecting San Francisco and Oakland with an 8.25 mile double-deck link across the San Francisco Bay at a cost of $77 million. Today, 270,000 cars and trucks cross the bridge daily. During the 1989 Loma Prieta earthquake, a fifty-foot section of the upper deck collapsed. A replacement bridge is being constructed next to it at a cost of $6.3 billion and is scheduled to open in 2013.

1937 — Golden Gate Bridge opens, connecting San Francisco and Mann County with, at the time, the longest suspension bridge in the world. The 1.7 mile bridge spans the mouth of San Francisco Bay. It cost $35 million to construct. Because of its graceful art deco design, it becomes recognized as the iconic symbol of San Francisco.

1939 — *The Grapes of Wrath* by John Stein beck is published. The gritty novel of the plight of Oklahoma farm workers who migrated to California because of drought and depression reflects many of the actual conditions existing at the time. In 1940, it was made into an award-winning film by Twentieth-Century Fox.

1940 — First McDonald's restaurant opens in San Bernardino, California. Founded by brothers Richard and Maurice "Mac" McDonald in 1948, they pioneer a food assembly line process that allows orders to be filled in less than one minute. Although the restaurant is very successful, Ray Kroc is the driving force behind the franchising of the business and he helps turn the company into a leading international force in the food industry that today has 31,000 restaurants in 119 countries.

1940 — Census records the state population of California as 6,907,387.

1940 — Kings Canyon National Park is created. Located east of Fresno in the southern Sierra Nevada, the 461,901-acre park features the General Grant Grove of giant sequoias as well as one of the deepest canyons in the United States.

1941 — Federal Bureau of Investigation, four days after Japan's attack at Pearl Harbor, Hawaii, arrests 1,370 Japanese Americans in California classified as "dangerous enemy aliens."

1942 — Urban Mexican population of Los Angeles is second only to Mexico City.

1942 — Zoot Suit Riots begin in Los Angeles with several nights of street brawls between white sailors and soldiers stationed in the city and Mexican American (and some African American) youths. The riots were largely the product of an insecure and charged war atmosphere, coupled with a police department that was institutionally racist.

1942 — Executive Order 9066 is signed by President Franklin Roosevelt, authorizing the secretary of war to define military areas "from which any or all persons may be excluded as deemed necessary or desirable."

1942 — Japanese submarine fires at an oil field near Goleta. Although all twenty-five shells miss their target in the three-minute bombardment and cause almost no damage, it is the first time the United States mainland has been attacked since the War of 1812.

1942 — Internment of Japanese Americans begins after General J. L. DeWitt issues order creating military areas in Washington, Oregon, California, and parts of Arizona and declaring the right to remove German and Italian aliens and anyone of "Japanese ancestry" from the proscribed areas. In less than two months, 120,000 Japanese Americans (most citizens) are forcibly evacuated from their homes and relocated in a series of inland U.S. internment camps.

1942 — "Bracero program" begins under the Emergency Labor Program. Due to severe labor shortages brought on by World War II, the program allows the importation of tens of thousands of people from Mexico, many coming to California farms, to work for a designated period of time and then be returned home. Although the program is intended to be temporary, California growers in particular successfully lobby for its extension and the program continues until 1963.

1945 — Shipyards in the San Francisco Bay Area employ more than 240,000 people during World War II, many of them minorities and women. Using mass-production techniques, workers build 4,600 ships, nearly half of all the cargo vessels and warships produced in the United States for the war effort.

1945 — Nearly 500,000 African Americans move to California during World War II as part of the largest internal migration in United States history.

1945 — Population of California, between 1940 and 1945, grows 35.7 percent as more than 2.5 million people move into the state during World War II.

1945 — United Nations Charter, the constitutional document that governs the new organization, is signed in San Francisco by fifty of the founding nations.

1947 — *Mendez v. Westminster School District,* the U.S. Court of Appeals in San Francisco, in a legal precedent, rules that segregation of Mexican American students in "Mexican schools" is a violation of the Fourteenth Amendment. Later that year, all remaining school segregation in the state is outlawed in the California Education Code.

1948 — *Oyama v. California,* the U.S. Supreme Court rules the Alien Land Laws violate the Fourteenth Amendment rights of Japanese American citizens.

1948 — *Perez v. Sharp*, the Supreme Court of California rules the state's anti-miscegenation law, in place since 1850, is a violation of the Fourteenth Amendment. California becomes the first state in the country to allow interracial marriages.

1948 — Evacuation Claims Act is signed by President Harry Truman, authorizing payments to Japanese Americans who suffered economic loss as a result of their being placed in internment camps during World War IL A total of $38 million is paid as the provisions of the law only return ten cents for every one dollar of provable loss.

1950 — Census records the state population of California as 10,586,223.

1951 — *Stoumen v. Reilly,* the legal right to operate a "gay business" is affirmed for the first time as the California Supreme Court rules that the liquor license of Sol Stoumen, owner of the Black Cat Cafe, one of the first gay bars in the Castro district of San Francisco, could not be revoked by the State Alcoholic Beverage Commission simply because the bar catered to homosexuals.

1953 — Earl Warren is selected by President Dwight Eisenhower to be Chief Justice of the United States Supreme Court. Warren is the first, and to date, only Californian to be Chief Justice and third overall to sit on the court. The state's only three-time elected governor, Warren is considered to be moderately conservative when appointed. He proves to be a progressive liberal and presides over some of the most significant court cases of the century, including *Brown v. Board of Education* (banning racial segregation in public schools), *Gideon v. Wainwright* (requires free legal counsel to destitute defendants), *Miranda v. Arizona* (requires the reading of rights to a person in police custody), and *Loving v. Virginia* (allows inter-racial marriage, overturning a 1924 law that banned it). He retires in 1969 as one of the most significant justices in the court's history.

1954 — KQED, one of the first public television companies in the United States, begins broadcasting in the Bay area.

1955 — Disneyland Park opens in Anaheim, California. The only theme park designed under the direct supervision of Walt Disney, today it is one of the best known and most visited entertainment sites in the world with more than 650 million visitors since it opened.

1955 — *Howl,* an epic poem by Allen Ginsberg, is read in public for the first time in San Francisco at the City Lights Bookstore. In 1956, City Lights publishes *Howl and Other Poems* where it becomes the subject of a long trial before a federal court rules the book is not obscene. The poem and trial bring attention to an emerging "beat" generation of writers.

1957 — *The Cat in the Hat* by Theodor Seuss Geisel is published. Born in Springfield, Massachusetts, Geisel lives in La Jolla (San Diego county) from 1948 until his death in 1991. The children's book, one of forty-four he publishes under the name Dr. Seuss, influences generations of children learning to read.

1957 — Brooklyn Dodgers and New York Giants relocate to Los Angeles and San Francisco respectively, prior to the start of the 1958 major league baseball season. California's third team, the Los Angeles Angels of Anaheim is an expansion team that begins play in 1961. The state's fourth team, the Oakland Athletics, move from Kansas City in 1967.

1960 — Census records the state population of California as 15,717,204.

1960 — Winter Olympics are held at the Squaw Valley Ski Resort, near Lake Tahoe, only the second time the winter games were held in the United States. The games are televised; one innovation that results is the use of the "instant replay."

1960 — Master Plan for Higher Education adopted by California to coordinate the state's postsecondary education systems to cope with an emerging surge in high school graduates who are part of the "baby boom" that follows World War II. The plan's arrangement of the state's colleges and universities into a pyramid-shaped organization remains largely in effect today with the 10 University of California (UC) schools serving as a "top tier" of education and research, the 23 California State University (CSU) schools focusing on undergraduate education, and the 110 California Community College

(CCC) schools providing vocational degrees and lower division course work to prepare students for transfer to universities.

1962 — California's population surpasses New York as the largest of any state in the United States. California's population continues to have net gains of approximately 1,000 people a day through the middle of the decade before the rate significantly slows.

1962 — Nobel Prize for Literature is awarded to John Steinbeck. The novelist, playwright, and essayist, born and raised in Salinas, authors twenty-five books, many considered twentieth-century classics, including *The Grapes of Wrath* and *East of Eden.*

1962 — United Farm Workers (UFW) is founded by Cesar Chavez, the first farm labor union, to improve the wages and working conditions of California's 250,00 farm workers. In the late 1960s, after years of labor strikes, consumer boycotts, and severe personal sacrifices, the union wins agreements to form collective bargaining contract with several large growers.

1962 — Three convicts escape from Alcatraz prison and disappear into San Francisco Bay, never to be seen again. Whether they reached the mainland or drowned has been debated since, and is the basis of a movie chronicling their ingenious break out.

1964 — UC Berkeley protests, the first major college student demonstrations of the decade, begin as several thousand students form a Free Speech Movement to challenge a university ban on all political activity on campus.

1965 — California Land and Conservation Act, commonly known as the Williamson Act, is passed. This landmark law in state farm preservation allows farmers and ranchers to enter into renewable contracts with their county government. In return for guaranteeing they will restrict the use of their land to agriculture or open-space (grazing) for at least ten years, the land will be taxed at a preferred, lower rate.

1965 — Watts Riot begins, the result of tensions between the Los Angeles police department, white business owners, and largely impoverished African Americans living in the Watts section of Los Angeles. The riots last six days during which 34 are killed and 1,000 injured.

1966 — Ronald Reagan, a former actor whose political views shifted from liberal to conservative during the Cold War, is elected to the first of two terms as governor.

1966 — Black Panther Party is founded by Huey Newton and Bobby Seale in Oakland. The group strikes a controversial mix of confrontational, paramilitary "Black Power," along with self-help and education programs within the black community.

1967 — Super Bowl I, the AFL-NFL Championship football game, is played in Los Angeles Memorial Coliseum with the Green Bay Packers defeating the Kansas City Chiefs. It is the only Super Bowl not to be sellout.

1967 — "Summer of Love," in San Francisco attracts tens of thousands of young people to the city and helps bring the counterculture movement, with its alternative living concepts and criticism of mainstream American society, widespread public attention.

1968 — Intel (Integrated Electronics) corporation, is founded in 1968 in Santa Clara. In 1971, it introduces the first microprocessor. It will become the world's largest semiconductor company.

1968 — Richard Nixon is elected 37th president of the United States, Born in Yorba Linda, Nixon is the first native Californian to hold that office. He is easily re-elected in 1972, but is a polarizing figure during the controversial era. Two years later, in 1974, as a result of the Watergate scandal, he becomes the first president in U.S. history to resign from the office. He faced certain impeachment on changes he obstructed justice by trying to cover-up a burglary of the Democratic national headquarters by men associated with the White House.

1968 — Student protests at San Francisco State University regarding a Eurocentric perspective of education, results in a five-month student and faculty strike, the longest such protest at an academic institution in the history of the United States. One result was the creation of an Ethnic Studies program and efforts to diversify the faculty.

1969 — Santa Barbara oil spill occurs less than a year after the controversial development of drilling rigs in the environmentally sensitive Santa Barbara Channel. The spill covers 850 square miles and decimates shore, bird, and sea life. It is the first ecological disaster to attract extended national attention and is part of the impetus to create many new environmental protections, including the national Environmental Protection Agency in 1970.

1969 — Altamont rock concert, in northern California, headlined by the Rolling Stones is scarred by fighting and four deaths, including the murder of a black man near the front of the stage by white Hells Angels hired as concert security. The disastrous concert undercuts the youth culture's "peace and love" image popularized at the Woodstock music festival just four months earlier.

1969 — American Indian activists seize Alcatraz Island, claiming the island and its former federal penitentiary, closed in 1963, as Indian property. The eighteen-month occupation brings widespread attention to the poor and politically neglected lives of many of the nation's two million living Indians.

1969 — Douglas Dollarhide is elected mayor of Compton and becomes California's first African American mayor.

1970 — Census records the state population of California as 19,971,069

1971 — "Silicon Valley" term is coined by journalist Dan Hoefler to describe the region around the Santa Clara Valley and southern end of the San Francisco peninsula where a developing semiconductor and computer industry is centered.

1971 — Sylmar earthquake kills 65 people and damages the Van Norman Dam, leading to the precautionary evacuation of 80,000 San Fernando Valley residents.

1971 — Lorette Wood is elected mayor of Santa Cruz and becomes California's first female mayor.

1972 — Bay Area Rapid Transit (BART) begins operation after eight years and $1.6 billion of construction. Built mostly underground, including under the San Francisco Bay, the 104-mile system today serves 350,000 riders a day.

1972 — California Coastal Commission is created by the voters' approval of Proposition 20. Conceived in an era of heightened awareness of the human impact on the ecosystem, the commission is authorized to regulate the use and development of land and water along the state's coastal regions.

1972 — "Slow growth" measures, the first in California history, are enacted by Petaluma, in Sonoma County, in response to its quickly rising population. The number of new housing units the city allows to be built is severely limited. The measures are upheld in the course of several court challenges.

1973 — Tom Bradley, whose grandparents were slaves and parents were sharecroppers, elected the first African American mayor of Los Angeles. He is re-elected four times; at twenty years he is the longest serving mayor in city history.

1977 — Harvey Milk becomes the first openly gay person elected to public office when he wins a seat on the San Francisco Board of Supervisors. In 1978, he, along with Mayor George Moscone are assassinated by Dan White, a former supervisor. In 2009, Milk is awarded the Presidential Medal of Freedom by Barack Obama.

1977 — Apple II, the world's first commercially successful personal computer, is introduced by the Apple Computer Company, headquartered in Cupertino, in Santa Clara Valley. It initially cost $2,638 for a model with 48K RAM. More than two million units are sold before it is discontinued in 1993.

1978 — ***Bakke v. the Regents of the University of California,*** U.S. Supreme Court declares using racial quotas in college admissions to be unconstitutional.

1978 — **Proposition 13** is overwhelmingly approved. This landmark tax measure limits property taxes, which had been rising sharply during the decade, to one percent of the purchase price of a house, with no more than a two percent increase per year. Among its many significant effects, property taxes drop by 57 percent the following year and school districts that depend heavily on these taxes lose $6 billion in funding.

1980 — **Ronald Reagan** elected the 40th president of the United States, the second Californian to hold the office. He is re-elected in 1984. His enormous popularity among Republicans helps inspire a conservative movement that continues for years to come.

1980 — **Census** records the state population of California as 23,667,764.

1984 — **Summer Olympics** are held in Los Angeles. Although 6,829 athletes from 140 nations attend, the Soviet Union and thirteen of its allies do not, in retaliation for the United States' boycott of the 1980 games held in Moscow. As a result, American competitors win 174 medals, more than three times the number won by medal count runner-up Romania, the only Soviet ally to participate. The games make a profit of $215 million, only the second time that has happened—the other being the 1932 Olympics, also held in Los Angeles.

1984 — **Proposition 37** passes, creating a state lottery system. With 34% of its revenue to be used to supplement public education, the lottery is intended to generate money for schools without imposing more taxes.

1984 — **Prison construction** begins a vast expansion with thirty-three new prisons being constructed by 2004. Between 1852 and 1984, only twelve prisons were built in the state.

1987 — **Project AIDS Memorial Quilt** is created in San Francisco to remember people who died from the disease. There were 4,135 AIDS-related deaths in the United States that year, and a total of 20,436 had occurred since 1981. The quilt is made of personalized, individual panels that are sewn together in twelve-foot square sections. Eventually, the quilt has more than 40,000 panels.

1988 — **Anthony Kennedy** is selected by President Ronald Reagan to be associate justice of the United States Supreme Court. His nomination comes after two earlier choices by Reagan, Robert Bork and Douglas Ginsberg, are unsuccessful. Born in Sacramento, Kennedy is the first native-born Californian to sit on the U.S. Supreme Court and fourth overall. He is considered a conservative but not a rigid ideologue. As a consequence, he is often a "swing vote" in 5-4 decisions.

1988 — The Civil Liberties Act of 1988 empowers the federal government to grant reparations of $20,000 to each Japanese American who had been forced into internment camps during World War II as a result of "race prejudice, war hysteria, and failure in political leadership."

1989 — Loma Prieta Earthquake strikes, measuring a magnitude 6.9 it is centered about sixty miles south of San Francisco in the Santa Cruz Mountains. The twenty-second quake is felt as far away as San Diego and western Nevada. It causes sixty-three deaths and $6 billion in property damage.

1990 — Census records the state population of California as 29,760,021.

1991 — Migration out of California in substantial numbers occurs for the first time in state history as more then one million people leave between 1991 and 1994, in great part due to a prolonged recession.

1992 — Los Angeles Riots occur after four white Los Angeles police officers are acquitted of charges in a videotaped beating of an African American, Rodney King. Rioting in South Central Los Angeles leaves fifty-four people dead and causes an estimated one billion dollars in damage.

1992 — Election of Barbara Boxer and Dianne Feinstein to the U.S. Senate makes California the first state to be represented by two female senators at the same time.

1994 — Northridge Earthquake occurs in the Reseda area of Los Angeles. Measuring a magnitude 6.7, the fifteen-second quake causes fifty-seven deaths and $20 billion in property damage, making it the most expensive natural disaster in the United States up to that time.

1994 — Proposition 184 is approved by California voters. Popularly known as "three strikes, you're out," the measure mandates that a person convicted of two or more violent or serious felonies, who then commits any new felony, automatically receives a prison sentence of twenty-five years to life in prison.

1994 — Proposition 187 approved by California voters in a move to stop undocumented immigrants from having access to public schools and medical care, and other social services. By 1999, federal and state courts declare most of the provisions of the proposition to be unconstitutional. However, by then, federal laws require all states to deny welfare benefits and most health benefits to all people who cannot verify they are legally in the United States.

1996 — O.J. Simpson is tried and acquitted of the murders of his former wife, Nicole Brown Simpson, and Ronald Goldman, in a Los Angeles trial that is described as the most publicized criminal case in U.S. history.

1996 — California's total output of goods and services is more than $1 trillion. It is the world's seventh largest economy after the United States, Japan, Germany, France, Italy, and the United Kingdom.

1996 — Proposition 209 enacted as California voters prohibit the use of racial and sex-based preferences by public institutions in making decisions such as college admissions. Initially blocked by a federal judge, in 1997 a federal appeals court rules the proposition is constitutional.

2000 — Sesquicentennial celebrating California history concludes on the 150th anniversary of the state admission day. Official ceremonies began in January 1998 marking the discovery of gold by James Marshall at the American River in Coloma in 1848.

2000 — Proposition 39 passes and improves the likelihood of school construction bonds being approved by reducing the required "yes" vote from a two-thirds "super-majority" to 55 percent. In the next two years, the passage rate for school bond measures is 84 percent, as compared to 56 percent during the previous fourteen years.

2000 — Census records the state population of California as 33,871,648.

2001 — California's total output of goods and services tops $1.3 trillion. It is the world's fifth largest economy after the United States, Japan, Germany, and the United Kingdom.

2003 — First successful recall of a governor in California occurs and Gray Davis is replaced by actor Arnold Schwarzenegger as governor of the state.

2005 — Antonio Villaraigosa is elected mayor of Los Angeles and becomes the first Latino to serve in this office since 1872.

2006 — Number of Inmates in California state prisons is a record 172,000 and causing overcrowding of facilities. In 1980, there were 27,916 inmates in state prisons, or 177 per 100,000 people. In 2004, there were 164,169 inmates, or 686 per 100,000.

2006 — Water returns to Owens River for the first time since 1913 as Los Angeles allows 1/20 of the original volume to flow along the sixty-two mile riverbed. The symbolic gesture to the residents of Owens Valley is the culmination of a thirty-year legal battle between Inyo and Los Angeles counties.

2007 — Statewide median price for a house or condominium rose to a record $554,00 in February. It is estimated that the number of Californians who can afford to pay the mortgage on an entry-level home is 24 percent—down from 44 percent in 2003.

2008 — First Natural Landmark in California is 40,000 acres of Orange County parkland, much of it surrounding Irvine. The designation places the land on a statewide registry. It does not provide regulatory protection or require the land to be permanently protected, but it is intended to raise public awareness of its environmental significance.

2008 — Proposition 8 passes and eliminates the legal right of same sex couples to marry in California.

2009 — Statewide median price for a house or condominium falls to $249,000. This is a 45 percent decline from its peak two years earlier.

2009 — Building projects are delayed or cancelled for the first time in state history due to a lack of long-term supplies of water. The restriction is the result of a 2001 law requiring developers to offer proof of a twenty-year water supply for a new building. This followed a serious two-year state drought, and a much longer drought affecting the Colorado River, a major source of water for Southern California.

2010 — Census records the state population of California as 37,253,956.

2010 — California's total output of goods and services tops $1.9 trillion, or 13% of the United State's Gross Domestic Product.

2011 — Steve Jobs dies, co-founder of Apple Inc., and a leading pioneer in the computing industry. Born in San Francisco, under his leadership, Apple inventions include the iPod, iPhone, iPad, MacBook Air, and the OS X computer operating system.

2012 — Housing foreclosures figures show California has nine of the top ten hardest hit cities in the country. Worst off is Stockton, where one out of every 140 houses is in foreclosure.

2012 — Bankruptcy protection is sought by the municipalities of Mammoth Lakes, San Bernardino, and Stockton, the largest U.S city to ever declare itself bankrupt.

2012 — California residents living in poverty rose for the 5th year in a row. Nearly 6.4 million people, 1 in every 6 residents lived on incomes below the federal poverty line. That rate of 16.9 percent is the highest since 1996.

2014 — A statewide drought entered its fourth year with 58 percent of California classified as in "exceptional drought." Governor Jerry Brown imposed a series of mandatory water cutbacks, as did municipalities across the state.

2016 — California has the 6th largest economy compared to all the nations in the world, with $2.4 trillion in Gross Domestic Product.

2017 — The state minimum wage, currently set $10.50 per hour, is scheduled to rise until 2023 when it will be $15.00 per hour. This will make California the first state to reach that benchmark in pay.

2017 — St. Thomas Fire, in Ventura and Santa Barbara counties, becomes the largest fire in state history as it burns 281,893 acres (440 square miles). Driven by Santa Ana winds, at its height, the fire consumes one acre per second. It takes 8,500 firefighters six weeks to extinguish the blaze.

2018 — Wildfire insurance claims for the year exceed $11.8 billion, the most costly in state history and more than four times greater than the previous most expensive fire season in 1991.

2018 — Gold recovered from the wreck of the SS *Central America*, which sunk in a hurricane in September, 1857 as it traveled from San Francisco to Panama, is publically displayed for the first time. Four-hundred and twenty-five people died with the sinking of the sidewheel steamer and the loss of its 9.1 tons of gold cargo helped initiate a devastating financial panic across the United States. The wreck was discovered in 1988 but its salvage was held up for years as a result of legal battles over who had the right to own the gold, worth $300 million in today's money.

2018 — California has the 5th largest economy compared to all the nations in the world, with $2.7 trillion in Gross Domestic Product.

2018 — An estimated 34,000 homeless people live in Los Angeles, the largest concentration of homeless in the United States. The city announced a $430 million plan to provide some housing and other services for what is called the city's greatest humanitarian crisis.

The Land and Geography

A Fortunate Nature

A study of the physical features of California reveals key aspects that geography has played in the history of the state. First, simply by its westernmost position on the Pacific coast, California was long isolated, initially from European colonists who developed the eastern shores of the North American continent, and later from the United States during its first half-century of existence. Far from the U.S. and even farther from Europe and the Atlantic trade, California remained unknown to non-natives for a very long time. The first non-native Americans did not reach California until 1826, when Jedediah Smith and a group of trappers first arrived from an overland route to explore the region. This geographic isolation was intensified by the fact that the eastern edge of California is lined by either an imposingly tall mountain ranges or wide and forbidding deserts. Arriving by land was certainly no easy proposition.

The long period of isolation had another profound effect of the region. It led to the proliferation of an incredible range of biodiversity that gave rise of a mixture of animals and plants un-matched in other states. Land that included prairie, marshes, sagebrush, chaparral, woodlands, forest, and alpine supported a corresponding mélange of species of life.

"In many ways, California looks like the country, if in the extreme. By its sheer size, California carries special weight. If the Pilgrims had landed in Santa Monica Bay, there'd be something like 13 states in California."

—Kevin Starr, Author and Professor of History

California's Regions

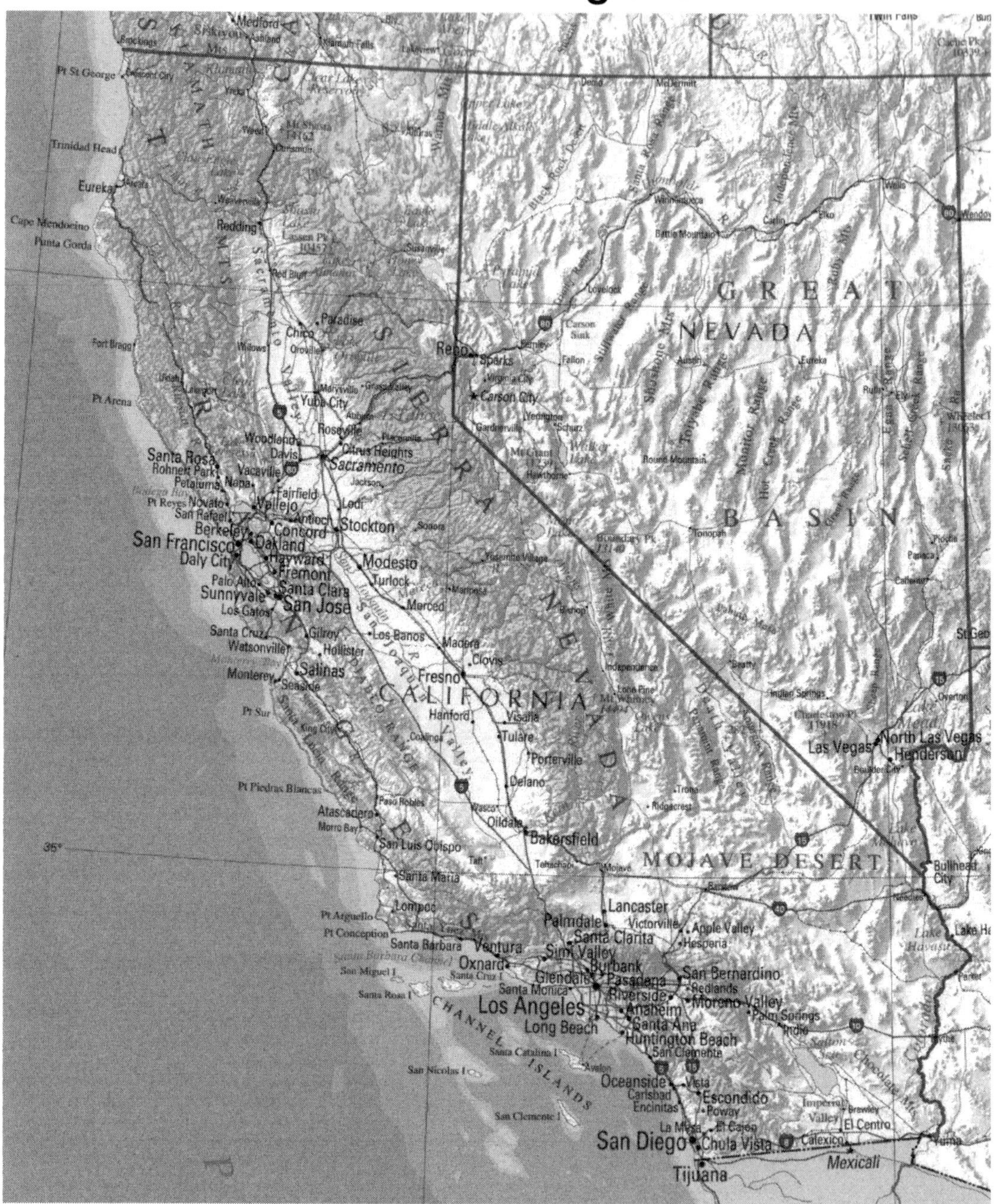

U.S. Geology Survey.

Sizing up the State

California is the 3rd largest state in the United States

Total Area:	163,707 square miles (155,973 square miles of land, 7,734 square miles inland water)
Longitude:	120° 4.9'W
Latitude:	36° 57.9'N
Northern border:	Oregon
Southern border:	Mexico
Eastern border:	Nevada and Arizona
Western border:	Pacific Ocean
Coastline:	840 miles
Width:	250 miles at its widest point
Geographic Center:	North Fork, a small town 38 miles north of Madera
Highest Elevation:	Mount Whitney 14,494 feet above sea level (highest point in the contiguous 48 states of United States)
Lowest Elevation:	Badwater, Death Valley –282 feet below sea level (lowest point in the United States)
Mean Elevation:	2,900 feet above sea level
Active Volcanoes:	Lassen Peak, last erupted 1915 (one of two active volcanoes in United States outside of Alaska and Hawaii)
Major Rivers:	American, Colorado, Eel, Feather, Klamath, Sacramento, San Joaquin, Trinity
Major Lakes:	Clear, Eagle, Mammoth, Mono, Owens (dry), Salton Sea, Tahoe

Note: The state's largest lake, the Salton Sea, located between Anza-Borrego Desert State Park and Joshua Tree National Park near Coachella in the Imperial Valley, is actually a lake made by human error. While dredging for the All American canal in the early 1905, construction workers accidently opened a breach, according to Doug Barnum, USGS science coordinator in the Salton Sea Science Office. For 18 months, the Colorado River flowed into the Salton sink and created the lake, before the canal breach could be fixed. More recently, water restrictions on the Colorado River has lessened flow into the lake and Salton has seen its water level steadily decline. In turn, this has increased water salinity, which is prompting a decline in the fish migratory bird population, potentially destroying a major stopping point in the Pacific bird migration route. (source Reuters.com/article/environmentnews, 2009)

Climate

Given the size of the state, particularly, its north-south extremes, one can experience wide variances in weather. Still, there are some common points. Most of California experiences only two distinct seasons; a rainy season and a dry season. The rainy season occurs from October to April in Northern California and from November to March or April in Southern California. In the south, from the late spring through the entire summer, there is very little, if any, precipitation. The Los Angeles Basin, for example, will average a mere 2.5 inches of rain in total for the five months between May and September, while areas along the northwest coast receive more than 100 inches of rain each year. The average annual precipitation for the entire state is 23.88 inches.

What Accounts for California's "Desirable Climate?"

The answer, of course, depends on what part of California you are referring to, and defining the term "desirable." Human preferences for environmental conditions are as varied as there are climates. If the goal is to live in moderate, relatively unchallenging weather, it is easy to understand why many people enjoy the Mediterranean climate. It is one of the state's most appealing and enduring attractions. This mood-enhancing atmospheric condition found in parts of California exists in only four other regions of the world: the southern tip of Africa, central Chile, southern Australia, and along the perimeters of the Mediterranean Sea in Europe and the Middle East. All of these lands are located along or near to either the 40° S latitude, or 40° N latitude, as is California. They are all coastal lands as well. A Mediterranean climate is characterized by its lack of many of the harsh extremes that weather conditions can produce, especially when it comes to cold temperature. There is little freezing and even less snow. Winters are cool and wet, while the low-humidity summers range from warm to very hot and are dry and quite sunny. For these reasons most of the world's citrus is grown in these regions.

Trade winds and westerlies (west-blowing winds) are the primary reason for these conditions. In the winter, low-pressure cells traveling along California's Pacific-facing west coast result in precipitation. In the spring and summer, high-pressure cells centered off the upper coast steer storms north toward Oregon and Washington, allowing central and southern California weeks of dry and sun-filled days. Along the coast, air moving inland after being cooled by deep ocean water combines with the Mediterranean climate to keep temperatures mild during the summer. In San Diego, the typical day temperature in July is 70°. In comparison, Charleston, South Carolina, at roughly the same latitude as San Diego, but three thousand miles to the east, is typically 82°. San Diego averages 146 clear days a year, six more weeks than Charleston. Santa Maria has 176 clear days, Los Angeles 186, and Sacramento 188. The state's sunniest city is Fresno with 194 clear days and sunshine 79 percent of its daylight hours.

Diversity

California's large size and predominately north-south orientation helps explain the great variation of its geography. This, in turn, contributes to its extraordinary mix of climates. Four of the five major climates that exist in the world—Mediterranean (mild, wet winters; warm to hot dry summers), temperate rain forest (warm and wet throughout the year), arctic (long, cold winters; short, cool summers) alpine (mountain climate above tree-line), and semi-arid desert (low precipitation year-round) are found here. Only the hot, rainy tropical climate is not represented. Climate, alone, sets the state apart from all others. But that is only one aspect of its diversity.

The unique and diverse character of California's geography, topography, and geology led some inhabitants to realize early on that the state contained an incredible array of natural treasures. California has more unique plants and animals than any other state. In fact, it is one of the most biologically diverse areas in the world. There are more than 5,000 native plant species in the state. This is more variety than exists in all of the northeastern United States and Canada *combined.* One-third of these plant species are found nowhere else in the world. Within the land itself 1,688 different soils have been identified. California is also home to a range of exclusive and rare fauna. This helps explain why there are more then 30,000 species of insects.

The wildlife is equally as varied. There are 961 native vertebrates (animals with a backbone of spinal column), two-thirds of which are not found outside of the state. One can find more then 200 types of mammals, In the forested areas, there are elk, deer, squirrels, bears, red foxes, and bighorn sheep. Until 1922 when they were hunted to extinction, there was the grizzly, the largest bear in North America.

In rivers there are 47 amphibians including salamander and 83 species of fish such as rainbow or golden trout, and salmon. Along the coastline there are sea bass, yellow fin tuna, barracuda, sea lions, grey whales, and a variety of shorebirds.

In the desert there is the kangaroo rat, Mohave ground squirrel, pocket mouse, jackrabbit, and 77 reptiles such as the desert tortoise, and horned toad. In northern California there are nearly three dozen species of snakes—six types of rattlesnakes alone, along with the sidewinder, and garter snake to name just a few.

In the air, one may find 540 bird species, the largest being the California condor, narrowly saved from extinction in the mid-20th century. One of the smallest, the hummingbird, can be found in 14 species.

All things considered, it is not surprising that California became one of the birthplaces of the conservation movement sparked, in part, by the work and words of naturalist John Muir, who became impassioned with Yosemite Valley after he spent the summer of 1869 herding sheep in the Sierras. Today, scores of areas of the state are legally preserved and have varying levels of restrictions on human use and development.

A sizable portion of the land of California have been legally preserved and have varying levels of restriction of use and development. There are key legal distinctions between the types of protection afforded to these designated areas.

National Parks

A natural landmark or a structure or site of historic interest set aside by the federal government and maintained for public enjoyment or study. (The years noted are the dates each received their nationally designated status. Some locations had previous other designations.)

Channel Islands (1980)	249,353 acres
Death Valley (1994)	3,367,627 acres
Joshua Tree (1994)	1,022,967 acres
Kings Canyon (1940)	461,901 acres
Lassen Volcanic (1916)	106,372 acres
Redwood (1968)	105,516 acres
Sequoia (1890)	402,510 acres
Yosemite (1890)	761,266 acres

National Monuments

Cabrillo (1913)	162 acres
Devil's Postpile (1911)	798 acres

Lava Beds (1972)	46,559 acres
Muir Woods (1908)	553 acres
Pinnacles (1908)	22,353 acres

Seashores

Land by the ocean that is set aside by the federal government and maintained by the National Park Service.

Point Reyes (1962)	71,059 acres

Preserve

An area maintained for the protection of wildlife or natural resources.

Mojave (1994)	1,553,815 acres (source: National Park Index, 2001–2003)

The California State Park system manages 278 sites that encompass an additional 1.4 million acres as parks, recreation areas, and reserves. This includes one-third of California's beaches and coastline.

The state also has ten designated Wilderness Areas, land that has not been significantly altered from its natural condition and is now managed to maintain that status. These sites total 466,320 acres.

California's Big Trees

It should come as no surprise that the diversity of California's geography and climate gives rise to a varied, sometimes unique, array of plant and animal life. One such example is the native **California redwoods**, also known as coast redwoods. They are the tallest trees on the earth and among the oldest. Their longevity and size owes much to their having very thick bark with little resin. This makes them remarkably fire-tolerant and long-lived; some have been proven to be more than 2,200 years old and are thought to be even much older.

Redwood forests were once wide-spread but today, after decades of extensive logging, only 2 percent of the original old growth forest is left. Much of what remains is now within national and state parks. Redwoods grow naturally only in a narrow belt of land, 450 miles long and from 5 to 50 miles wide, between southern Oregon and Monterey County. They are primarily located in Del Norte and Humboldt counties in northern California. The elevation of the land ranges from near sea level to 3,000 feet. The trees thrive in this moderate climate, where winter rains and summer fog provide an even temperature and a high level of moisture year-round. The tallest of these majestic trees are over 350 feet.

A close relative of the coast redwoods are the **giant sequoias** found in the Sierra Nevada Mountains. These trees are somewhat shorter but are more massive and can be even longer-lived. They are, in fact, the largest living organisms, by mass, on earth. Named for a Cherokee Indian chief, Sequoyah, giant sequoias are found only on the western side of the central Sierra range. They live primarily between 5,000 - 7,000 feet elevation, much higher than the coastal redwoods. Many of the largest are 250 feet tall (equal to a 26-story building) and are commonly over 2,000 years old. A few are as much as 3,000 years old. Their hardiness comes, in part from the presence of tannic acids which helps them resist fungal rot and wood-boring beetles. Their bark is as much as three feet thick, making the tree much more resistant to fire. Their width is as much as 26 feet across. The largest alive today, named the "General Sherman," is estimated to weigh 2.7 million pounds. One of these giants could supply enough wood to build five, 5-room houses. Although they were logged in the 19th century, their wood is brittle and does not make for good commercial lumber. In 1937, the California Redwood was designated the official state tree.

Mountain Ranges

Much of California is covered by a series of mountain ranges, most of which run north-south for much of the present-day eastern border of the state. For many decades, these mountains both helped to isolate the region from European and United States exploration and settlement, as well as to attract vast numbers of people, such as during the gold rush in the 1850s.

About 35 percent of the total surface area of the state is covered by forest. California contains more forestland, in total area, than any other state except Alaska. The U.S. Forest Service manages more than twenty million acres of this land. Most of the forest is found in two areas: the northwestern part of the state and along the western slope of the Sierra Nevada range.

About 25 percent of the total surface area of the state is covered by desert. In the southeastern section of the state, butting against the boundary with Nevada, there are three major deserts: the Mojave, Great Basin, and Sonoran. Further north, but still on the east side of the state, is the much larger desert of Death Valley, famous for having the lowest point of elevation in the nation, as well as being the hottest place in all of North America, averaging over 100° for its summer months with highs over 120°. Death Valley is also one of the driest spots on the earth, averaging less than two inches of rain a year.

Almost the entire southeastern border region of the state is arid and hot, with the Coachella Valley and Imperial Valley routinely experiencing extreme high temperatures during the summer. Yet, even further south, below Palm Springs in the Imperial Valley is the Salton Sea. At 376 square miles, it is the largest lake in California. It is also 228 feet below sea level.

Klamath Mountains: These are located in the northwest region of the state. They consist of numerous small forest-covered ranges separated by deep canyons. The Klamath and Trinity are two of its notable rivers. With upper elevations ranging between 6,000 to 8,000 feet above sea level, the Klamath Mountains are higher than the coastal mountain ranges to the south. They peak with Mount Eddy at 9,038 feet, located near Mt. Shasta.

Cascade Mountains: This range extends north from the Sierra Nevada. The range is approximately two hundred miles inland from the Pacific Ocean and receives most of the moisture which passes over the lower coastal range. The full range continues through Oregon and Washington where it is home to the snowiest region in the United States. In the California portion, some areas collect up to 150 inches of precipitation a year. Unlike the other mountain ranges in California, the Cascade Range was formed by volcanic activity and is part of what is called the Pacific Ring of Fire. The area is renowned for its robust seismic activity. The range includes Mount Shasta, rising 14,162 feet above sea level, and Mount Lassen at 10,457 feet. Both are volcanic peaks, with Lassen still active, last erupting between 1914–1917, with a particularly violent outburst in May, 1915 when it threw volcanic ash more than 200 miles from its peak.

Coastal Ranges: These ranges extend 20 to 30 miles inland and run between the Klamath Mountains in the north to Santa Barbara in the south. The Coastal Ranges consist of numerous chains of low mountain ranges (most are under 4,000 in height) that include the Diablo and Santa Cruz Mountains. The Coastal Ranges include the remaining groves of the California Redwoods, which are some of the tallest (some are more than 400 foot) and largest (by mass) living things in the world. Another feature of the ranges is the San Andreas Fault zone, a six hundred-mile long series of deep geological fractures which mark the boundary between the Pacific and North American continental plates. Some of the valleys found among the Coastal Ranges are Napa, north of San Francisco, and Santa Clara and Salinas in the south.

Sierra Nevada: This mountain range extends 430 miles from north to south, with fifteen peaks, led by Mount Whitney, rising to over 14,000 feet above sea level. The range is generally between 40 to 70 miles wide. Streams and glaciers have created deep valleys into the western part of the Sierras, with Yosemite Valley being the most noteworthy. Of the 7,000 species of plants found in California, half of them exist in the Sierras, with 20 percent in Yosemite alone. It also contains an unusually large number of species of animals with 112 mammals, 32 reptiles, and 25 types of amphibians. It is a migratory route for birds travelling between South America and Alaska. As a consequence, it provides habitat for 276 species of birds.

The western side of the range gently rises from foothills to mountains from the **Central Valley**. Also called the Great Valley, it actually consists of two smaller valleys, the Sacramento Valley in the north, and the San Joaquin Valley in the south. The Central Valley is about 450 miles long and runs north to south. It lies between the Coastal Range and the Sierra Nevada. A flat, broad plain made from sediment over 100 million years old and up to 60,000 thousand feet deep, the Central Valley is extremely fertile and the most important farming area in the United States west of the Rocky Mountains, producing about three-fifths of California's agricultural output.

On the sharply rising eastern side of the range is **Owens Valley**, part of the Great Basin. Here, the land is drier, and the population, as a result is much more sparse. Further east are the **White Mountains** where ancient bristlecone pines grow. At more than 4,000 years of age, these are the oldest living organisms in the world. Earth's oldest living inhabitant is a bristlecone named "Methuselah" that, in 1957, was found to be 4,723 years old. That is more than 1,000 older than any other known tree on the planet.

The Sierra Nevada, which translates as "snow-covered mountain range," is one of the snowiest places on earth when measured in feet of snow per square mile. In record periods, more than 20 feet of snow have fallen in a single month. Not surprisingly, the Sierras are the primary source of water for much of the state. Much of the snowmelt is collected through the **California State Water Project**, a complex system of 21 dams and more then 700 miles of canals, tunnels and pipelines. This system serves central and southern California (as far south as San Diego) as well as the bay area, distributing on average, 2.4 million-acre feet of water.

Basin and Range Region: This region makes up part of California's southeastern deserts. The Basin and Range Region extends into Nevada, Oregon, and other states. In the north, much of the area is a lava plateau. This was formed thousands of years ago when the region was flooded with molten lava flowing out of cracks in the earth's surface. In the south, a good deal of the area is arid and includes the Mojave and Colorado deserts. Death Valley, with some of the harshest terrain in the world, lies near the California-Nevada border. Some sections of the Basin and Range Region have become important agricultural areas due to large irrigation projects. Two of these areas are the Imperial and the Coachella valleys near the California border with Mexico.

Transverse Ranges: These ranges get their name because they run east to west, rather than north to south. They lie between Santa Barbara and San Diego counties and include the Santa Ynez, Santa Monica, San Gabriel, and San Bernardino mountains. They run along the Coachella and Imperial valley. They have peaks over 10,000 feet tall.

Peninsular Ranges: These ranges are located south of the Los Angeles Basin. They cover most of San Diego County and the southwestern corner of California. They include the Agua Tibia, Laguna, and Vallecito mountains and extend southward into the Mexican peninsula of Baja California. The land is semi-arid and contains an abundance of chaparral and hardy stands of drought-resistant pines.

(source for mountains: www.netstate.com)

Native Peoples, Early Europeans, and Land

Did Native Americans walk lightly on the earth? Were they people who led lives of such primitive simplicity they existed seamlessly in a natural paradise, taking only what they needed and sustaining a pristine wilderness? Did they act out the very ideals found in the modern-day conservation movement? It is an appealing notion held by some environmentalists and more widely in the general public. The image of Natives as stewards of nature, undoubtedly, is shaped by their long and immediate relationship to the natural world. Because they survived on what the physical world offered, tribes, universally, held an unquestioned belief that perpetuating nature as it existed was a defining principle of life. It was, in fact, essential to their lives, as tribes maintained themselves in step with the rhythms of the annual seasons. If the cycle of sustainability was broken by over-hunting, or exhausting the soil, it would be the natives themselves who would suffer. There was no logic to that proposition.

In contrast to the Native American narrative is what happened to the natural world in North America with the arrival of Europeans in the last years of the fifteenth century, first as explorers, then as maritime traders, and finally, a century later, as conquering colonists. If natives were the responsible environmentalists, so goes the story, the Europeans were the indiscriminate developers and careless polluters. Within their more invasive and powerful tools, they cut, dug, planted, burned, removed, and killed everything they could, including the natives themselves, in a single-minded and heedless pursuit of profit. Over time, the tremendous, and frequently awful consequences of this plundering of the land, along with the fish, fowl, and other marketable natural fare, would become plainly evident.

These versions of two very different groups of people are broad enough to contain many elements of truth. But these stories also do a disservice to both groups as well for they can create perceptions that are over-simplified caricatures. Native Americans were not simple people but tough and clever humans who had amassed the knowledge and devised the ways to maintain a prehistoric existence for thousands of years. For their part, Europeans were clever people too. Their movement into the New World expanded the human world's knowledge of itself, and initiated a radically new global dynamic for trade, politics, and culture. The trans-Atlantic trade they fostered improved technology and enriched the diets for countless millions on both sides of the ocean. Their brutal quest for wealth, however, was real, as evidenced by the emergence of an enormous and ghastly slave trade. And their biological differences with the natives would so devastate thousands of tribes that between 1492 and 1650 an estimated 20 percent of the world's population would perish in a massive dying from disease. Slavery and disease are two immense elements of the European appearance in the New World. How they impacted the land is another.

European Attitudes Toward Nature

It is clear that in the colonial world, the Native American and European attitudes regarding the natural world greatly diverged. In fact, it was one of their most distinct features. This is largely due to the profoundly different cultural and intellectual backgrounds of the two groups.

By the time Europeans—Spain, England, France, and the Netherlands being most prominent--began a significant effort to establish colonies on the eastern shore of North America around 1600, their minds were already filled with dreams of mastering the lands and many of the people around the globe. This audacious ambition was the product of many factors. Throughout the fifteenth century Europeans experienced the development of more stable nations with defined borders and inhabitants who coalesced around a more or less unified identity. Added to this was mercantilism, the economic theory that trade was the primary generator of wealth which was further stimulated by having surpluses in production. Therefore, whatever nation controlled the most gold, silver, or other precious products would end up being the richest, and from that would come power and influence. These two factors, nationalism and mercantilism, contributed in intensified international competition in the New World.

There was also zeal in colonization for Christian missionary work. At the dawn of the seventeenth century, and for the previous thousand years, to be a European was near-universally equated with being a Christian. Even after the Reformation, with its divisions of the Church of Rome and the rise of Protestantism and sects within it, Europeans were nearly all still Christian. And to the great, majority of them, a non-Christian was a heathen, an inferior being, and a clear threat.

One should include too the fact that many Europeans had the very human desire for personal distinction and achievement, and they lived in a culture of violence that readily accepted war as a suitable means to these ends. Wrapped up in these impulses were myths and stories of what might found in the interior of North America. Legends fanned their passion for gold, silver, jewels, spices, and other riches. The shorthand expression was that colonial Europeans were on a quest for "God, Gold, and Glory."

Finally, the influence of classical Greek philosophy on Renaissance thought, coupled with the Christian tradition that preached a dualistic separation of man from nature, resulted in Europeans perceiving themselves as apart from the natural world. In their thought, humans were superior to nature because they had a thinking mind and spirit. Nature did not have an intrinsic spiritual meaning as it did in some other cultures. European people did believe, however, that nature existed for their benefit and that its worth was tangible.

The Forest Myth

Prior to European contact, the eastern third of what is today the United States had the most abundant food resources of any region of the continent. Much of this area of 360 million acres was covered in forests which provided a rich and diverse array of natural resources that enabled tribes to simultaneously farm, hunt, gather, and fish. But to European colonists, forests were lands defined by mythology. Old folk legends were repeatedly set in forests that were invariably mysterious, largely unknown, and full of real and imagined threats.

While the actual frontier woods of North America did contain dangers, bears, wolves, mountain lions, and of course, native peoples, to this European mythology added werewolves, ogres, witches, and child-eating monsters. Through well-known tales such as Hansel and Gretel, Little Red Riding Hood, Sleeping Beauty, and Snow White, the message was the same—forests were full of unpleasant surprises. There would be little interest in preserving or conserving such places. Just as people today associate civilization with paved ground and controlled climates with artificial lighting, the objective for colonists was to use the forests' resources, to clear its land of native plants and wild animals, and transform it into farms and towns, connected by roads.

The European economy was "cash-based" and driven by the acquisition production of commodities. The desire for profit meant that nature was, in a sense, itemized, and each natural "product" was assessed by its potential value as a commodity. Was it a tree or a finished piece of lumber? Was it a beaver or felted fur to make a hat? The for-profit economy required the creation of material surpluses that could be sold. But capitalism, being inherently competitive, meant that, as there was no limit to the extent of wealth one might collect, there was, at the same time, the continual potential for economic failure and ruin. It was from this perspective that colonists looked anxiously at the land in the New World and at its indigenous people they had carelessly misnamed Indians.

Native American Attitudes Toward Nature

The difference in perspectives on nature could not have been greater for Native Americans. From their view, the natural world and humans were tightly bound and integrated: people, animals, and plants all shared the same interconnected realm. There were no boundaries between the natural and supernatural either. Thus, for example, when a native hunter killed a deer or a bear he might apologize or say a prayer asking for forgiveness for taking its life. After all, that animal might contain the spirit of a dead relation. Tribes based their origin stories, their oral traditions, their faiths, and their understanding of all they knew and saw on their physical environment. In sum, unlike Europeans, natives did not seek mastery over nature but coexistence. They did not understand and often failed to appreciate the insatiable European demand for new lands to control and develop. Sometimes colonists who were killed by natives were found with their mouths stuffed with dirt as a final reminder they had always wanted more land.

Native tribes were intimately aware of their environs and the rituals they took part in often emphasized their recognition of their dependence on the continuation of nature; as it had been before was how it should continue to be. While there was no singular faith in North America, certain common religious beliefs were widely shared. Most important was the belief in a mysterious force in nature. Some tribes believed in an especially powerful god, but the great god belief was always accompanied by a belief in many other spirits. Native Americans depended on these spirit powers for success in the search for food, in healing the sick, and victory in war. Many of these rituals were designed to ensure that the people had enough food. Hunting tribes performed ceremonies to keep game plentiful. Farming tribes held planting ceremonies, rain dances, and harvest festivals.

Legends, stories, rituals involving nature were passed through the generations. They formed the basis of many important ceremonies and were part of the foundation of their culture. Natives knew from these accounts what the world had been like before it had people. They knew of the origin of their tribes, and tales of their tribal heroes. Again, a continuous relationship between the land and the people who lived on it was evident.

Still, it would be a perception, not a fact, to conclude that Native Americans different attitudes and treatment of their ecosystem was due to a higher moral standing than found among Europeans. If they were to survive, tribes had no choice but to live through sustainability. Their prehistoric status meant they lacked the tools that would allow them to live apart from the natural world (as most people in the western world do very easily today). They did not have the means to create large surpluses of production either; consequently, they thrived with an economic cycle that was expected to repeat each year.

Native Use of Land

It is incorrect to think that Native Americans were benign in their interactions with their environment. They held in in respect, to be sure, but they realized its value to their needs could be enhanced through human manipulations. There is ample evidence they did exploit the land to an extent that things could still be maintained. Ironically, while the native ability to improve their conditions by actively modifying nature was noted at the time by seventeenth century Europeans, it would not be widely noted, much less appreciated, for a long portion of United States history.

Fire

The uses of fire represented some of the most significant impact Native Americans would have the natural world. By 1500, large parts of the North American continent had been radically transformed to what one New England Puritan described as, "the thin Timber in many places, like our Parkes in England." Similar observations were made elsewhere. In 1538, Hernando de Soto and his expedition spent three-years exploring large portions of the South—what later were Georgia, Alabama, Mississippi, Arkansas, and Louisiana—they found the land—except for swamps—to be quite unobstructed. An English traveler on the Potomac River in 1633 wrote the forest "was not choked with the undergrowth of brambles and bushes, but laid out in a manner so open, you might freely drive a four-horse wagon in midst of the trees."

Native tribes had different reasons for so much burning. Land that had been thinned made for easier travel, hunting, and fending off surprise attack from animal or human aggressors. In the American South, it was a defense against fleas, biting flies, mosquitoes, and ticks. In the East, burnt land created an "edge effect," an open meadow that met forest—an attractive place for game such as deer, elk, turkey, and quail. On the Great Plains fires signaled the discovery of buffalo, or the approach of enemies. Burning the land opened the soil to sunlight, promoted grasses and plantings to grow, increasing the yields.

Fire was used in actual hunting as well. Animals were surrounded by a circle of fire with only one exit from the flames, making for easy killing as they ran through. Bison had a dread fear of fire and would crowd together on the grasslands. Men would rush at the panicked herds and could quickly kill large numbers.

In California, tribes such as the Yukuts and Timbisha Shoshones set fire to marshes, to encourage new growths of reeds and other plants for game to eat. At the same time the fires opened space for more waterfowl nesting, thus, increasing both the diversity of species and their overall numbers. Throughout the state, Indians had burned land to foster seedlings to grow and to increase the variety of plants. In the foothills, they maintained areas with a park-like environment of large spaced trees spread over sunny grasslands.

Trade

Trading goods was an important and vigorous activity. Throughout the Americas, trade routes existed thousands of years before the Europeans arrived. Salt was a staple trade product in agricultural areas. Across the Americas, tobacco was bartered wherever it could not be grown From Central and South America came precious metals and gems. Black volcanic obsidian was carried from the Rocky and Cascade Mountains; flint came from Ohio and southern Canada, copper from Lake Superior, mica from North Carolina, and shells from all the coasts around North America.

For the most part, native tribes traded goods and services for other goods or services. There was no formal system of money however, in some areas, the Native Americans used certain objects much as money is used today. In California, the Northwest Coastal tribes used sea shells called *dentalia* or tooth shells which were divided into five sizes. The longer the shell, the greater was its value. Central Coast Natives, such as the Chumash, used olivella shells from a marine snail also called the Purple Olive. In eastern North America, tribes sometimes used wampum. Wampum, a combination of purple and white beads made from shells, was strung into necklaces or belts. It served mainly as a means of keeping records or recording treaties. But because it had value, it was also used as money.

California Natives

By the end of the Ice Age, more than 10,000 years ago, the vast bulk of large mammals that existed in the Americas had been exterminated. Of the fourteen species of large, domesticated animals found in the world today, such as horses, cows, pigs sheep, and goats, only one, the llama, came from the Americas.

Thus, the typical California tribe depended for its subsistence on hunting, fishing, and gathering what generally were abundant natural sources for food. Only in a few instances, notably along the Colorado River, did people engage in agriculture. Reflecting the mild climate of that area, their housing and dress were often minimal. The basic unit of political organization was the village community, consisting of several small villages, or the family unit. For the most part, these were sedentary people: they occupied village sites for generations and warred with their neighbors only sporadically.

It is a challenge to estimate the native populations anywhere in North America because none of these societies existing in what is now the United States kept written records and the information they did pass on in the form of art or oral stories certainly did not include population totals or other demographic data. As a result, there is wide variance among researchers today what the total population may have been. Estimates for all of North America range from one million to twelve million. For California, the consensus a common estimate is that in 1770 the native population was about 300,000 inhabitants. This means that California natives had a greater population density (1.5 people per square mile) than anywhere else in North America. It is thought that perhaps one out of ten of all natives in North American lived in California.

This large California population was divided into at least 105 separate tribes or nations speaking at least 100 different languages and dialects, about 70 percent of which were as mutually unintelligible as English and Chinese. No area of comparable size in North America, and perhaps the world, contained a greater variety of native languages and cultures than did aboriginal California.

Whatever the precise California native population was in 1770, it is clear that the decades that followed were a titanic disaster for tribes. In 1847, after the rise and fall of the Spanish mission system and the formal transfer by treaty of California from Mexico to the United States, the population had declined to an estimated 100,000. About 60 percent of this decline was due to the introduction of new diseases. Epidemics of cholera, malaria, measles, and smallpox ravaged natives in

Image courtesy of the Ethnic Studies Library and the California Indian Collection, University of California, Berkeley.

seemingly unending waves of misery. But poor diet, hard work, and sometimes-oppressive living conditions and severe punishments, also contributed to the deaths. Compounding the decline was the fact that, compared to Europeans, natives historically had a lower birth rate. And adding that was the reality that for some individuals, mission life became simply too much to bear. Church records list numerous Native American suicides and even infanticides. In sum, it is difficult not to see the Spanish mission system, despite its altruistic intentions, as being a cataclysmic disaster to California tribes.

The misery did not end with the collapse of the missions. The population of California tribes continued to plummet throughout the 19th century. Just between 1847 and 1870, the Native population declined by 70 percent to a total of fewer than 30,000. Not all of these deaths can be attributed to natural causes, either. During its first twenty years as a state, California recorded the killing of more than 4,500 Natives by whites in both random acts of violence, and organized campaigns of extermination. Indians were kidnapped, beaten, and terrorized by organized groups who gave themselves names such as the Humbolt Home Guard, the Eel River Minutemen, and the Placer Blades. Tribes were forcibly dispossessed of millions of acres of land, were subject to wholesale relocations, and were turned into indentured servants through a series of laws passed by the new California legislature. By 1900, their total presence in California had been reduced to a meager 15,000 people, 5 percent of what it had been in 1770.

The Chumash

When examining the specifics of prehistoric peoples, perhaps one of the more helpful points to keep in mind is that the current knowledge is quite fragmented. While a contemporary historical understanding of prehistoric peoples has been increased by work done in the fields of archeology and anthropology, a considerable portion of our knowledge continues to rely on often spotty European recordkeeping, such as journals made by European explorers and early settlers. One result of this is that some historical insights are derived from conflicting information and differing interpretations. In the absence of systematic record keeping by the natives themselves, we simply do not have a complete picture.

Archaeological evidence indicates that people had been in living in some regions of California for more than 12,000 years. There were hundreds of tribes and most numbered under 500 people. The largest of the tribal populations were the Chumash. The term Chumash refers to their language group. They were not wholly united as eight distinct language dialects were spoken. They lived in village settlements that date back as much as 10,000 years, though it is uncertain if the earliest of these people were Chumash or not. At their peak, some 2,000 years ago, between 15,000 to 20,000 Chumash lived in 75 to 150 of these settlements. Small villages might have 12 to 15 families. Larger ones contained 50 to 60 families. The largest of these, near present-day Santa Barbara, contained upwards of 1,000 people. Their population density is thought to have ranged between ten to twenty persons per square mile in the settled regions. This was hardly the "empty land" that many Europeans, and later Americans, would claim.

The traditional Chumash homeland existed in a rich and varied environment. When the Spanish arrived off the California coast in 1542, the Chumash occupied an area that extended more than two hundred miles north to south, from San Luis Obispo, Santa Barbara, and Ventura counties, to as far as Malibu Canyon in the Los Angeles area. In addition, there was the year-round occupation of the rugged Channel Islands of San Miguel, Santa Rosa, and Santa Cruz. Anacapa Island, having no dependable source of fresh water, was occupied seasonally. In total, more than 7,000 square miles were Chumash land.

These regions incorporated diverse microenvironments. Along the ocean coast, Chumash lived near sandy beaches, sheltered lagoons, and rocky shores. Here the climate was dry with 10 to 15 inches of annual precipitation. The climate was moderate with temperatures between 50 and 75 degrees much of the year. Further inland, from the Carrizo Plain to the western edge of the San Joaquin Valley, Chumash lived on flat terraces separated by small streams and gently rolling hills and valleys. Rainfall was heavier than on the coast and the climate more extreme with temperatures ranging between the low 30s in the winter and 100 degrees in the summer. At the easternmost border, the hills graded into steep mountains up to 5,000 feet high.

Like most California natives, despite engaging in trade, the Chumash had provincial lives that were in general isolation from other tribes. The barrier of different tribal languages was reinforced by strong geographical limitations on mobility and communication. It would be common for a person to be born and die on the same stretch of riverbank or near the same hill. One might travel but did not relocate unless forced to do so. With a few exceptions, such as the Mojave and Yuma tribes, the largest collective sense of themselves did not extend beyond the village. The village community, therefore, was usually the highest political unit. There was no broad cultural identification—no collective "national consciousness" with other tribes such as the Europeans had developed by the sixteenth century.

Spanish explorers described the Chumash as physically attractive, strong, graceful, inventive, and industrious. Men were generally between five and six feet tall, and women stood between four and a half and five feet tall, taller than the Spanish themselves. Although the native life expectancy is difficult to assess--their European counter-parts lived about thirty-five to forty years—the Spanish considered the Chumash health to be generally good and estimated that some tribal elders were over the age of seventy.

Recent scholarship divides the Chumash into nine subgroups speaking one of six languages in the Hokan language family. The Indians who lived on the Santa Cruz Channel Island specialized in making the bead money, or *anchum* (roughly meaning "bead money makers" or "shell beads"). The name Chumash and *anchum* are related words and the Spanish universally applied "Chumash" to all nine subgroups—the kind of misidentification that was common among early Europeans. It is thought the Chumash previously called themselves a term that would translate as "the first people" but the exact term has been lost to history. Today, while Chumash is commonly used, the name they have for themselves is Samala. In 2008, the first Chumash "Samala-English" dictionary was published with more than 4,000 entries.

Although Spanish explorers generally looked down on the Chumash culture as inferior to their own, they did express admiration for native skills in hunting, trade systems, construction of villages, canoes, tools, and more. They favorably commented on their physical prowess and found them to be proud and confident as a people, while friendly and generous as individuals.

Diet

The Chumash did not farm and depended on natural sources for their food. Although their diets could be varied, not surprisingly, island and coastal natives ate vast quantities of fish, often dried, and shellfish such as mussels, clams, barnacles, and abalone. Over time, discarded shell grew into mounds as high as thirty feet. As with 75 percent of all California Natives, the inland Chumash relied heavily on acorns as a staple food. Plentiful in number, high in fat (18 percent), protein (6 percent), and carbohydrates (68 percent), they would husk the acorns and either parch or boil out the bitter tannic acid. Using a stone mortar and pestle, the nuts were ground into flour that was then sifted through a shallow basket. The flour was made into porridge or bread—both flavored with grass seeds and other nuts. They also hunted deer, using stone-tipped spears or, after 500 AD, the bow and arrow. Small game such as rabbits and squirrels were killed with throwing clubs, slingshots, nets, and loop traps. Coyotes, gray foxes, badgers, skunks, mountain lions, bobcats, and bears were eaten. So were turtles, frogs, lizards, and snakes. Ducks and geese were caught using decoys and nets.

Tools

One pejorative term the Spanish applied to the Chumash meant "diggers." They observed the Indians using sticks to dig in the soil around the base of plants and trees. The Spanish mistakenly concluded they were searching for worms, grubs, or even roots that they intended to eat. In reality, the Chumash were collecting plant fibers for basket making, something they were experts at doing. Tribes pruned shrubs for basket-making materials only during a plants dormant fall or winter period so not to hurt its health. They produced baskets for a wide array of purposes, including as trays, bowls, sieves, fish traps, cradles, and hats. A cooking basket was so tightly woven it would hold liquids. Some basket containers were coated with pitch of tar to make them watertight. Not only could liquids be contained, water could be boiled as fire-heated rocks were placed inside the basket. There are only a few hundred Chumash baskets known to exist. The Santa Barbara Museum of Natural History has the largest collection of Chumash baskets in the world.

In addition to their fine craft abilities in basket making, the Chumash were skilled jewelers and artists. Their rock paintings are considered to be among the most spectacular and elaborate of any still existing in the United States. Colors were made from minerals. Red was made from an iron oxide called hematite. White came from gypsum or diatomaceous earth. Black was made from charcoal. These pigments were mixed with a binder such as animal fat, or plant juices, to make the paint. They were applied by fingers or with brushes made from animal tails.

Like the naturally occurring tar, obsidian rock and quartz were used to make the sharp heads for arrows and knives. These tools were for hunting; the Chumash had few weapons for fighting other people. They made hooks, nets, and harpoons for fishing.

They were skilled as well in working with wood. Whalebone was used to split wood which was then carved using sharp edges on abalone, flint, or obsidian. Pieces were fitted together with fibrous reeds as they did not nails. They made wooden boxes, plates and bowls.

Some Chumash made ocean-going canoes called tomols. These were not dugouts but used plank construction. Gaps between the planks were sealed with natural tar. Today, large tar-like asphaltum deposits can still be found near the Carpinteria State Beach campgrounds. The largest tomols were thirty feet and could carry as many as ten people at a time. As a note, in 2006, a group of descendants from several Chumash tribes made a ceremonial eleven-hour crossing of the Santa Barbara channel in a traditional tomol, only the fourth such crossing in the past 150 years. Weather permitting, it has become an annual event and an important revival of the native culture.

Dwellings

Most Chumash lived in groups of simple dome-shaped houses made out of plants such as tule or grasses. Easily constructed, they would last up to a few years. Long willow branches were cut to provide the framework; they were then bent and tied together at the top to form the dome. Then smaller branches were tied across for support. The structure was then covered with tule, bulrush, or cattails, which were attached in overlapping rows to keep out rain and wind. In addition to a doorway, a hole was left in the top of the dome for light and ventilation and to allow smoke from fires to escape. These dwellings varied in size, the larger ones, as much as 50 feet across, were capable of holding dozens of people at a time.

Unlike most California tribes, the Chumash did not sleep on the floor of their houses. They slept on beds that were raised off the ground by wood frames. They covered themselves with animal skins for warmth. Sometimes woven reed mats were used as screens and were placed between the beds for privacy.

There were also buildings for specific uses. One was the "sweat house," or temescal, as the Spanish called it. Reserved for adult men, the building was partly underground and was heated by a large open fire. Fully enclosed, there was a door in the roof and men used a ladder to climb down. Heated rocks helped dry the air and increase the temperature. Sweating was both a ceremonial purification of the body and a practical way to remove scent prior to hunting game. After sweating, men would immerse themselves in a cold stream or lake and then repeat the process.

Clothing

The diversity of land and climate within the Chumash region of California played a major role in what people wore. Men, if the weather permitted, often had on little or no clothes save a belt or rope for carrying items. The Spanish were particularly bothered by this customary nudity, considering it "sinful." Chumash women often wore a two-piece apron and top outfit made from deer and rabbit animal skin. Often these were decorated with fringed edges with shells ties on the ends. In colder weather, the skin of the sea otter was prized for its warmth. Body paint, necklaces, earrings were common decorations with each tribe have its own distinctive designs. Elaborate hairstyles were also common among both men and women.

Family and Society

Social classes were not especially strong but divided families between the elite and the commoner. Families that had members who attained particular skills, such as in boat construction, formed an intermediate class. Slavery was absent from all but a few tribes in the northwest regions. The family, by far, was the most important social institution and was matriarchal. Marriage was often arranged and was usually by purchase. Polygamy was practiced, in part, as having multiple wives was a sign of wealth.

The Chumash tribal chief need not be a military leader. Warfare, when it did flare up, was on a small, limited scale, frequently little more than a revenge feuds. Trespassing or poaching were the common type of localized causes of fighting.

Compared to Europeans at the time, the native birth rate was lower. Prostitution, apparently, did not exist. Adultery did occur and was considered more of an economic than social crime. Redress to the husband by the adulterer could be made in the form of a financial payment. For the most part, goods and services were bartered, but money did exist in the form of strings of fine beads or shells. Sea Shells called dentalia or tooth shells were divided by size. The longer the shell, the greater its value. The Olivella shell, a purple marine snail was commonly used to make bead money.

Religion

The Chumash, like all North American people who lived prior to European contact, were not Christian. Thus, they had no western world concept of sin, Heaven or Hell, no belief in predestination, and no organized hierarchal system of church. They worshipped multiple gods and had a strong belief in the intertwined forces of nature with their faiths. The natives considered themselves dependent on these spirit powers for their survival and successes and their rituals often emphasized their environmental connections.

The Chumash developed an extensive astronomical knowledge that was incorporated into their religion. They would study the sun and stars to predict seasonal changes in weather. Important points in the year, such as fall harvest and winter solstice, were marked by ceremonies.

Shamans were religious leaders and also medical practitioners. Illness was thought to be caused by foreign objects entering the body or by an illness of the spirit. The shaman would attempt the drive the objects out or correct the spirit with chants, dancing, and prayers. In addition, more than one hundred native plants were used as medicines. Religious rituals might include drinking a drink derived from the Jimson weed. Its narcotic effect was said to induce sacred visions.

Like their European counter-parts, there were many annual celebrations and occasions; birth, the attaining of adolescence, and death were noted times. The arrival of the first fruit of the season, the return of the salmon, and the onset of the acorn harvest were marked with ritual celebrations.

Games

The playing of games had many purposes. Games requiring coordination could help teach one to hunt. Games of chance were for gambling and sport. All games offered opportunities for recreation, socializing and, of course, could simply be played for the element of fun. One of the more popular traditional games of California natives that survived the arrival of the Europeans was the "hand game" (also called bone game or *Peone*). This was a game of individual will and perception. Two players sat facing each other, making no facial expressions. Each player kept his hands concealed under a small cloth. Also hidden were two small bones, a few inches long. One bone was plain while the other had a string tied around it. When one player was ready, he raised his hands, clenched as fists. The other player was to guess which hand held the unmarked bone. Spectators would talk, sing, and make bets. A single round could last for quite a few minutes. Players would look at body language, consider the past behavior of an opponent, and use intuition. Sometimes false gestures were made to see how a competitor reacted—a good player would nearly always be right.

Dice games were another popular native pastime played by most California tribes. One Chumash dice game was *pi,* a simple contest with many variations played with walnut shells. The shells were split open and the nuts were removed. Teams of players were each given three shell halves which they would roll to see how many would land on their back or with the flat side down. Before each roll, one team player would choose to be "odd" or "even." Betting was often involved.

They were musical as well. In addition to singing, they played flutes made of wood or bone, bows, rattles, and whistles. However, did not have drums.

Contact by Europeans

The initial contacts between the Chumash and European were sporadic and of short duration. Therefore, they had minimal impact on Chumash society. But in 1769, the Spanish began a long-term colonization effort with the establishment of the series of mission outposts, the first one being in San Diego. That same year, a Spanish land expedition, led by Gaspar de Portola, traveled north from Baja California to the Santa Barbara Channel. Eventually, five of the twenty-one missions founded by Spanish Franciscans were established in Chumash territory: San Luis Obispo de Tolosa (San Luis Obispo) 1772, San Buenaventura (Ventura) 1782, Santa Barbara 1786, La Purísima Concepción (Lompoc) 1787, and Santa Inés (Solvang) 1804.

These missions were more than just religious institutions. One principal concern of all missionaries was to convert the Indians to Christianity and, in total, more than 88,000 baptisms were performed at all missions by 1835. The Franciscans also sought to bring about a rapid and thorough cultural transformation of the Indian world. They were taught to perform a wide variety of tasks new to them: making bricks, tiles, pottery, shoes, saddles, wine, candles, and soap; herding horses, cattle, sheep, and goats; and planting, irrigating, and harvesting.

The Chumash, like all California Natives, were used by the Spanish as the essential labor supply for the missions on their lands. They were decimated, largely European diseases. In 1770, there were about 10,000 Chumash. In 1831, as the Spanish mission period was ending, the number of mission-registered Chumash was 2,788. The decline continued through the era of Mexican control, and, later, the United States. In the U.S. Census of 1910, there were 74 Chumash. It would not be hyperbole to state the Chumash people came close to extinction.

After mission secularization in 1835, lands formerly under mission control were given to Spanish families loyal to the Mexican government. Retiring Spanish soldiers were often granted small parcels of land by their commanders. Other larger tracts of land were sold or given to prominent individuals as land grants. The modern-day towns of Santa Barbara, Montecito, Summerland, and Carpinteria were established on traditional Chumash lands. Mexican authorities made little headway in distributing the remaining land among the surviving Chumash who had lived and worked at the missions, causing further decline in their economic status and population. Most of the Chumash who remained in the area survived through menial work on area farms and ranches. The last full-blooded island Chumash died in Santa Barbara in 1915.

In 1901, the Santa Ynez Reservation in Santa Barbara County and was established for members of the Santa Ynez Band of Chumash Indians. It is the only Chumash tribe among the 562 federally recognized tribes in the United States. Today, there are 14 bands of Chumash people.

Although there are 154 enrolled tribal members, an estimated 2,000-5,000 people identify themselves as Chumash.

A Postscript

Today, many Californians are more familiar with Native tribes through their association with gambling. In 1988, Congress enacted the Indian Gaming Regulatory Act which allowed limited gambling operations on Indian lands as a way of promoting economic development for tribes. Since that legislation was created, Indian casinos have boomed in California, in part, because of its past as a far-western territory. The state has the most federally recognized tribes living on federally recognized tribal land, two chief requirements for native gambling casinos. The fact that, today, California is the most populated state with a large tourism industry, has made it an attractive alternative to traditional gambling destinations such as Las Vegas. In 2006, California had fifty-three Indian gambling operations, the second-most number of casinos in any state, trailing only Nevada. Altogether, these casinos employed more than 50,000 workers and, in 2005, collected in excess of $7 billion in revenue, much of it from people playing slot machines. One of these casinos is operated by the Chumash tribe in Santa Ynez. The Chumash Casino is one of the most profitable gambling operations in the state. In 2006, each of the then-152 enrolled tribal members received $428,969 in annual casino profits.

In 2018, the casino and resort attracted an average 7,900 visitors a day. It operates 24 hours a day, 7 days a week. There is a 328-room hotel, three restaurants, and a 1,400 seat-concert venue. There are 94,000 square feet dedicated to gambling: 2,300 slot machines, 50 table games, poker, and bingo. The resort employs nearly 1,700 people and generated an estimated economic sales impact in Santa Barbara County of more than $350 million, though the operation is exempt from federal, state, and local taxation.

The United States Takes California

Two and a half centuries after being first discovered by the Spanish explorer Juan Rodriquez Cabrillo, and more than thirty years after Spain began an effort at colonization, California remained isolated and ignored by most of the western world. It was too far away, too expensive to reach, and offered too little incentive to attract substantial attention by Europe or the United States. While those circumstances had not changed much by 1800, during the first half of the 19th century, the possession of California would fairly quickly pass between three countries: Spain, Mexico, and the United States. Another country, France, would play a significant, though completely unintentional, role in the handing off of the region. Throughout, the interests of the tens of thousands of California Natives Americans were ignored as seemingly unrelated events elsewhere eventually aligned themselves into one of the greatest gains in land and resources for the United States.

The Troubled Spanish Missions

In 1800, Spain had established eighteen missions in Alta California in thirty-one years. But their overall status was not what the home government had hoped for. Spain's plan to integrate the Native tribes into their realm had encountered serious problems. The Franciscan Friars saw the Natives as inferior beings who needed to be "saved" by becoming, more or less, Spanish. Once baptized, these "neophytes" (new believers) were to adopt to Catholicism & speak Spanish. They were to cleave to the culture of Spain, while leaving behind nearly everything from their own past. They were also to become the primary source of labor in the missions, even if by force. Daily life for the mission Indians was routinized. Activities, including waking, eating, and and sleeping, were marked by the ringing of bells. Natives spent their days with their time divided by working at a variety of jobs (for which they were not paid), prayer, attending religious services, and social activities.

Unsurprisingly, many of them resisted. Mission records reveal there was considerable instability and worse. At any given time, an estimated 10 percent of mission natives were considered runaways. Men and resources had to be allocated in efforts to retrieve these recalcitrant, who were likely top be punished with beatings, whippings, or denial of food. Sometimes logs were tied to the leg of the Natives so they could work but not leave.

Despite prohibitions on speaking in Native tongues, or practicing traditional religions, both were done. The records note Native complaints regarding food shortages, health problems, working conditions, and the punishments meted out by particular Spaniards. In some cases, these complaints became violent and deadly. Perhaps more distressing were the incidents of native infanticide & suicide. They were plain indications of the sorrow and hopeless that had burrowed into the minds and hearts of the Natives. Clearly, the mission system was exacting a vicious toll as it destroyed much of the indigenous culture and turned large portions of tribes into an exploited and degraded laboring people.

Apart from these serious problems, the mission system had other persistent difficulties. There was the geographical separation. California was far from the growing United States whose population in 1800 had passed five million. It would be another a quarter of a century before the first American came on foot overland into the region. Of course, it was even further from the European markets and its 150 million people. The only route was by sea, a voyage of six months or more. Trade was dismal. Between 1769 and 1824 an average of fewer than three ships a year came to California. There were two major reasons for this pathetic traffic. First, Spain's government is partly to blame as it acted to control trade by limiting it to Spanish ships. Second, the missions had little anyone wanted, and certainly nothing that could not be gotten elsewhere and likely for less cost. Gold had yet to be discovered in California and there was no transformative product, such as tobacco had been for the English colonies on the eastern side of the continent.

In looking back to 1800, one can see the signs of failure for the missions decades before their final collapse. In the next few years a string of events would begin which, by their conclusion, saw Spain left out of California entirely.

1803–1808

In 1802, James Monroe and Robert Livingstone traveled to Paris to see if they could purchase New Orleans from France. The city controlled access to the Mississippi River and was an important agricultural port. Monroe and Livingstone represented President Thomas Jefferson, who like many Americans, had been upset in 1795 after Spain reneged on a treaty with the United States and prohibited U.S. ships from stopping in New Orleans. Although Spain reversed course in 1801, it had been learned that France had taken possession of the city from Spain the year before. Jefferson hoped that to a successful acquisition would allay the fears of another port embargo and would spur the western development of the United States.

To the president's surprise, the negotiations between the two countries led France to offer to sell all of Louisiana—its entire North American possessions—a vast area running from New Orleans to near the Canadian border. The French ruler, Napoleon Bonaparte, had his focus on empire-building in Europe. He did not need tensions with the United States, but he did need money to fund his massive military ambitions. The greatest real estate deal in history soon took shape. It was so large Jefferson debated whether he had the political authority to agree to the deal.

In overcoming his own doubts, as well as a variety of skeptics and critics, the president agreed to these terms: the United States' compensation to France totaled $15 million for 820,000 square miles, or 524 million acres of land—a paltry 2.8 cents per acre. The price was incredibly cheap and was, arguably, the greatest land sale in U.S. history. And accomplished with the stroke of a pen, not the firing of guns. By comparison, the U.S. Land Act of 1796 (and 1804) set the sale of public land to farmers at a minimum of $2 per acre. The Louisiana Purchase doubled the physical size of the United States and the country, at least on paper, became hundreds of miles closer to California. Straightaway American settlers moved into the new lands. In 1804 Congress established a territorial government. Eight years later, Louisiana became the 18th state in the Union, and the first one to come from the Purchase. Eventually, the land Napoleon did not want would become all or part of fifteen U.S. states.

Napoleon's second inadvertent contribution to the fate of California was more direct. While he used all his Louisiana Purchase money to mount a war against Great Britain, in 1808, he also acted against Spain, an ally to that point. Early in the year, under the pretext of subduing Portugal, French troops were sent into Spain where they seized key locations. Spain's king, Charles IV. was forced to abdicate. Napoleon soon replaced him with his brother, Joseph Bonaparte. This was an intolerable situation for many Spaniards. Thus, began six years of bloody guerrilla ("little war") fighting between Spanish rebels and the French Army. Violence raged across the country. A cycle of back-and-forth brutality set in. Attacks by Spanish civilians on French soldiers were met with wholesale massacres of hundreds of noncombatants. The future of the royal family was undetermined. This much was certain; Spain had no time to tend to its far western American colonies. And than Mexico took action.

The Mexican War for Independence

Spain had a presence in Mexico since it conquered the Aztec empire in 1521. In 1810, Miguel de Hildalgo y Costilla, a Mexican priest with a strong egalitarian streak, saw Spain's immense troubles with France, formally known as the Peninsular War, as an opportunity to overthrow Spain's long-enduring oppressive colonial government. With other conspirators, he ignited the Mexican War for Independence. It began as a peasant's rebellion; it would end as a guerrilla insurgency. Hildalgo did not live to see much of it. Although he lacked any real skills as a general, for a time he led a ragtag force to capture several cities. It did not last. He was captured and executed in 1811 by Spanish authorities who had his body mutilated as a warning to other rebels. Despite this loss and atrocity, there were others who assumed leadership and the conflict became a protracted series of fights from town to town between Mexican irregulars and Royal Spanish troops. As in the American Revolution, the revolutionaries did not have to win as many battles as much as they needed simply to survive, persist, and inflict damage in the hope of wearing down the opposition.

Even with end French rule in 1813, and the restoration of King Ferdinand VII to the Spanish throne, the rebel's efforts at independence in Mexicowere able to continue. The Spanish government was in disarray. It was nearly broke, still faced foreign interference, and was very divided politically. In 1820, a civil war erupted in Spain between Monarchists who supported the royal government, and Liberals who wanted to implement a constitutional government. Again, the fate of the government was unclear (in 1823 the Monarchists prevailed.) It was the final blow to Spain's effort to keep Mexico under colonial control. By the time the war ended in 1821, at least 23,000 people had been killed (in the absence of a systematic recordkeeping, it is impossible to accurately calculate the true count. A few estimates place the deaths as high as 10 percent of the population.) The Treaty of Cordoba established Mexico as an independent empire that covered more than a third of the North American continent. It gave Mexico's 5.5 million citizens, not only their first chance at greater autonomy, but also control of California.

Note: Spain made one last attempt to reclaim Mexico. In 1829, an expedition of Spanish troops was launched from Cuba and landed in the southeastern port city of Tampico. Within weeks they were forced to surrender to Mexican forces under the command of General Santa Anna. Moreover, the Mexican government expelled thousands of Spaniards as punishment.

Mexico's Uneasy Hold on California

Mexico got its independence but not peace. Instability continued for years as factions fought for control of the country. Its struggle to shed its deep roots of the Spanish colonial system and form a unified federal nation would be long and turbulent. By 1848, it endured forty changes of government, and average of one every eight months. And as had been Spain's situation during the Peninsular Wars, in its first decade of independence, Mexico did not have the ability focus much attention on the northern region of its country. The capital of Alta California, Monterey, was more than 2,100 miles from Mexico City and travel between the two cities was took weeks by ship, months by land.

During its control, Spain had viewed the California region of New Spain as a buffer between European (and the United States) encroachments to Spain's valuable holdings in central Mexico. Now with Mexico in control, it faced much larger problems in this vast and sparsely populated region. In 1821, there were only about 3,200 Mexicans living there. California's twenty-one missions were being run by 142 priests, roughly 150 soldiers, and about 53,600 Natives. Not surprisingly, the region produced little or no tax revenue. It had been seven years since the soldiers and priests had been paid. Each mission was more like its own inward-looking community and lacked a broader sense of connection with the new Mexican authority. With the onset of independence, there were calls for privatization of the missions and a break-up of their vast land-holdings. This secularization would begin in 1834 and eventually more than 500 land grants would be established out of mission properties.

Mexico was particularly concerned about U.S. expansion into Texas. Although the U.S. had renounced any claim to Texas with the 1819 Adams-Onís Treaty, some Americans considered it (wrongly) to be a part of the Louisiana Purchase and, by extension, a part of the United States. Compounding this situation was that both and Mexico had offered tax exemptions and low-priced land in an effort to attract foreign immigrants into Texas. As a result, large numbers of U.S. citizens came to Texas, many with slaves. By the 1820s Americans in Texas outnumbered Mexicans two to one.

Efforts by Mexico to weaken the American influence (prohibitions on more Americans from entering Texas, abolishing slavery, and requiring Mexican states send colonists to the region), largely failed and Americans continued to move in. By the middle of the 1830s, the 30,000 Americans in Texas outnumbered Mexicans four to one. Then, in 1835, Texas declared itself a nation, independent from Mexico. Although it never accepted this proclamation, Mexico was unable to reclaim the region by military force. In Mexico City, concern rose that the United States would annex Texas. A decade later, in 1845, those fears were realized when Texas voted to allow annexation to happen. By the end of the year, it became the 28th state to join the Union. Soon after, President James Polk, an ardent advocate of expansion, attempted to buy California and New Mexico and offered $25 million to Mexico.

Polk's enthusiasm for enlarging his country was a view widely shared by many Americans. The same year he proposed to purchase California, John O'Sullivan, editor of the New York newspaper, *The Morning Post,* had published what would become one of the most repeated pronouncements of American exceptionalism. He wrote, "(It is) . . . our manifest destiny to over spread and to possess the whole of the continent which Providence has given us for the development of the great experiment of liberty." The ethnocentric and rather self-serving premise of O'Sullivan's claim that the United States was on a mission and had a destiny to fulfill, dove-tailed perfectly with the American notion that the west's tremendous natural resources would be harnessed and utilized to their full capacity only by the United States. Nevertheless, Polk's offer for California and New Mexico was rejected by Mexico, still very much upset by the loss of Texas.

The Mexican War

Rebuffed at the bargaining table, the aggressive Polk shifted toward military action to get what he wanted. In early 1846, he massed 4,000 soldiers at the Rio Grande. In May, the president prepared to ask Congress for a declaration of war against Mexico on the basis of some unpaid debt and Mexico's refusal to sell its northern lands. Mexican soldiers saved him the trouble by attacking first, killing eleven American troops in a skirmish on the land between the Nueces River and the Rio Grande.

The war lasted sixteen months and the United States dominated most of it. The main American strategy was to take control of land and important cities. U.S. troops, led by General Zachary Taylor, drove west to Monterrey, which it captured in September 1846, and southward toward Mexico's capital. Within a year, the U.S. controlled both the northwest and northeast regions of Mexico. In the first month of the war, in California, where opinion on the war ran strongly in its favor, American settlers were able to seize a garrison in Sonoma, in the Sacramento River Valley, without firing a shot. They declared themselves free from Mexico and raised a homemade flag emblazoned with a single star, a grizzly bear, and the words "California Republic." The Bear Flag Revolt, as it came to be known, was short-lived; within a month the "Republic" disbanded and threw its support toward the U.S. in waging war.

In the spring of 1847, Commanding General Winfield Scott took the important port city of Veracruz, located on the Bay of Campeche in the Gulf of Mexico, after a two-week siege. Now with this vital supply base in hand, just 260 miles from Mexico City, he moved west and followed the route Hernando Cortes had taken centuries earlier when he defeated the Aztecs at Tenochtitlan. By September, U.S. soldiers had fought their way to the outskirts of Mexico City. Scott anticipated that the assault on the city would require house-to-house conflict and a siege of the civilian population. Their capital surrounded, Mexican leaders concluded the war was lost. Any further fighting would simply inflict more death and destruction on their people to no purpose. A peace delegation of Mexican officials met with Scott and surrendered unconditionally. U.S. troops marched triumphantly into the city, victory in hand.

The New United States

The Treaty of Guadalupe Hidalgo that concluded the Mexican War dramatically reshaped both nations. Signed in February 1848, the treaty reflected the terms dictated by the victorious Americans. Mexico was forced to cede 525,000 square miles, or 336 million acres of land. Initially, the lands included Baja California, but that claim was later dropped. For what later became all or part of seven states, the United States paid $15 million, or 4.4 cents per acre. Mexico lost 55 percent of its country. It would be a bitter blow. Mexico would remain an under-developed country well into the 20th century while the United States emerged as a world power. The humiliation of having to submit to U.S. aggression and the treaty would forever mark Mexico's self-image and relationship with it northern neighbor. In some ways, it did bolster Mexican nationalism among those who adopted a "never again" attitude and who acted to reform and strengthen it political institutions.

As far as California was concerned, Spain was out, Mexico was out, the United States in. Although the treaty had included a provision that allowed U.S. citizenship to Mexicans and Natives who were living in California in 1848, this would not happen until the 1930s. Both groups were universally considered to be foreigners by white American settlers. The new California government enshrined this racist view into law by limiting all political power, including voting rights, to white, male U.S. citizens. As a result, both Mexican-Americans and Natives became a disenfranchised and poverty-stricken minority in a place they had each once controlled.

But California is now the far west of the United States and just as hard as ever to get to. Overland travel had begun in 1841, but the six-month journey, fraught with hardships and dangers, had only been accepted by a only a few thousand hardy persons each year. And than the region so long neglected would suddenly transform itself and once more. In an amazing coincidence of timing, nine days before Mexico signed away California, James Marshall accidently discovered placer gold while working in the American River. Although broad public awareness of his discovery was months away, it is worth speculating how the history of Mexico and the United States might have been altered had the news reached them sooner. This much is certain; the subsequent placer and hard-rock mining that took place in the next few years revealed that Mexico had lost to the United States an *El Dorado* of gold, copper, and silver.

The California Gold Rush

During the last Ice Age 10,000-15,000 years ago, in the Sierra Nevada mountain range (and the Rockies) the granite and metamorphic rocks were broken apart, allowing metallic minerals to push into the faults left behind. In some areas, the sand and gravel beds of rivers contained large quantities of valuable minerals. In a 130-mile belt in the foothill deposits of gold, silver, silica, zinc, lead, and copper were pushed up through cracks and fissures close to the surface of the earth. Erosion loosened the minerals where they settled in river beds, some mere inches from the surface. When found, these placer deposits could be mined with relative ease. Or so it seemed.

The Desirability of Gold

Explaining just why people covet gold is somewhat difficult as human values are subjective. But because it is desired, it is regarded as precious. There is no question people have sought to possess this metal throughout human civilization. There is evidence that gold was mined up to 6,000 years ago. The color of gold, lustrous deep yellow or yellow-brown, is no doubt a factor in its perceived attractiveness. One of its most notable features, certainly one that has added to its allure, is that it is very rare. Gold is found throughout nature, even in the oceans, but it is elusive. It makes up only five ten-millionths (.0000005) of the outer layer of the Earth. A one-ounce nugget of gold is more uncommon then a five-carat diamond. And despite being pursued by humans for several millennia, it is believed that most of the gold which exists on earth, perhaps 75 percent, is still in the ground.

As a metal, it has certain properties that gives it a respected cachet. Of the 118 elements in the periodic table, Au, or gold, has been the one globally accepted as a monetary object. And that has been the case for thousands of years. It lends itself to that purpose as it is easy to carry, store, and divide. Unlike iron or silver, it does not rust, tarnish, or decay. Gold coins have been recovered after being submerged in salt water for hundreds of years looking brand new.

Gold is heavy, twice as heavy as lead. It is durable but also quite malleable. It can be hammered into sheets transparent enough that light can shine through. It is also very ductile, meaning it can be shaped into wire. A single ounce of gold can be drawn out into a fine wire more than forty miles long. Delicate "gold leaf" has long been used for jewelry and ornamentation of much less costly materials. The melting point for gold is 1945° Fahrenheit. As comparison, the melting point for platinum, which is also harder to extract, is 3214° Fahrenheit. Gold will usually be alloyed with other metals. This is done to increase the hardness of the metal and decrease the cost. Pure gold is twenty-four karats (999 parts per thousand). Eighteen karat gold (75 percent pure) has six parts metal; fourteen karat gold (58 percent pure) has ten parts metal, and so on. In sum, all factors considered, gold has been the most preferred of the possible choices of elements.

The California gold rush is the *event of California's history. There is no denying it has had a certain historical panache. Where the Franciscan priests in the Spanish missions were sedate and pious, the miners (called "forty-niners") who rushed to the California gold fields were wild and swashbuckling. Part of the mystique of the rush is how it happened. Writers had imagined the gold and explorers had searched for it, but when it was finally, actually found, the discovery was a complete accident. But in an unhappy twist of fate many of the discoverers, those who were in the best position to benefit from the gold, did not. For some, the discovery would be their ruin.*

Key Figures in the Discovery

(Johann) John Sutter (1803–1880)

A native of Switzerland, he came to New York in 1834. He left behind in Europe a large number of debts, a warrant for his arrest, a wife and four children (he would send for his family in 1850). For the next several years, he spent time in Missouri, New Mexico, Oregon, Hawaii, and Alaska, before arriving in California in 1839. He became a Mexican citizen so he could acquire land. He asked for and received from the Mexican governor of California, Juan Bautista Alvarado, the rights to a large tract in the Sacramento Valley. He was tentatively granted 48,000 acres, or about 76 square miles. Sutter named it New Helvetia, Latin for Switzerland. He built a fort and armed it with cannons he bought from Russian fur traders.

As a protected place not far from the western foothills of the Sierras, Sutter's fort would soon become a natural destination for American settlers coming into

California and a general rendezvous for just about everyone else. Sutter had many business interests. His fort was more of a trading post. Nearby he raised cattle and planted crops. Part of the development of his budding domain required more lumber then he could contract and he decided he needed a sawmill. After choosing a site on the south fork of the American River (where modern-day Coloma is), Sutter hired James Marshall to oversee its construction.

James Marshall (1810–1885)

A bachelor from New Jersey, Marshall had learned the carpentry trade from his father. In his twenties he had started out west, living for periods in Ohio, Missouri, and Oregon. In 1845, he moved to California where he tried and failed to ranch in the Sacramento Valley. In 1848, now working for Sutter, he was in charge of building a sawmill 45-miles from Sutter's fort. He had a work crew of thirteen men. They were all Mormons, part of a larger contingent of several hundred who had come from Salt Lake City to fight in the Mexican War. During their return back to Utah, they had stopped at Sutter's Fort and eighty of them had agreed to stay and work for Sutter in exchange for a payment in horses and cattle.

Peter L. Wimmer (1810-1892) and Elizabeth (Jennie) Wimmer (1822–1885)

In addition to the Mormons, Sutter also employed Maidu Indians whose native home was between the American and Feather Rivers. Sutter employed Peter to oversee a crew of them to do the initial digging needed at the sawmill site. Peter's wife, Elizabeth was employed as a cook and laundress. The Wimmers had come to Sutter's Fort by wagon on the overland trail, arriving in November 1846, just days before the Donner Party became trapped in the Sierras.

Sam Brannan (1819–1889)

Originally from Maine, Brannan moved to Ohio in his teens. After his sister married a Mormon missionary, Brannan converted to Mormonism and helped build a temple. He also learned the printing trade. He was later sent to New York City to publish church literature in *The New York Messenger.* There he made valuable business contacts which he used to make himself well off by the time he was twenty-five. In 1844, anti-Mormonism led to the murder of Joseph Smith, the church's founder, in Carthage, Illinois. Brannan, now a church Elder, and more than 200 other Mormons sailed around Cape Horn, arriving in Yerba Buena (San Francisco) in the summer of 1846. Brannan had brought a printing press with him and was soon publishing *The California Star,* the second newspaper in San Francisco. An ambitious and talented entrepreneur, by 1847 Brannan had opened a hotel, a flour-mill, and several general stores, including one next to Sutter's Fort.

James K. Polk 1795–1849)

The eleventh president of the United States. Born in North Carolina, Polk lived his adult life in Tennessee and he represented that state. He was an ardent expansionist and a firm believer in Manifest Destiny, the idea the United States had a divine right, even an obligation, to spread into the western frontier. He had supported fellow Tennessean, Andrew Jackson, the seventh president who also considered the physical spread of the United States essential to its future. Polk's ability to bring in new land to the nation was spectacular, and would prove to be second only to Thomas Jefferson in terms of size. In his own single term, Polk added over 800,000 square miles to the nation, as much land as the Louisiana Purchase. His administration was able to negotiate an agreement with England that gave the United States both Washington and Oregon. When Polk failed to entice Mexico to sell Texas, he provoked the Mexican War (1846-1848), which ended with the United States gaining 525,000 square miles of land, including California.

The Find

It is a familiar story. On January 24, 1848, James Marshall was on the American River, in charge of building a sawmill for his employer, John Sutter. With the mill nearly complete, Marshall was making his regular daily inspection when he caught sight of something gleaming in a water-filled ditch where the Maidu workers had recently been digging. He scooped it up and saw he had a pebble-sized nugget that was gold in color. There were smaller flakes as well. Marshall was excited but unsure if it was actual gold or iron pyrite—fool's gold, so named because it resembles gold as it is shiny and can be in shades of yellow.

Marshall showed his find to the other mill workers. No one was sure if it was gold so they subjected it to a series of primitive tests. The nugget was compared visually to a gold coin someone had in their possession. Marshall knew that real gold was malleable so he bit it. He pounded it with a hammer. It flattened out but did not shatter or break apart. Still, there were questions raised about its luster. Marshall took it to Peter Wimmer who, in turn, showed it to his wife, Elizabeth. She may well have been the only person there who had actually seen gold in its natural condition. She had lived in Georgia where there was mining and her father had been a gold prospector. She knew of another test. Gold did not tarnish or corrode. She placed the nugget in a kettle of soap and cooked it overnight. Soap contains potassium carbonate that produces a caustic alkaline (high pH) solution. The next morning, the piece was examined. It was not corroded and was as bright as it had been the previous day. Although the tests were not definitive, the nugget had passed all of them and Marshall was convinced he had found real gold.

Marshall and some of his workers collected additional gold flakes and dust and then he traveled from the sawmill site to Sutter's Fort, arriving in a driving rainstorm. Sutter, startled to see his carpenter away from his job, was even more surprised after Marshall requested that the office door be locked. After Marshall showed Sutter the nugget, the two men spent the next several hours again trying to determine if the gold was indeed genuine. They read about gold in Sutter's *American Encyclopedia.* They preformed numerous experiments, including once again hitting it with a hammer. They poured nitric acid on it to see if it would tarnish. It did not. They weighed it against silver three times. They placed a set of scales in a bucket of water to see if the nugget had a greater specific gravity and sank to the bottom. It did. Finally, Sutter, as had Marshall, concluded it was a nearly pure lump of gold.

Sutter's initial thought was to keep the discovery quiet. A small find of gold was not necessarily a harbinger that more discoveries would follow. Besides, he was building an agricultural and mercantile business and he did not want to lose his labor force. He rode with Marshall back to the sawmill the next day and asked the workers to keep the knowledge of the gold a secret. He allowed that they could prospect on Sunday, their day off, should they feel the urge. For a short time, things were fairly quiet. But some events cannot be kept unmentioned for very long, and this was one of them. Elizabeth told a teamster named Jacob Wittner about the find and when the man expressed doubt, she showed him the gold. Wittner drove his wagon on to Sutter's Fort and told others what he had been shown. By spring, the news had reached San Francisco.

The Rush is Created

Why did the gold rush not begin in earnest in 1848? Marshall's find was in January, after all. As it turned out, "gold fever" needed some promotion and crafty advertising. At first, news of the discovery at Sutter's mill was treated as yet another nonsense story that had long been part of the lore of California. As recently as 1842, claims had been made of gold fields in the mountains around Los Angeles but little had come of it. San Francisco's two newspapers, *The Californian* and *The California Star* both treated the story without any significance.

However, the *Star's* publisher, Sam Brannan, was much more interested than he allowed in his newspaper. As a Mormon Elder, Brannan had collected tithes that were supposed to be sent to the Mormon Church in Salt Lake City. But now

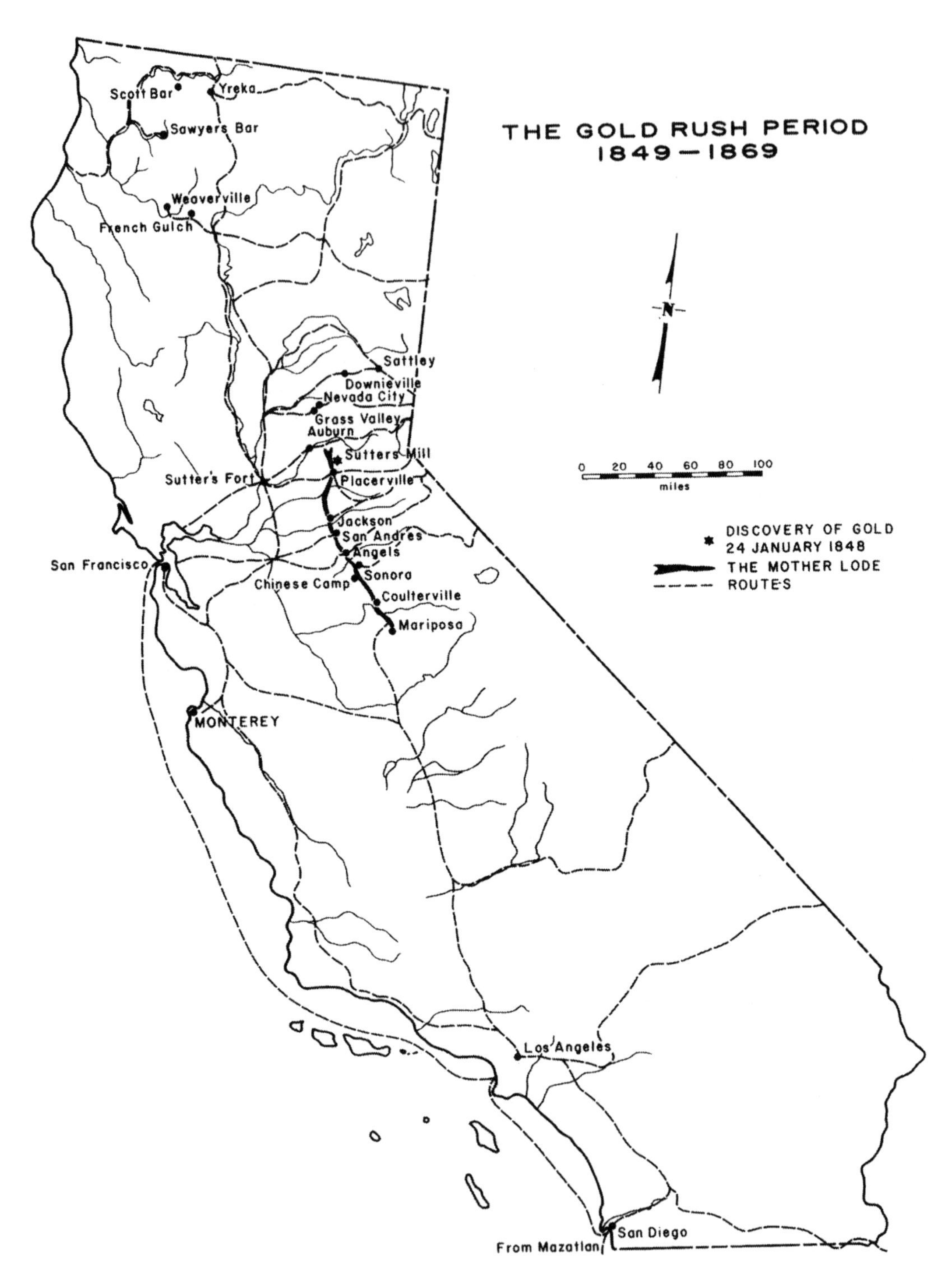

From Historical Atlas of California by Warren A. Beck and Ynez D. Haase, 1974. Reprinted by permission of University of Oklahoma Press.

he envisioned other uses for the money. He spent it in preparation for a surge in mining that he planned on creating. He began to buy and hoard any item a likely gold prospector would need: picks, shovels, pans, clothing, hats, cookware, and foodstuffs. These items he planned to sell at ten to fifteen times their cost. He even gained control of the landings used by steamboats coming to Sacramento. His preparations completed, in May 1848, Brannan returned to San Francisco. He brought with him a small bottle of gold dust. There had already been prospecting since January The gold had come from Sutter's Mormon employees who used it to make purchases at Brannon's store at the fort. Standing on a corner at Portsmouth Square, Brannan shouted, "Gold! Gold! Gold from the American River!" He walked the streets, waved his hat, and kept repeating his line, showing the curious the shiny specks in his bottle.

Within two weeks of Brannan's appearance and "one-man parade," nearly all of the male population of San Francisco was heading towards the rivers and mountains near Sutter's mill. They were quickly joined by scores of sailors and soldiers who, upon taking in the frenzied activity of the civilians, deserted their positions in San Francisco's port and elsewhere. In all it only added up to a few hundred men and it was very local, but the rush had a start. What it needed now was national attention. It is doubtful even Brannan could imagine what was soon to happen.

On December 5, 1848, President James K. Polk gave the annual State of the Union Address to a joint session of Congress. It was a long speech, 21,300 words in all. The most, perhaps only, well-quoted line was this: "*The accounts of the abundance of gold in that territory are of such an extraordinary character as would scarcely command belief were they not corroborated by the authentic reports of officers in the public service who have visited the mineral district and derived the facts which they detail from personal observation.*" If he said nothing else, this single sentence made Polk a major factor in the origins of the California gold rush. His stature as chief executive, coupled with the importance of what was always a widely- reported address, was enough to convince thousands of men that stories and rumors coming out of California about gold strikes were this time based in fact, not fable.

It is worth noting that Polk said much more on the subject in his address. Before he mentioned the gold, he offered a detailed accounting of the acreage of the various lands the nation had recently gained, primarily through the Mexican War. The president had received criticism for his aggressive actions against Mexico, and for the costs of both the war, and the terms of the treaty that had followed it. California's gold gave him a chance to justify his actions, albeit after the fact, and, perhaps to reduce the financial price tag as well.

Therefore, Polk did not just offer the one sentence regarding verified accounts of an abundance of gold. Several paragraphs of his speech were devoted to the subject. He stated there were 4,000 men already in the gold fields and that more were coming. He said the "supply is very large and that gold is found at various places in an extensive district of country." Polk noted that quicksilver (mercury) was also being extracted in a mine "believed to be among the most productive in the world." He pointed out the high prices heedlessly being paid for supplies, the high wages being paid labor, and the fact that sailors could only be kept from abandoning their ships by receiving "a large increase of pay."

Like Brannan, Polk shrewdly promoted the gold rush but for different purposes. Brannan coveted personal wealth. The president may have wanted personal political glory, but the financial gain was to be the nations'. He called for the building of a U.S. mint in California. He said it would attract bullion from Central and South America that currently went to Great Britain where it was coined and used in the English banking system. Polk envisioned California gold enriching American banks and cities. The gold would develop new trade in China and other parts of Asia. It would create new markets for American businesses around the country. From the American perspective, it was quite a thrilling prospect. Congress would agree with Polk and in 1852 approved a new U.S. Mint in San Francisco. It opened two years later and soon was converting millions of dollars of gold into coins.

Polk's State of the Union Address gave political gravitas to the beginning of the gold rush. And it offered another motive as well. One could conclude from the president's words that the pursuit of gold was not simply a selfish desire for individual riches. It was an act of patriotism that would strengthen and benefit the institutions of the nation and, by extension, all Americans. And his words had the effect he sought. In the month following the speech, more than 3,000 people, nearly all men, sailed away from ports on the eastern shores of the country, bound for California. By the end of the year, that number would balloon to 40,000. Others, an estimated 30,000, decided to prepare for the journey on the overland trail in the coming spring when the earth was firm enough and the grass tall enough for the livestock to begin their 2,000-mile trip. However, Polk was dead before most of the people he inspired had arrived in the gold fields. He left office in March 1849, and within a few months contracted cholera. He died June 15, 1849, at the age of fifty-three.

Getting to El Dorado

There were three primary routes to get to California's gold country, but there was no easy way. And one has to remember the "rush" was often more in a miner's heart and head. His feet moved as slow as ever. For most forty-niners, a trip to California would take months.

There was the land route. Since 1841, when the Bidwell-Bartleson party emigrated to Oregon and California, there was an established overland trail that could be travelled by wagon, horseback, or foot. The well-reported disaster of the Donner party in 1846-1847 had resulted in a sharp drop-off in the number of people who took the trail. Now, thousands began to push across to the West. More than nine out of every ten persons were male. Few traveled alone. It was too expensive and far too risky. Almost no one had been to California and many had never been on the frontier. Most joined informal wagon trains, or signed on as passengers with the few companies that began offering service. While some made it in a relatively quick eight to twelve weeks, more often a journey took between four and six months.

Many people feared encounters with natives, although the fact is that attacks were rare. The much greater threat was Asiatic cholera, which was contracted by eating food or drinking water that was contaminated with the bacteria. It was quick and deadly; a victim could die in less than a day. The afflicted suffered diarrhea, cramps, and vomiting, all of which led to severe dehydration. Their faces turned blue, their skin crinkled and cracked, and their fingers and toes went cold. The incubation period was between one to three days with no outward symptoms. Thus it was all too easy to be in close contact with someone who looked healthy but was already infected. The problem was compounded because no one knew what caused the sickness. People did blame food and water, but they also suspected alcohol, the night air, limestone in the soil, fate—anything and everything. In actuality, the disease thrived on the human filth that was common on the trail. There were plenty of travelers but no sewer systems. The deadly organism was spread by feces, flies, contaminated watering holes, and the emigrants themselves as they moved from camp to camp. The Oregon Trail became marked with hundreds of crosses bearing a name and the word "cholera."

Thus, many people chose to bypass the land route in favor of going by ship. It was more expensive to travel by ship, between $300 and $1,000. Depending on one's occupation, the cost to California could be equal to one or two, or even three year's income. In 1849, the traditional sea route to California took one down around the tip of South America and through Drake's Passage around Cape Horn. This was a well-known and charted course but it was famous for the appearance of icebergs, mammoth waves, and great winds. It also had the obvious drawback of being very long. It was approximately 14,000 nautical miles (one nautical mile is 2,025 yards compared to 1,760 yards in one land mile) between New York harbor and San

Francisco Bay. A fast trip was considered to be five months. A more typical voyage took six months. In that much time, any trip could be a harrowing experience fraught with storms and disease. Even the best of trips would include bad food, seasickness, and a lot of boredom.

Given the drawbacks of the overland trail and the Cape Horn route, it is not surprising that a third route soon attracted men anxious to get to the gold fields. In 1849, 6,000 of them took another sea route that cut off thousands of miles and weeks of time. They sailed south to the town of Chagres on the Atlantic side of the Isthmus of Panama. From there, one had to cross just fifty miles of mountainous jungle before reaching the Pacific side and the port town of Panama City. From there, one would board another ship and sail to San Francisco. By taking this route, a traveler reduced the distance at sea by 9,000 nautical miles. With good fortune, one could usually complete the trip in about two months.

However, there were major problems. One could not bypass disease. The wet and humid jungles of Panama were breeding grounds for the mosquitoes that carried the malaria parasite and yellow fever virus, two diseases that were as devastating as cholera. And again, people did not know the source of the diseases, nor how to treat its victims, or adequately shield the healthy from the sick.

Rapid passage through Panama would be the best preventive to illness but often that was not possible. The fact was the unexpected swarm of forty-niners quickly exceeded the capacity of available ships to convey them. There were many more and larger vessels on the Atlantic side than on the Pacific side. As a result, a bottleneck quickly emerged. If one was unlucky or lacked enough money to bribe a ship captain, he could become trapped. Frustrated men found themselves stuck in Panama City for weeks, or even months, trying to complete the last leg of the journey. Waiting lists for a ship on the Pacific side were as long as two thousand names. And all the while, more people kept arriving from the Atlantic side.

The congestion was also due to the fact that, despite what it looked like on a map, a direct voyage north from Panama City to San Francisco in a sailing ship was not possible. The prevailing winds and ocean currents required ships to begin the trip by sailing straight west out to sea away from the continent until the vessel was as far out as the longitude of the Hawaiian Islands. Only then could they turn northeast and sail toward San Francisco. Not surprisingly, the combination of limited supply and overwhelming demand dramatically pushed up ticket prices for the Pacific side ships. Prices rose more than 50 percent in the first year of the rush and the cheapest steerage accommodation cost $150, easily six months income to a working man.

In the years that followed, despite the hardships and deadly risks, all three routes were used by many thousands. Another 24,000 people crossed north of Panama in Nicaragua, where all but twelve miles of the isthmus could be traveled by boat across Lake Nicaragua. But Panama took the lion's share of everything. Backed by capital from New York investors, in 1855 a rail track had been laid across most of Panama and for a $25 ticket one could go from the Atlantic to the Pacific in three hours. By 1859, 196,000 people had done so. Heading past them going east would be $300 million in gold bullion. The train would also haul 100,000 bags of mail. The Panama Railroad was only fifty miles long, but it made $6 million in profit during this period. At one point, it had the highest priced stock on the New York Exchange.

The Fates of the Discoverers

As it has been noted, President Polk did not live to learn much beyond the initial reports of the first gold find. He holds the dubious record for shortest post-presidency life-103 days.

As for the others, Peter and Elizabeth Wimmer never struck it rich in the rush. Peter did prospect but soon gave up. The couple moved up and down California, eventually settling in Valley Center, in San Diego County, where they farmed on 165 acres. Elizabeth died at the age of sixty-three. Peter moved again and lived another seven years before dying in San Luis Obispo County in 1892.

For John Sutter, the discovery of gold would prove to be a personal disaster. His decade of work on his land grant was soon all for nothing. Foremost, he lost his workers to the gold fields, including many of the Maidu natives. He was unable to harvest more than a fraction of his crops, most of which rotted in the fields. His trading post lost its blacksmith, its wheelwright, its cooper, and most everyone else. He had to give it up. Briefly, he partnered with Peter Wimmer in some prospecting but that only cost him more money. He and his family moved north to his Hock Farm, which he had planned to use in his retirement. In the next years, he also lost the farm to squatters who simply took over much of the property. Sutter spent years in court pursuing compensation for his losses from the State Legislature. In 1865, he lost his house to a deliberately set fire. The next year Sutter traveled to Washington D.C. where he petitioned Congress, asking $50,000 in compensation for all the losses at the hands of gold miners. In 1866, he wrote his account of the origin of the rush. In 1871, he settled in Lititz, Pennsylvania. In 1880, he died of a heart attack in a Washington hotel, never having received any money from Congress. He was buried in Lititz.

James Marshall became a tragic celebrity. In most accounts of the origins of the rush, he was depicted as the central figure in the discovery. He was hounded by miners who wanted him to show them how to strike it rich. He could not even do that for himself. His own partnership in a gold mine near the town of Kelsey in El Dorado County, was a bust and he nearly went bankrupt. His property was stolen and his cabin was burned. He became bitter and reclusive. For a period of the 1870s he received a $200-a month pension from the state legislature, in recognition of his contribution to California, but it lapsed in 1878 and Marshall was again destitute. He lived out his life in a small cabin in Kelsey growing vegetables in a small garden. After he died in 1885, his body was brought back to Coloma where it was buried on a hill overlooking the American River and the site of Sutter's sawmill. Five years later, a tall monument was built directly over his grave. On top was placed a tawny bronze statue of Marshall, with his arm and index finger extended, pointing down to the river to the spot where, for him, many of his troubles began.

In the 1850s, Sam Brannon turned himself into a land baron. He owned large sections of San Francisco and Sacramento. He bought land in Hawaii. In 1868, he purchased 160,000 acres in Los Angeles County. He became the major landholder in Calistoga in Napa, which he tried to develop as a resort. But bad investments, a bitter divorce, and a growing addiction to alcohol eventually led to his financial and personal ruin. Brannon died on May 14, 1889 in Escondido, California (San Diego County) at age seventy. He had no money to pay for a funeral and his body lay in a receiving vault for a year before being interred.

The Gold that Started It All

Much of the story of the beginning of the gold rush is straightforward. Still, there are disagreements on some details that set off this thunderous event in the history of the United States, let alone California. Gold rush enthusiasts differ on whether James Marshall was alone when he made the find, or if one or both of the Wimmers were with him. Most historical accounts seem in agreement, whoever was present, there was more than a single piece of gold found, though descriptions of the size of the larger nugget vary from as small as a pea to as large as a dime.

That more substantial nugget was given by Marshall to Elizabeth who kept it for years, allowing it to be publicly displayed from time to time. It is unclear when the "naming" of the nugget occurred. It does raise the question of whether Marshall was the one true discoverer and the nugget should, by all rights, bear his name. Or have the less-known Wimmers been slighted and they should share the historical stage with Marshall? As for the gold itself, today, it is kept in the permanent exhibition collection of the Bancroft Library in Berkeley. The nugget weighs about one-third of an ounce. At the time it was found, it had a value of $5.12, a few days earning for a farmer in those years.

Sutter turned the other gold from the initial discovery over to Army Captain Joseph Folsom in order to validate the gold claim for the federal government. The gold was taken to Washington by way of Panama and New Orleans and overland. In 1861, a flake was donated to the Smithsonian Institution, where it is kept today.

A First American Description of California During the Gold Rush

Aside from the Civil War, no 19th century event was more written about than the Gold Rush. Thousands of the tens of thousands of immigrants wrote letters home describing their experiences, the land, and the people on, what for most, was the greatest adventure of their lives. The enormous national interest in the events happening in such a far-off area drew dozens of professional writers to California, as well. One of the earliest these writers was Bayard Taylor. His 1850 accounts, published as El Dorado, *was a best seller that sold many thousands of copies and went through ten editions in thirty years. The title, literally translated from Spanish, means "the gilded one" and refers to the thirty-mile wide region in the western foothills of the Sierra Nevada where most of the elusive metal was found. Ironically, little of the book actually dealt with gold mining itself Taylor paid more attention to the informal society that the gold had created. He marveled at how men collaborated and dealt with problems in places that had no formal government and very little restraint. The book has been reissued and is in print today. It may well be the single most important publication of the rush. Not only does Taylor offer a first-hand account of California during its first year as a state in the midst of phenomenal change, but alsoß helped shape a depiction of the gold years that carries down to the present.*

Eldorado: Adventures in the Path of Empire, Bayard Taylor

Chapter 5: "The Coast of California"

"There is California!" as the cry next morning at sunrise. "Where?" "Off the starboard bow." I rose on my bunk in one of the deck staterooms, and looking out of the window, watched the purple mountains of the Peninsula, as they arose in the fresh, inspiring air. We were opposite its southern extremity, and I scanned the brown and sterile coast with a glass, searching for anything like vegetation. The whole country appeared to be a mass of nearly naked rock, nourishing only a few cacti and some stunted shrubs. At the extreme end of the Peninsula the valley of San Jose opens inland between two ranges of lofty granite mountains. Its beautiful green level, several miles in width, stretched back as far as the eye could reach. The town lies near the sea; it is noted for the siege sustained by Lieutenant Haywood and a small body of American troops during the war. Lying deep amid the most frightfully barren and rugged mountains I ever saw, the valley of San Jose, which is watered by a small river, might be made a paradise. The scenery around it corresponded strikingly with descriptions of Syria and Palestine. The bare, yellow crags glowed in the sun with dazzling intensity, and a chain of splintered peaks in the distance wore the softest shade of violet. In spite of the forbidding appearance of the coast, a more peculiar and interesting picture than it gave can hardly be found on the Pacific. Cape San Lucas, which we passed toward evening, is a bold bluff of native granite, broken into isolated rocks at its points, which present the appearance of three distinct and perfectly formed pyramids. The white, glistening rock is pierced at its base by hollow caverns and arches, some of which are fifteen or twenty feet high, giving glimpses of the ocean beyond. The structure of this cape is very similar to that of the Needles of the Isle of Wight.

On the 12th of August we passed the island of Santa Marguerita, lying across the mouth of a bay, the upper extremity of which is called Point San Lazaro. . . The coast, as far as I could see with a good glass, presented an unbroken level of glaring white sand, which must extend inland for fifty or sixty miles, since, under the clearest of skies, no sign of rock or distant peak was visible. The appearance of the whole Peninsula, in passing—the alternations of bleak mountains, blooming plain, and wide salt desert—the rumors of vast mineral wealth in its unknown interior and the general want of intelligence in relations to it—conspire to excite in me a strong wish to transverse it from end to end.

Chapter 6: "First Impressions of San Francisco"

Thus, braced against the fog and raw temperature, we sallied out for a night-view of San Francisco, then even more peculiar than its daylight look. Business was over about the usual hour, and then the harvest-time of gamblers commenced. Every "hell" in the place, and I did not pretend to number them, was crowded, and immense sums were staked at the monte and faro tables (card games). A boy of fifteen, in one place, won about $500, which he coolly pocketed and carried off. One of the gang we brought in the Panama won $1,500 in the course of the evening, and another lost $2,400. A fortunate miner made himself conspicuous by betting large piles of ounces on a single throw. His last stake of a hundred ounces was lost, and I saw him the following morning dashing through the streets, trying to break his own neck of that of the magnificent garanon (stallion) he bestrode.

Walking through the town the next day, I was quite amazed to find a dozen persons busily employed in the street before the United States Hotel, digging up the earth with knives and crumbling it in their hands. They were actual gold-hunters, who obtained in this way about $5 a day. After blowing the fine dirt carefully in their hands, a few specks of gold were left, which they placed in a piece of white paper. A number of children were engaged in the same business, picking out the fine grains by applying them to the head of a pin, moistened in their mouths. I was told of a small boy having taken home $14 as the result of one day's labor. On climbing the hill to the Post Office, I observed in places, where the wind had swept away the sand, several glittering dots of the real metal, but, like the Irishman who kicked the dollar out of his way, concluded to wait till I should reach the heap. The presence of gold in the streets was probably occasioned by the leakings from the miners' bags and the sweepings of stores, though it may also be, to a slight extent, native in the earth, particles having been found in the clay thrown up from a deep well.

Chapter 9: "The Diggings on Mokelumne River"

There is more gold in California than ever was said or imagined; ages will not exhaust the supply. From what I saw on the Mokelumne, I was convinced that the fables Cibao of Columbus, splendid as it seemed to his eager imagination, is more than realized there.

I went up in the ravines one morning, for about two miles, looking for game. It was too late in the day for deer, and I saw but one antelope, which fled like the wind over the top of the mountain. I started a fine hare, similar in appearance to the European, but of larger size. A man riding down the trail from the double Spring, told us he had counted seven deer early in the morning, besides numbers of antelopes and partridges. The grizzly bear and large mountain wolf are frequently seen in the more thickly timbered ravines. The principal growth of the mountains is oak and the California pine, which rises like a spire to the height of two hundred feet. The pinons, or cones, are much larger and of finer flavor than those of the Italian stone pine. As far as I could see from the ridges which I climbed, the mountains were well timbered as the soil and climate will allow. A little more rain would support as fine forests as the world can produce. The earth was baked to a cinder, and from 11 a.m. to 4 p.m. the mercury ranged between 98 and 110 degrees.

There was no end to the stories told by the diggers, of their own and others' experiences in gold hunting. I could readily have made up a small volume from those I heard during the four days I spent on the Mokelumne. In the dry diggings especially, where the metal frequently lies deep, many instances are told of men who have dug for two or three days and given up in despair, while others, coming after them and working the same holes, have taken out thousands of dollars in a short time. I saw a man who came to the river three weeks before my visit, without money, to dig in the dry gulch. Being very lazy, he chose a spot under a shady tree, and dug leisurely for two days without making a cent. He then gave up the place, when a little German jumped into his tracks and after a day's hard work weighed out $800. The unlucky digger than borrowed five ounces and started a boarding house. The town increased so fast that the night I arrived he sold out his share (on third) of the concern for $1,200. Men were not troubled by the ordinary ups and downs of business, when it was so easy for one of any enterprise to recover his foothold. If a person lost his all, he was perfectly indifferent; two weeks of hard work gave him enough to start on, and tow months, with the usual luck, quite reinstated him.

The largest piece found in the rich gulch weighed eleven pounds. Mr. James, who had been on the river since April, showed me a lump weighing sixty-two ounces—pure, unadulterated gold. We had a visit one day from Don Andres Pico, commander of the California forces during the (Mexican) war. He had a company of men digging at the Middle Bar, about a mile above. He is an urbane, intelligent man, of medium stature, and of a natural gentility of character which made him quite popular among the emigrants.

From all that I saw and heard, while at the Mokelumne Diggings, I judged there was as much order and security as could be attained without a civil organization. The inhabitants had elected one of their own number Alcalde (magistrate or mayor), before whom all culprits were tried by a jury selected for the purpose. Several thefts had occurred, and the offending parties had been severely punished after a fair trial. Some had been whipped and cropped, or maimed in some other way, and one of two of them hung. Two or three who had stolen largely had been shot down by the injured party, the general feeling among the miners justifying such a course when no other seemed available. We met near Livermore's Ranch, on the way to

Stockton, a man whose head had been shaved and his ears cut off, after receiving one hundred lashes, for stealing ninety-eight pounds of gold. It may conflict with popular ideas of morality, but, nevertheless, this extreme course appeared to have produced good results. In fact, in a country without not only bolts and bars, but any effective system of law and government, this Spartan severity of discipline seemed the only security against the most frightful disorder. The result was that, except some petty acts of larceny, thefts were rare. Horses and mules were sometimes taken, but the risk was so great that such plunder could not be carried on to any extent. The camp or tent was held inviolate, and like the patriarchal times of old, its cover protected all it enclosed.

Chapter 10: "A Gallop to Stockton"

The history of law and society in California, from the period of the golden discoveries, would furnish many instructive lessons to the philosopher and statesman. The first consequence of the unprecedented rush of emigration from all parts of the world into a country almost unknown and but half reclaimed from its original barbarism was to render all virtually null, and bring the established authorities to depend entirely on the humor of the population for the observance of their orders. The countries which were nearest the gold coast—Mexico, Peru, Chile, China, and the Sandwich Islands (later, Hawaiian Islands)-sent forth their thousands of ignorant adventurers, whom speedily outnumbered the American population. Another fact, which none the less threatened serious consequences, was the readiness with which the worthless and depraved class of our own country came to the Pacific coast. From the beginning, a state of things little short of anarchy might have been reasonably awaited.

Instead of this, a disposition to maintain order and secure the rights of all was shown throughout the mining districts. In the absence of all law or available protection, the people met and adopted rules for their mutual security—rules adapted to their situation, where they had neither guards nor prisons, and where the slightest license given to crime or trespass of any kind must inevitably have led to terrible disorders. Small thefts were punished by banishment from the places, while for those of large amounts or for more serious crimes, there was the single alternative of hanging. These regulations, with slight change, had been continued up to the time of my visit to the country. In proportion as the emigration from our own States increased, and the digging community assumed a more orderly and intelligent aspect, their severity had been relaxed, though punishment was still strictly administered for all offenses. There had been, as nearly as I could learn, not more than twelve or fifteen executions in all, about half of which were inflicted for the crime of murder. This awful responsibility had not been assumed lightly, but after a fair trial and a full and clear conviction, to which was added, I believe in every instance, the confession of the criminal.

In the large digging districts, which had been worked for some time, there were established regulations, which were faithfully observed. Alcades were elected, who decided on all disputes of right or complaints of trespass, and who had power to summon juries for criminal trials. When a new placer or gulch was discovered, the first thing done was to elect officers and extend the area of order. The result was that in a district five hundred miles long, and inhabited by a hundred thousand people, who had neither government, regular laws, rules, military or civil protection, nor even locks or bolts, and a great part of whom possessed wealth enough to tempt the vicious and depraved, the was as much security to life and property as in any part of the Union, and as small a proportion of crime. The capacity of a people for self-government was never so triumphantly illustrated. Never, perhaps, was there a community formed of more unpropitious elements; yet from all this seeming chaos grew a harmony beyond what the most sanguine apostle of Progress could have expected.

The rights of the diggers were no less definitely marked and strictly observed. Among the hundreds I saw on the Mokelumne and among the gulches, I did not see a single dispute nor hear a word of complaint. A company of men might mark out a race of any length and turn the current of the river to get at the bed, possessing the exclusive right to that part of it, so long as their undertaking lasted. A man might dig a hole in the dry ravines, and as long as he left a shovel, pick, or crowbar to show that he still intended working it, he was safe from trespass. His tools might remain there for months without being disturbed. I have seen many such places, miles from any camp or tent, which the digger had left in perfect confidence that he should find all right on his return. There were of course exceptions to these rules—the diggings would be a Utopia if it were not so—but they were not frequent. The Alcaldes sometimes made awkward decisions, from inexperience, but they were none the less implicitly obeyed. I heard of one instance in which a case of trespass was settled to the satisfaction of both parties and the Sheriff ordered to pay the costs of court—about $40. The astonished functionary remonstrated, but the power of the Alcalde was supreme and he was obliged to suffer. . .

Abundance of gold does always beget, as moralists tell us, a grasping and avaricious spirit.

The principles of hospitality were as faithfully observed in the rude tents of the diggers as they could be by the thrifty farmers of the North and West. The cosmopolitan cast of society in California, resulting from the commingling of so many races and the primitive mode of life, gave a character of good-fellowship to all its members; and in no of the world have I ever seen help more freely given to the needy, or more ready cooperation in any humane proposition. Personally, I can safely say that I have never met with such unvarying kindness from comparative strangers.

Chapter 30: "Society in California"

There are some features of society in California which I have hitherto failed to touch upon in my narrative, but which deserve a passing notice before I take my final leave of that wonderful land. The direct effect of the state of things growing out of the discovery of the placers was to develop new qualities and traits of character, not in single individuals, but in every individual of the entire community—traits frequently most unlooked for in those who exhibited them in the most marked degree. Society, therefore, was for the time cast into new forms, or, rather, deprived of any fazed form. A man coming to California could not more expect to retain his old nature unchanged than he could retain in his lungs the air he had inhaled on the Atlantic shore.

The most immediate and striking change which came upon the greater portion of the emigrants was an increase of activity, and proportionately of reckless and daring spirit. It was curious to see how men hitherto noted for their prudence and caution took sudden leave of those qualities, to all appearance, yet only prospered the more thereby. Perhaps there was at bottom a vein of keen, shrewd calculation which directed their seemingly heedless movements; certain it is, at least, that for a long time the rashest speculators were the most fortunate. It was this fact, no doubt, that seemed so alarming to persons newly arrived, that gave rise to unnumbered predictions of the speedy and ruinous crash of the whole business fabric of San Francisco. But nothing is more contagious than this spirit of daring and independent action, and the most doleful prophets were, ere long, swallowed up in the same whirlpool against which they had warned others.

The emigrants who arrive in California very soon divide into two distinct classes. About two thirds or possibly three fourths of them are active, hopeful, and industrious. They feel this singular intoxication of society and go to work at something, no matter what, by which they hope to thrive.

The remaining portion see everything "through a glass, darkly." Their first bright anticipation are unrealized; the horrid winds of San Francisco during the dry season chill or unnerve them; or, if they go to the placers, the severe labor and the ill success of inexperienced hands complete their disgust. They commit a multitude of sins in the shape of curses upon everyone who has ever written or spoken favorable of California. Some of them return home without having seen the country at all, and others, even if they obtain profitable situations, labor without a will. It is no place for a slow, an over-cautious, or a desponding man. The emigrant should be willing to work, not only at one business, but many, if need be; the grumbler of the idler had far better stay at home.

It cannot be denied that the very activity of California society created a spirit of excitement which frequently led to dangerous excesses. The habits of emigrants, never, even at home, very slow and deliberate, branched into all kinds of wild offshoots, the necessary effect of the sudden glow and expansion which they experienced. Those who retained their health seemed to revel in an exuberance of animal spirits, which carried them with scarce a jar over barriers and obstacles that would have brought others to a full stand. There was something exceedingly hearty, cordial, and encouraging in the character of social intercourse. The ordinary forms of courtesy were flung aside with a bluntness of good-fellowship infinitely preferable, under the circumstances. I was constantly reminded of the stories of northern history—of the stout Vikings and Jarls who exulted in their very passions and made their heroes of those who were most jovial at the feast and most easily kindled with the rage of battle. Indeed, it required but little effort of the imagination to revive those iron ages, when the rugged gold-diggers, with their long hair and unshorn beards, were grouped around some mountain camp-fire, reveling in the ruddy light and giving full play to a mirth so powerful and profound that it would not have shamed the Berserkers.

Taking Part in the Rush

In 1850, Bayard Taylor wrote, "Age will not exhaust the supply" of gold in California. The dream of striking it rich had a powerful effect on people. People from across the state, across the country, and around the world were caught up in the vision of undertaking an adventure that would culminate with the acquisition of easy wealth. Men closed their shops, quit their jobs, and left their farms and families to make their way to the hills and streams of northern California. From Latin America, large numbers came from Mexico, Peru, and Chile. From Europe, there concentrations of people came from Ireland, Germany, and Belgium. Thousands of Chinese men, seeking escape from civil strife and poverty that wracked parts of their country, came to the place they called "gold mountain." Wherever they came from, for most, the first destination in California was San Francisco.

Nothing, it seemed, could stop the great California migration. Consider that San Francisco had a population of fewer than 1,000 residents when word of James Marshall's discovery was first proclaimed on the town's dusty streets by the merchant Sam Brannon in 1849. Within five years, the city had mushroomed to a population of 50,000 people. By comparison, it took New York City 190 years to reach that size.

Most of these people were "greenhorns," newcomers who knew little about California and were unfamiliar with living in frontier conditions. While all of them shared the general dream of getting rich, most knew little or nothing at all about mining. For the great majority, they did not initially plan on remaining very long. California was too remote and distant; it had few towns and fewer cities. It seemed to exist beyond the edge of civilized society. Unlike the settlers who had been arriving in a gradual stream during the 1840s, most 49ers saw their journey to California as a two-way trip.

Their anticipation of securing easy and rapid wealth was not rooted in fact, but hope. Compounding their task, it was difficult to foresee just how expensive life in California would be. Scarcity of food, tools, and other basic needs was an inherent characteristic of the western frontier. As illustrated by Bernard Reid's experience (later in this section), this situation was made much worse by the surge of people converging into the same locations at the same time.

The exorbitant prices demanded for all manner of products and services was tolerated because, for one thing, there was no alternative, and also because millions of dollars were being made. Without question, there truly were significant deposits of gold. Just how much money was made, however, cannot be precisely determined as there was no systematic record-keeping. Additionally, the value of gold fluctuated between $12 and $35 per ounce depending on the year and who was the buyer. One estimate of how much money was being made would be to use the New York Exchange. Between 1840 and 1860, the price of gold on the Exchange was fixed at $21 per ounce. Using that figure:

Total dollar value of gold extracted by year

1848:	$5.69 million
1849:	$12.48 million
1850:	$53.02 million
1851:	$64.68 million
1852:	$66.64 million

In 1853 alone, 2.7 million troy ounces of gold was taken from the Sierras. A troy ounce is 480 grains; twelve troy ounces equal one pound. By then, however, the competition for it was terrific. The sheer numbers of gold seekers greatly diluted any individual's chance of getting rich. As a result, it is not surprising that most did not "pan out."

Mining Devices: The Pan

One iconic image of the gold rush is that of a solitary man, working on the edge of a stream, bending down over a slightly curved, broad pan that he has dipped through the water to collect gravel that he will carefully wash away, leaving behind, with any luck, glittering copper-yellow flakes and pieces of gold clinging to the sides of the pan. The scene has its appeal. The process looks simple enough, and it is clearly a low-cost venture. It looks like an investment requiring more of time than brains or physical strength. In short, it was the everyman's method to getting rich in the rush. There was such a sense of democratic fairness about it. Even taking into consideration the ecological sensibilities of today's society, there appears to be no significant degradation of the environment as a result of panning, though looks can be deceiving. In the early 1850s, to the arriving prospector with no experience and little capital, panning for gold was something that could be started right away. But one fact would be immediately evident: panning was physically hard work that followed a woefully inefficient method.

At that time, the mining pan was commonly called a "gold dish." Some pans were carved out of wood which was smoothed by rubbing with fine gravel. It was desirable to leave some texture in a pan to catch the fragments of gold. Nevertheless, metal pans were more popular. They had to be hand-forged by a blacksmith (unlike later pans that were manufactured on a lathe that spun the metal). They cost more than wood pans, but they lasted longer. The size of a pan varied from eight to eighteen inches. The larger ones were naturally heavier and more tiring to use. Also, as they held more rock and water, more skill was required in handling. Generally, miners preferred pans that were twelve to fourteen inches.

Panning started by picking a location to work. Since a detailed knowledge of the geology of the Sierras was well beyond nearly all forty-niners, the choice of site to pan might be decided by what others had found. It could be influenced by gossip or "perhaps-it-might-be-true" stories of strikes. Possibly, the decision could simply come from a hunch. A good spot would be near the edge of a stream where the water was at least six inches deep and flowing fast enough to quickly carry away disturbed mud so one could see the river bottom. Having a comfortable place to sit would have been nice, but the miner usually would be stooping or squatting above the water as he worked. He would probably use a shovel to fill the pan three-fourths full with gravel and dirt and then, holding it under the surface of the water, would make several vigorous shakes side-to-side so the small but heavy materials would settle on the bottom of the pan. This was followed with a more gentle circular motion to carry out much of the dirt, clay, or plant debris. The process of shaking followed by swirling was repeated to encourage small but heavy materials toward the pan's bottom.

Next, the pan, still under water and held at a slight tilt, was swirled around and forward to push the lighter gravel up and over the edge. This process was continued until only a couple of cups of heavier material, called black sand or concentrate, remained.

The pan was raised out of the stream and most of the water poured out while the black sand was retained. The remaining water was slowly swirled to spread the black sand across the sides of the pan. If gold was present, it would be removed at this point. To minimize the loss of gold, miners would often coat the pan with mercury. The mercury would bind with the gold making it easier to capture gold and increase the speed of their work.

After this, the pan was refilled and the process started over. It would take several minutes for a single panning to be completed. An experienced prospector could process about fifty pans, or about one cubic yard of material, a day. By comparison, mining companies today use super-sized dump trucks to move 400 tons in a single load of rock and dirt to be processed for gold.

Panning for gold did make money for some, but it required time, physical finesse, and often, simple luck. It inefficiently processed relatively small amounts of material. Unless one was extraordinarily fortunate to uncover sizable flakes or pieces, the accumulation of gold dust by panning did not pay well, based on the amount of money made when looked at on an hourly basis. A year into the rush much of the easiest-to-find surface gold had been collected. Yet more miners kept arriving, many of them coming to work over already-played-out rivers and streams.

Other Mining Devices

Panning was an example of placer (sediment) mining, the extraction of gold from a bed of sand or gravel in a river or lake. The technology was simple. A miner would rely on moving water and the heaviness of gold to settle to the bottom of a collection device. Soon, other more efficient contraptions for capturing the gold in this way were developed. There was the "rocker" or "cradle," a large wooden box several feet long, with riffles (ridges) on the bottom that would be rocked back and forth as dirt or stream gravel was shoveled in and water poured over it. A mesh screen allowed the small material to pass through to the bottom of the device. After several passes of material and water, what remained was panned for gold. Most rockers were homemade. Still, with this machine, even an inexperienced miner could process a cubic yard in about an hour.

Another device was called a "long tom," a ten- to fifteen-foot long sloped metal bottom trough with a sieve and a ripple box at one end. As dirt was shoveled in, diverted stream water would rinse away lighter materials. The sand concentrate that remained was collected in the ripple box to be processed later. A long torn operated on the same principle as panning, but six to eight men were needed to make full use of its capacity. The "toms" would evolve into much longer sluices, some of which took weeks to construct.

Today, most of the world's gold comes from "hard rock" mining. This is where seams of gold are trapped in layers of solid rock and are extracted by tunneling and drilling. Such was the case in the 1850s. During the rush, a good hard rock miner was likely to be skilled at handling explosives. He blasted with black powder (a combination of charcoal, potassium nitrate, and sulfur) inserted into drill holes in the mine shafts. The rubble would be processed through stamp mills that crushed and pulverized the quartz rock into small pieces the size of sand and pebbles. As a final step, the remains were chemically treated with mercury to coax out the gold. One advantage of hard-rock mining was that no water was necessary for the processing. A single stamp mill could weigh more than 1,000 pounds. The din of many assembled machines could be overwhelming and would reverberate for miles. Of course, to the miners, it was the sound of money being made.

Individuals Miners Versus Mining Companies

In 1853, the *Placerville Herald* published "The Miner's Ten Commandments," written by James Hutchings. The first commandment was "Thou shalt have no other claim than one." It is not surprising that this idea was given such prominence. It spoke to one of the essential beliefs that the gold rush was equalitarian in nature—everyone should have a reasonable shot at finding their share of gold and no one should take more than what was fair to the others.

Although the "pick and shovel" period of placer mining, work that could be preformed by a single individual, continues to be a well-remembered image of

California, its dominance in the gold rush was relatively brief. Each progression in gold mining was more expensive and required more cooperation and organization among the miners. With the more sophisticated equipment, gold mining quickly became a business monopolized by companies that drew upon large amounts of investment capital.

In 1851 and 1852, nearly three dozen mining corporations were formed out of the pooled financial resources of large investors. Some businesses were able to secure hundreds of mining claims, giving them control over thousands of acres of land. Thus, in the space of just a few years, the changing scale of mining economics demanded the extraction of gold on a much greater scale. By the time of Hutchings' commandments, many of the independent miners were losing their claims and their livelihood to mining companies who, in turn, ended up employing many of them to carry-out what proved to be the most effective, and environmentally damaging method of gold extraction. In the next thirty years, hydraulic mining would deliver more than 90 percent of California's gold.

Hydraulic Mining

The use of water in extracting minerals from the earth goes far back in the history of mining. Ancient Chinese "mined" briny water from shafts they dug hundreds of feet into the earth in order to reap salt as the liquid evaporated. Using gravity and its own weight as the force, Romans used water to wash away rocks and sediment to expose desired metals. In California, the use of hydraulics (also spelled hydraulicking at the time) was first large-scale mining in the region. It was first used in April 1852 at American Hill, north of Nevada City, in Placer County. The first hoses were made of canvas. Later, a tapered iron metal nozzle, also called a monitor, was added to increase the water pressure. To reduce the frequency of burst hoses, rubber sleeves sometimes covered the canvas. When aimed at beds of gravel, it quickly became evident that the force of water could do in hours what it took shovels and picks weeks to accomplish.

This form of mining was not cheap. It required a large initial capital investment. Elaborate systems to transport water had to be constructed on rugged topography that rose sharply up hills and mountains and slid steeply into valleys and streambeds. Reservoirs were constructed to maintain the water supply during the dry summer months Over a thirty-year period, 5,276 miles of flumes, canals, and ditches were built throughout the Sierras. It is estimated that $110 million was invested in hydraulic mining in the state. At one time, as many as 20,000 men worked in the industry.

Certainly, this method of mining could be sustained only by companies with considerable capital assets. By the late 1850s, the hydraulic mining business along the American, Bear, Feather, and Yuba rivers had only two main competitors, the South Yuba Water Company and the Eureka Lake and Yuba Canal Company. Within a few years, these two companies had displaced 684 million yards of gravel in the Yuba watershed, 257 and 254 million yards along the American and Bear watersheds respectively, and more than 100 million yards of material along the Feather. Despite the obvious destruction being done to the environment, with some negative consequences soon evident, there was no public oversight of hydraulic mining and nothing was done to stop the lucrative practice.

As a consequence, gold regions were ravaged. The titanic volumes of water tore away the soil, sand, and gravel, exposing the bedrock beneath. Over time, larger monitors were developed. The biggest of these "little giants" were seventeen feet long. Water could be shot four to five hundred feet through the air in torrents so powerful they could kill a man if he had the misfortune to step into its stream. Monitors were aimed along crest lines and ridges. Thousands of yards of cliffs and banks would dissolve into muck and mud and run down through long lines of sluice boxes where the gold could be recovered. The profits were so high, as much as 300 percent, that some companies operated monitors twenty-four hours a day, using torches to see at night. In later years, black powder detonations were made before the water was applied to help break up the land more quickly. Other improvements in extraction included wrapping the hoses with coils of iron for a dramatic increase in pressure. With the enhanced equipment and technique, entire hillsides would be washed away in a matter of a few days.

One troublesome by-product of hydraulic mining was that it moved enormous volumes of thick mud and silt as the hills disintegrated. Where that huge mass went was the result of both humans and nature. In today's gold mining, five tons of material needs to be processed to extract one ounce of gold. During the three decades that hydraulic mining was extensively used in the Sierras, it is estimated that more than 1.5 billion cubic yards of soil and rock were washed down from the hillsides. This was eight times the volume of material excavated during the digging of the Panama Canal. The hundreds of millions of tons of debris and water were channeled though mountain streams that fed rivers flowing into the Sacramento Valley. Some streams were buried under one hundred feet of sediment, permanently altering the landscape. This had a devastating effect on both the natural environment and agriculture. Streams ran brown with mining waste called "slickens." Rivers were choked, fish died, and wildlife was driven away. The Sacramento River's once prodigious salmon run was decimated, and so were those of most of the rest of the streams that flowed into the San Francisco Bay. For these reasons, Native Americans too, could not remain in areas in which hydraulic mining was utilized. Sadly, their displacement was another ignored consequence of mining.

Once the mud-laden mountain waters reached a flat valley, its speed lessened and the sediment it carried dropped to the bottom. An estimated 685 million cubic feet of mining debris was dumped from the Oroville and Malakoff mines into the Yuba River alone, clogging it with mud and gravel. Because there was so much debris, the riverbed filled up and the channels widened, causing the water to rise, overflow its banks, forcing it to dig new channels into the earth. The result was major flooding, particularly during the spring snowmelt. For years, flooding in the rich agricultural areas of the northern Central Valley caused millions of dollars in damages.

One town greatly affected by this was Marysville, forty miles from Sacramento, where the Yuba and Feather Rivers met. Marysville was a "jumping off" point for miners heading into the foothills, and it quickly became a major transportation and supply center. In 1853, its population passed 10,000, making it California's third-largest town, after San Francisco and Sacramento. By the 1870s, the hydraulic waste had raised the Yuba riverbed so high that townspeople had to build a complex levee system to protect them from flooding. Ironically, Marysville was also a manufacturing center for tools needed by the miners, including, hydraulic monitors, the very equipment that brought the threat of inundation to the town.

The Use of Mercury

Mercury is a chemical element. It is a heavy metal, like arsenic, copper, lead, and zinc. One shared characteristic of these elements is they are not easily excreted from the human body and will remain for a long time. Mercury is the only metal that is in a liquid state at ordinary "room" temperature. If left open to the air, a significant amount of vaporization will occur. This makes working in its fumes dangerous as it can cause acute poisoning of the lungs. Modern handling of the chemical would include the use of latex gloves and breathing masks, two protections not available to men in the 1850s.

Any amount of exposure can result in health problems. Mercury is easily absorbed through the skin. Its compounds can be extremely toxic. The ingestion of large amounts of mercury, an uncommon occurrence, can cause heart failure and immediate death. Symptoms from acute poisoning include headaches, severe abdominal pains, vomiting, and diarrhea. It can cause hair loss, loose teeth, and kidney damage. Sustained exposure to even small amounts of mercury can lead to neurological disorders such as fatigue, memory loss, tremors, blindness, and mental disturbances. For most people, the most likely contact with mercury comes through consumption of certain fish.

Like gold, mercury (also called quicksilver) was mined in California. And like water, mercury has been used in gold mining for centuries. (Because of its effectiveness, it is still widely used today in many countries even where it is banned.) The region's first mercury mines opened in the early 1840s in the Santa Cruz Mountains. When James Marshall discovered gold in the American River, he helped create a large, relatively close market with a high demand for mercury. Despite the risks, mercury is an excellent substance for the recovery of gold flakes.

When mercury and gold come into contact, mercury immediately begins to penetrate into the gold. A blend, or amalgam, of the two metals is the result. Given enough time, mercury would entirely absorb the gold but it is a slow process. The amalgam is the consistency of soft clay. Because of the very high surface tension of mercury, it holds the gold particles in place, making it easier for miners to recover the gold and lose less of it in the process. The amalgam could later be heated to separate the gold from the mercury. There was no regulation on the use of mercury. From the miners' point of view, it was a very useful product that made them more money—and that was a good thing. As a consequence, huge amounts of mercury were both mined from, and used in, California.

Placer miners would combine globules of mercury with diluted nitric acid and swab the surface of their pans with the mixture. In hydraulic mining, the volume of water that carried along the gold-bearing sediment through wooden sluice boxes was so great that mercury was poured directly into the sluice from containers that held as much seventy-five pounds of the element. An estimated 10 to 30 percent of the mercury escaped into the environment during this process. Over the course of time, that loss totaled ten million pounds, or five thousand tons, of mercury. Hydraulic mining in California between 1852 through 1884 captured an estimated eleven million troy ounces, or 458 tons, of gold. In other words, more than ten times as much mercury was carelessly introduced into the California ecosystem than gold was carefully taken out. The mercury ended up where all the other mining waste finally settled—on river bottoms, in farming valleys, and in the San Francisco Bay.

Because it does not break down, much of the mercury that washed down the Sierras more than a century ago is still where it settled. Today, mercury concentrations in the fish and wildlife that eat fish caught in and around San Francisco Bay continue to have much higher than average levels of the toxin. Not all of the mercury is attributed to the gold rush. There are hundreds of contemporary sources of mercury pollution, including ongoing mining operations. Still, the environmental damage caused in the 1850s continues to be a part of the problem. In 2007, the California State Water Resources Control Board adopted a plan to reduce the mercury levels in the Bay low enough to make fish caught in its waters safe to eat. The project is a combination of cleaning up old sources of the chemical along with reducing the introduction of new contaminate. The official estimate of how long the plan will need to be in effect to reach its goals is seventy years.

A Partial End of Hydraulic Mining & the Beginning of Environmental Law: The Sawyer Decision

> *The first treasure California began to surrender after the Gold Rush was her oldest: her land.*
>
> —John Jakes, author

In 1878, farmers in Yuba City whose land and businesses had been hurt by hydraulic mining formed the Anti-Debris Association to challenge the mining industry. A number of lawsuits were filed. In one suit, a lone farmer, Edward Woodruff, took on the state's largest hydraulic mining business, the North Bloomfield Mining and Gravel Company. North Bloomfield controlled the highly productive and extremely profitable Malakoff Mine. Over many years, the company had constructed a complex system of canals and flumes that included a drainage tunnel more than a mile long. By 1874, gravel deposits rich in gold at Malakoff were being attacked by seven hydraulic monitors that ran non-stop, seven days a week. Fifty thousand tons of gravel was processed each day, after which, everything but the gold was dumped directly into the South Yuba River. As the years of litigation passed, and the millions of pounds of mining waste accumulated, it began to look as if Malakoff and agriculture could not coexist.

In 1884, Lorenzo Sawyer, a federal judge in San Francisco, ruled in *Woodruff v. North Bloomfield* that hydraulic mining was a "public and private nuisance" and issued an injunction that banned any company from dumping debris into pubic waterways such as the Yuba River. Known as the Sawyer decision, it set an important precedent in environmental law in the United States by essentially stating that a grossly polluting industry could be shut down for the public good. The decision has been considered the first environmental protection law in the nation. There were legal challenges to the ruling, and injunctions against continued operations were ignored at first, but eventually the use of hydraulics throughout the Sierras ended.

It should be noted, however, that Sawyer's ruling did not apply to all of California, and hydraulic mining continued well into the mid-twentieth century. For example, the La Grange Hydraulic Gold Mining Company operated in the Klamath-Trinity

Mountains in the northwest area of the state. Between 1892 and 1918, using the same environmentally disruptive methods as North Bloomfield, the La Grange company displaced more than 34 million tons of earth as it extracted $3.5 million in gold.

Today, one can still see the vivid effect hydraulic mining had on the land. At the Malakoff Diggins State Historic Park, hillsides remain deeply rutted and denuded of trees and other plants. The Malakoff mine pit produced a canyon seven-thousand feet long and three-thousand feet wide, with a depth of nearly six hundred feet.

"Seeing the Elephant"

This was a popular saying among the people who joined the hurried exodus to California's gold country. The expression itself came from the time when a traveling circus had a parade through the town it was to perform in to draw the interest of the locals. Elephants, being large and exotic creatures from distant lands, had rarely been seen in person by Americans in the early 19th century, and were among the favored attractions. These huge animals were also used in helping to erect the circus tents. They were usually docile but, if angered or made afraid, they could get out of control. Thus, elephants were both admired and feared; they were thrilling and terrifying. "Seeing the elephant" or "going to see the elephant" was an apt metaphor for the Gold Rush as people had the adventure (or misadventure) of getting to California, where they entered into a society with a diversity of people, behaviors, and interests, unlike any they had ever experienced before.

A 49er Story: Bernard J. Reid

The literature on the gold rush is rich because many of those who participated kept written accounts of their experiences. With tens of thousands of people involved, a single story can only reveal a small part of the total event. Today, records list the locations of 546 different mining camps and diggings. Bernard Reid was, in some ways, a typical forty-niner, though he was better educated than most. He kept a diary of his effort to get to the gold fields of California, joining in with the first wave of would-be miners who descended on the region. The diary itself was not discovered until 1953. The story it told of that remarkable experience is summarized here.

In 1849, Bernard Reid, single and twenty-six years old, had several options for his career. He lived in St. Louis. He had arrived three years before from his home state of Pennsylvania where he had been a teacher, a surveyor, and, in Clarion, a small newspaper publisher. Lately he had worked in the office of the U.S. Surveyor

General. He decided to leave Missouri and seek his fortune as a gold miner in California. Reid did not have enough money to travel by himself. If he had, he could travel by train south from St. Louis and make his way to a gulf port city such as New Orleans and book passage on a ship that could sail to Panama. There, he could have transferred to a smaller ferry that could navigate the rivers that cut through the mountains and jungles until he arrived on the Pacific Ocean. (In 1850, construction began on a rail line across Panama. When completed in 1855, passengers could cross Panama from the Atlantic to the Pacific in three hours.) From Panama, another ship ticket would have to be purchased for the journey north to San Francisco Bay. This risky and uncertain trip was out of Reid's ability to afford.

Instead, to get to California, Reid would join with others and pool their resources for an overland crossing. This was not an easy proposition either. A journey of that length and duration would require an outlay of $200-300. As he could not afford to buy a wagon and supply it, he would have to join a group, likely as a hired hand. This group would perhaps follow a guidebook or a mutually agreed upon route. Other terms of the trip were daunting. There would be the months of long wagon drives through dust, rain, mud, and cold, keeping an anxious eye out for grass and water to keep the animals alive and pulling across hundreds of miles of lands that Reid had never seen and did not know. Reid must have thought there could be a better way to get himself west.

In need of a creative solution, Reid came across an advertisement for an outfit called the Pioneer Line—a wagon train transportation company with service west to California. The company was created by two St. Louis entrepreneurs, Thomas Turner and a man named Allen. Reid discovered a very favorable proposition in their company's advertisement. Leaving from Independence, Missouri, all the needs for the trip would be provided for $200 per passenger. Included services were the procurement of wagons, teams, drivers, even the handling of luggage. The most attention-getting claim was that the Pioneer wagons would complete the 1,515-mile journey to San Francisco in "a mind-boggling 55-60 days."

Perhaps in a period when there was not so much excitement about California rippling across the country, Reid might have given more consideration to what he read, and a more thorough examination of this fledgling transportation concern might have raised some vital questions among the clientele. Passengers might have inquired more deeply just how the Pioneer wagons would get them to their destination in half the time, even with an untroubled crossing. Simple calculations would have shown the Pioneer Line would have to cover an average of twenty-five miles every day on the trail without delay or rest. On the frontier that was asking a lot. Looking at it rationally, it did not seem to be possible. But people like Reid were in a hurry and apparently did not concern themselves with such questions. Turner and Allen were good marketers and told their customers what they wanted to hear. They had, after all, two dozen freight wagons and twenty passenger carriages, all emblazoned with the Pioneer name in large gold letters. Soon Reid and 160 others had signed up, paying in advance for their journey.

Advertised expectations soon met reality. From the start in mid-May, the forty badly overloaded wagons made headway at a terrible cost. Even with 300 mules, they could not handle the loads or the hectic pace at the outset. As the animals began to die, some wagons and baggage had to be abandoned. Many of the passengers, all of whom had been told they would ride in the carriages, would have to walk. Some refused, sticking to their contract, until other passengers threatened violence. Floundering on every count, fifteen people would die during the journey, nine from cholera, others from scurvy. Three passengers died just while crossing Kansas. Others became gravely ill from the shortage of food. As one traveler recounted in his journal of the trip, "Hutton is dead. Others are worse." Reid kept a diary of his own. In it he wrote the journey was "a long, dreadful dream."

After 138 days on the trail, Reid somehow managed to arrive in California in early October as cold weather set in. There, he found his hardships were not over and the gold prospects were decidedly mixed. One fact that escaped most aspiring miners was that there was a considerable amount of time in any year in which prospecting was not possible. Winter snows, storms, and extreme cold kept miners out of the high Sierras for months at a time. Seasonal dry periods made it impractical to try to mine with sluices that required large amounts of water to carry sediment in which the gold was trapped.

As a result, miners like Reid were forced out of the mountains and had to idle away their time and savings in places like San Francisco. While there were expensive diversions such as gambling and drinking, what was notably missing was the presence of women. Of the 41,000 people who sailed to California in 1849, only 800 were women, fewer then 2 percent of the total. (California's population would not reach numerical gender equality until 1900.) Like the great majority of men around him, they had come alone to California, many leaving behind spouses, families, and friends. Being homesick and lonely was a common condition.

While in San Francisco, Reid fell seriously ill. "It is a hard thing to be sick and alone in this country," he wrote in his diary. One California doctor reported that diarrhea and dysentery "was so general during the fall and winter months, and degenerated so frequently into chronic and fatal malady, that it has been popularly regarded as the disease of California."

After Reid recovered, he tried prospecting for the first time at Weber's Creek near Placerville. "Some of the miners are making good wages," he wrote, "others barely making expenses. All seems a lottery." Like most miners, Reid had neither the needed knowledge nor experience. One of the first lessons learned was it required a lot of hard, physical labor. Panning meant standing in snowmelt, often under a hot sun, while repeatedly bending and stooping. Although it did bring a return, it was inefficient work, given that a man could only sift through one plate-sized pan of small rock and sand with each scoop. Miners could join together and spend weeks building a flume or a ditch to redirect a stream, then watch their work dissolve in minutes in an unexpected flood.

In 1850, even an unlucky miner, one who didn't make a great strike, could expect to make at least $10-$25 a day, an excellent income for the time, much more than the $1.50 a day a skilled worker back East could make, or the $1 a day earned by a farmer. But the cost of living in California was staggering. The mining pan that cost 30 cents elsewhere, was $15 in California. A loaf of bread that sold for 4 cents in the East cost $1 in the mining camps. Dinner in a San Francisco restaurant could cost $25, a small fortune at the time. Prices fluctuated depending on the month and year but the one constant was they were extremely high. Below is a sample of some other goods and the prices they commanded in the mining camps:

Apples $1 each
Boots $100 a pair
Butcher knife $30
Candles $3 each
Coffee $5 lb.
Eggs $1 lb.
Flour $1 lb.
Ham $2 lb.
Salt Pork $1 lb.
Socks $3 per pair
Work Shirt $20

In return for months of effort, Reid ended up in debt to "my old friend and partner Mr. Hawxhurst" who had financed his prospecting. He returned again to San Francisco where he took a variety of jobs to pay off his debts. He shoveled sand as a day laborer, did some surveying, and worked as a typesetter in a newspaper office. Later he helped found, and joined as one of the first faculty, the newly opened Santa Clara College where he taught math, English, and Spanish. Built in

1777 as one of Spain's Franciscan missions, in 1851, Santa Clara became the first college in California.

Eventually, Reid paid off his mining debt and built up some modest savings. In 1852, he left California by ship and sailed back east by crossing the Isthmus in Panama. Reid had certainly "seen the elephant" in California, but had not found the riches he had expected would be his for the taking.

Part of Reid's struggle was that there were so many men like him who had labored in the same rivers and mountains as he had. In 1848, there were 6,000 miners who, all together, collected nearly $6 million worth of gold. In 1849, twice as much gold was collected, but its value was spread among more than 40,000 miners. In 1852, near the peak of production, more than 100,000 miners were competing with each other for the gold.

After Reid left California, he returned to Pennsylvania and settled in Clarion where he earned his law degree and became an attorney. In 1854, he married Letitia Farran. Together, they had nine children and remained married for fifty-eight years. During the Civil War, Reid served as Captain in the 63rd Regiment, Pennsylvania Volunteers.

In 1886, at the age of sixty-three, Reid travelled alone back to California. This time he came by train. He was overwhelmed by the changes he saw. He made three more visits to the state over the next seventeen years. In 1904, he died from pneumonia while living in Pittsburgh. He was eighty-one.

> *"I had comrades then, a saucy set, They were rough, I must confess,*
> *But staunch and brave, as true as steel, Like hunters from the west;*
> *But they, like many other fish, Have now run out their line;*
> *But like good old bricks, they stood the kicks, Of the days of forty-nine."*
> —*"The Days of 49"* A popular song of the Gold Rush

The Experiences of Women in the Gold Rush

Few women took part in the Gold Rush. Overall, they made up only about five percent of the population. Even fewer were prospectors. But those women who did come to California in the early 1850s did not play an insignificant role. Quite the opposite, their rarity gave them a special status in society they did not have back home. For some, the Gold Rush presented them a unique opportunity to run their own businesses and to make money on a level quite unimaginable elsewhere. For others, the lack of defined community standards allowed them to dress, act, and engage in activities with a much great degree of personal freedom.

In the 1840s, in the United States, there were clear, rigid social expectations placed on both sexes. Certainly, not all people, male or female, conformed to these "ideals." But while individual experiences varied, there was much less public tolerance for personal choice than one finds in today's society. Although the early stirrings of feminism surfaced in this decade, in the Victorian era, most people looked down on anyone who deviated from the social norm. The pressure to "behave" was powerful and was bolstered by custom and law.

Women were considered naturally weaker than men, squeamish, prone to hysteria, and unable to perform work that required a lot of muscular activity. In most preindustrial societies, for example, domestic chores were relegated to women, leaving "heavier" labor such as hunting and plowing to men. This ignored the fact that caring for children and doing tasks such as milking cows and washing clothes also required heavy, sustained labor.

Ironically, physiological tests today suggest that women have a greater tolerance for pain, and statistics clearly show that women live longer then men and are more resistant to many diseases.

There was also the strong conviction that men and women should and did live largely in "different spheres" within society. Men lived in the "public" sphere. They were the actors and the "doers." They were the soldiers and adventurers. They were expected to be strong and tough and engage in the fiercely competitive capitalist world of business and commerce. They were to be the financial provider and head of the family. As the only voters, they controlled government, politics, and law making. Not surprisingly, many of the laws they wrote gave themselves a distinct advantage and control over women. The same was true in the social arena where men generally accorded themselves greater latitude in defining what was acceptable moral behavior than was tolerated for women.

For their part, women were to live in the "private" sphere. They were considered "naturally" weaker than men and unable to perform work that demanded significant physical or intellectual abilities. As a consequence, they were expected to be passive, submissive, and supportive to the "superior" male. As child-birth was the natural biological role of women, traditionally, it was regarded as their major social role as well. The resulting stereotype was "a woman's place is in the home." They were wives and mothers who took care of the house and children. Unless compelled by necessity, they did not work for money outside the home. They were expected to be pious and exert a moral influence on the family. Legally, without the vote, women were highly dependent on men for financial support, and the laws of divorce, custody of property and children were skewed in favor of men.

For those women who came to California, many of these expectations and demands were left behind. In a land where the sense of community was weak and fragmented, it was not possible to impose much community pressure on individual behavior. And few people cared to try. In the rush for gold, it mattered less who or what you were, than what you had and could do.

Life could be exhilarating for women cut loose from the social constraints of the East. One woman wrote of California: "A smart woman can do very well in this country. True, there are not many comforts and one must work all the time and work hard, but there is plenty to do and good pay. . .It is the only country I ever was where a woman received anything like a just compensation for work."

There was more fluidity in society. A woman might do laundry during the day and then work in a saloon in the evening—whatever was required and earned the most. There were not the clear-cut divisions that typically separated people by both class and gender. Thus, there was greater opportunity to pursue work. Women worked in unconventional roles: a photographer, a barber, a bullfighter who entertained crowds, or a stagecoach driver. Some women ran strings of mules and sold supplies to miners in the mountain camps.

Women in the mining towns were more likely to be professional gamblers than prospectors. Gambling was a fixture in every mining town. Women who dealt cards or poured drinks in gambling houses were major attractions. Also highly valued were domestic skills. Because of the traditional divisions of labor based on gender, most men had little or no experience in work associated with running a household. A woman could earn as much if not more than miners by baking, sewing, cleaning, washing, ironing, and so on.

There were no standards in what a woman could charge. Everything was based on what the market would bear. Some women who operated their own boardinghouses made $100 a week. A cook could earn the staggering sum of $30 a day. There is an account of a woman who baked and sold pies to miners, hungry for a taste of home-cooking. She was said to have earned $18,000.

The scarcity of women had another consequence that was more emotional. "You see no women here," wrote James Pratt in 1849. In Nevada City, another man wrote, "Got nearer to a female this evening than I have been for six months. Came near fainting." The 1850 census documented just how few women there were. In Calaveras County, there were 16,617 men and 267 women. Yuba County was 78 percent male. Mariposa County was an incredible 98.5 percent male. Sacramento, the second largest city behind San Francisco, had only 615 women out of a population of 9,087.

Loneliness was a prevalent condition for many. One miner, Chauncey L. Canfield, spent $150 for new clothing and traveled 100 miles just to see a woman working in a saloon as a card dealer. He wrote in his diary, "She's got a voice like music and just speaking to me in that way put me all in a flutter." When a woman was near, staring was common. Eliza Farnham wrote in 1856, "Doorways filled instantly and little islands of men would cluster around. Men would stand immovable till the spectacle passed from their incredible gaze." In her diary, Eliza Ann McAuley described how, upon her arrival in 1852 from Iowa at her father's cabin in California, men came to pay respects, hoping to see her and her sisters. She wrote, "One enthusiastic miner declared he would give an ounce of gold dust for the sight of a woman's sunbonnet."

Of course, there were women who journeyed with their husbands to California, traveling together for months in covered wagons or by ship. Others who had seen their spouses set off alone, tired of waiting for them and came out to reunite with them. Some came with their children. Some came out single and got married. Others came out believing they were married only to discover their husbands had died. Perhaps one revealing example of the degree of freedom that existed was illustrated by the divorce rate in California that, in the 1850s, was the highest of any state in nation.

"Dame Shirley" Letters

Many people who were part of the gold rush wrote about what they saw, experienced, and heard about. Few of them, however, wrote as well as Louise Amelia Knapp Smith Clapp who personally experienced life in a mining camp in its first stage. In twenty-three letters she wrote to her adopted sister Molly in Massachusetts, Clapp created a vivid and enduring portrait of California mining life in 1851 and 1852. Her perceptive insights provide a wealth of detail, from the incessant noise of the mining activities to the appearance and daily habits of the Indians in the area. She described the types of food miners ate, the manner in which they treated each other, and a myriad of social activities. During her fifteen months in the Sierras, she described men who were full of optimism and hope, racism and intolerance, frustration and bitterness. She knew of those who were morally righteous and those who were criminally-minded. Adding to all of this was her being female, a quality that sometimes seemed as rare as the gold the miners sought.

Louise Amelia Knapp Smith Clapp was born in Elizabethtown, New Jersey in 1819. At the age of eight, her parents moved and she was raised in a middle-class home in Amherst, Massachusetts. Though her father, a mathematics professor, died when she was twelve—no doubt a traumatic event—her mother was left with enough money to support the family. Louise would be well educated for a typical young woman of the era. In 1848, she married Fayette Clapp who was just starting his career as a doctor. The next year the couple sailed for California, reaching San Francisco in January, 1850. Dr. Clapp did not come to mine for gold but to establish his medical practice. But it was his own health that soon needed attention. The wet, damp San Francisco climate did not suit him and he wanted to move away from the coast.

In early 1851, the Clapps took a steamboat to Marysville, an up-and-coming town due to its location on the Feather and Yuba Rivers, now swarming with gold miners. From there they moved to two mining camps, Indian Bar and the nearby Rich Bar, along the north fork of the Feather River, about 120 miles north of Sacramento. Dr. Clapp was still not a prospector but the fresh mountain air did improve his health somewhat (nevertheless he would die in early middle-age in 1864). By this time Louise, who aspired to be a professional writer, had already written poetry and something of her experiences in San Francisco, began a series of letters to Molly. These twenty-three letters proved to be her greatest legacy.

In 1854, the letters were published as a series, one per month, under her pen name, "Dame Shirley," in the short-lived literary journal, *The Pioneer.* Her publisher, perhaps seeking to assure readers of the authenticity of their content, stated the "Letters from the California Mines" were not originally intended for publication, and "have been inserted with scarcely an erasure from us." Clapp, who playfully called herself a "mineress," wrote in her first letter, "You have no idea of the hand to mouth sort of style in which most men in this country are in the habit of living." It would be the first of many times she would describe the constant shortages of food and other staples that were all too commonplace in California at that time. Still, she wrote, "Really, everybody ought to go to the mines just to see how little it takes to make people comfortable in the world."

As in Bayard Taylor's writing in *El Dorado,* Clapp told of astonishing successes. She wrote of miners who made $6,000 in two weeks, of men who collected over thirty pounds of gold in a single day, and of a miner who recovered $1,500 in gold from a single pan of dirt. But she also told of how these finds attracted hundreds of new miners, and of how some men lost their fortunes through drinking and gambling.

As mining was the singular activity most of the time, it is unsurprising that Clapp wrote of it often. She related in meticulous thoroughness of the design and action of mining devices, such as the "long torn," though, in this case, she was frustrated in her search to learn the origin of its name. Clapp had sympathy for many of the miners, aware of the tremendous labor they expended in their occupation. "Gold mining is nature's great lottery scheme," she wrote as she told of a miner of "intelligence and education" who worked a claim for six months, at the end of which he had but six ounces of gold to show for all his effort.

It is clear from the letters that life in the camps was truly untamed. There was considerable drunkenness and bloodshed. Though death for a few miners came from natural causes such as drowning or illness, lives were also lost from being stabbed, shot, or from being hung by a mob for committing a violent crime. She even recounted a deadly duel between a reluctant Englishman who was killed by his good friend after a dispute developed.

By November, 1852, it was all over at Indian Bar as the gold ran out. Within weeks, where there had been hundreds of men, only a few dozen remained. As the Clapps prepared to leave, Louise wrote her final letter. She was sentimental about the end. "My heart is heavy at the thought of departing from this place. I like this wild and barbarous life; I leave it with regret."

Clapp would remain in California for another quarter of a century, where she had a long career as a school teacher in San Francisco. After she retired she moved to Morristown, New Jersey, and lived there until the end of her life in 1906. Her letters have become a treasure trove for those interested in daily life in the mining camps. Her thoroughness created balance in her depictions. Bret Harte, an unsuccessful miner but a talented writer who penned "The Luck of Roaring Camp," and other gold rush stories, read the Shirley letters and credited them as a source for background information. Josiah Royce, another prominent nineteenth century writer, considered the letters "the best account of an early mining camp that is known to me." Today, the Shirley letters continue to be cited as among the best sources of primary information on life in the gold rush.

"The Soiled Doves"

California was a wild, open society in the early 1850s. The degree of social freedom that existed would be hard to find before or since. But freedom does not necessarily always mean something positive. For while there was the freedom to live as one chose, there was, at the same time, the freedom to exploit others. In these years, California held special challenges for women. Many men assumed "there was not an honest women (morally)

> *in the land." Women, particularly if married, had to prove their integrity to their marriage as well as their mettle to endure the daily hardships of the rough and tumble life. Women in the Gold Rush were pioneers and adventurers. Some were teachers, merchants, and of course, prospectors. But the fact was that the large majority of them were prostitutes.*

Prostitution is recorded in history as far back as the Sumerian Empire more than four thousand years ago. Through the centuries, it has been accepted or outlawed depending on where and when one looks over its long existence. In the Victorian United States of the 1840s, it was illegal but was widely in practice on the fringes of society. Because it existed "unofficially" the historical record is fragmented. Still, it is believed that many women who sold their sex, did so because of poverty, a lack of education, and limited options and opportunities in their lives.

Whereas early feminists in the United States saw women in prostitution as victims of shortcomings of society, or from men's desire to keep women oppressed, the prevalent social attitude regarding sexual behavior of the time assumed that a woman was either "good," that is moral and chaste, or she was "bad," immoral and promiscuous. She made a choice as to which she would be. These strict puritanical mores combined with a broader general disapproval of women to engage in many public pursuits such as in entertainment. Females as actors were not even common in American theaters at this time.

With the onset of the Gold Rush, thousands of healthy, robust men moved into California. They often lived in crude shelters--tents or shacks—for months at a time, isolated from all but other miners, they suffered from overwork, danger, fatigue, and intense economic competition. Since nineteen out of every twenty persons was male, unfulfilled sexual desires were rampant. Some letters from miners related how some of them struggled to contain their sexual appetites and stay faithful to their wives and girlfriends. Nevertheless, it seemed prostitution flourished wherever there were miners. And in California, at the time, it was legal.

It should be understood there was a distinction between women who engaged in prostitution and those who worked in saloons. Soon after the miners arrived, dance halls began to appear and spread throughout the region. In 1850, in San Francisco alone, their were 537 registered saloons. While saloons sold alcohol and usually offered gambling, their chief attraction was the simple presence of women. Customers generally paid a lot, 75 cents to $1.00, for a ticket to dance with one of the saloon's female employees. If the woman would steer her dance partner to the bar, she would make an additional commission from the sale of a drink.

Dancing usually began in the evening. They ranged from waltzes to schottisches with each "turn" lasting about fifteen minutes. A popular female could sometimes make more in a night than a man could make in a month. Dance hall women made enough money that it was very rare for them to double as a prostitute, in fact some women left prostitution for the dance hall for that very reason.

The gold rush women who sold their bodies for sex in the towns, the mining and logging camps, and army posts came to be known by many names. Miners labeled them "ladies of the line" and "sporting women." They were dubbed "soiled doves," "fallen angels," "daughters of sin," "scarlet ladies," and "painted cats." Their backgrounds were as diverse as the names they were called. It was said that by 1852, there was no country in the world not represented in San Francisco by at least one prostitute. While some who came to California were already in the trade, many were not. Other women came from foreign countries to escape poverty. They usually were uneducated and often spoke little or no English. Some were tricked or simply forced into the sex industry.

Equally varied were the circumstances under which they worked. A smaller number worked as "courtesans" or mistresses in "fancy houses," lavish parlor houses where music was played, and women wore the latest fashions and sipped drinks with their clients as they made small talk in prelude to going upstairs. A bouncer would maintain order. It is from these places a romanticized image of the trade would later emerge in popular culture. The business of prostitution was bawdy, but not so bad. There arose a popularized portrayal of the "hooker with the heart of gold," who, despite her occupation and the circumstances of her life, remained an optimistic and caring person. According to the cultural expectations at the time, this type of woman conformed to at least that part of the social standards that expected her gender to be nurturing and supportive.

As in any facet of society in which so many people took part, there were exceptions to the norm. The story of the prostitute who dressed in men's clothing, traveled between mining camps, and claimed to have made $50,000 in a year (the equivalent of $1,000,000 in today's money), has been told and retold in countless histories of the gold rush. Then there were the stories of prostitutes who married into "legitimate" society, those who used their earnings to start their own businesses, and those who got out of the sex industry with their bodies and spirit intact. Although true, these stories did not represent the typical life of a prostitute.

The sorry facts are that the vast majority of women who were prostitutes faced misery on a daily basis. They had meager control over their lives or their money.

The "house" took at least 50 percent of the money they made. Many women worked in brothels, which catered to a brisk trade and offered no amenities. The furniture was worn, sheets and pillowcases were not changed, and the women usually had to hawk for customers, sitting in windows or out front. There were few rules and little protection for the women. Men came to these places for one reason. In some red light areas, men could be seen lined up down a street and around the block waiting their turn to enter a brothel. The diary of one woman in such a place records that she sometimes had sex with twenty-five men in a single day. And rarely did men bother to fully disrobe. There are accounts by women who said they had sex with eighty men in a day—a few minutes with each.

All prostitutes feared unwanted pregnancies as much as venereal disease. They could not practice the common form of birth control of the time—abstinence or withdrawal. Many regularly used opiates that caused disruption or cessation of menstruation as a form of birth control. Drug addiction was common. When the opiates failed, the majority who got pregnant ended up with an abortionist or attempted to end the pregnancy themselves. Botched procedures would kill some and leave many more sterile.

Thousands of women from Latin America and China were recruited into the sex trade. Some were indentured for their passage and housed in brothels supposedly to pay off their debts. Many girls and women were tricked into the trade. Recruiters in China, for instance, might tell the parents of a girl that they would take their daughter to California to find her a Chinese husband. Instead, on arrival in San Francisco, the girl would find herself sold at auction, right on the pier, to a pimp. It has been estimated that for a cost of about $100 a year to feed and house a girl, she could make $700 a year for a brothel as a prostitute. Locked in basements, abused and brutalized, exposed to disease and physical attack, many of these girls died young. In the 1870 census, 60 percent of the Chinese women in California listed their occupation as "prostitute."

Everything in California revolved around making money as quickly as possible. The consequences, whether for the ecosystem, the land, or the people involved did not appear to matter to most. Few planned on staying in California so the desire to improve situations for a long-term good held little interest. As the violence, drug addiction, suicide, and death became evident features of the sex trade, no significant actions were taken to prevent the conditions from continuing.

Legacy and Assessment of the Gold Rush

In sum, was the California Gold Rush a positive or negative event? Would California have been better if it did not have any gold? In formulating a response to these questions, one should include the immediate perceptions written at time of the Rush, as well as the long-term assessments of its impact. If nothing else, it should be apparent there are arguments to support a variety of conclusions.

The Case for the Gold Rush

The rush "made" California in many ways. Of course, it rapidly brought hundreds of thousands of people from around the world to a region that for centuries had meant nothing except to its native inhabitants. Even more quickly, it resulted in statehood and entry into the United States. That, in turn, led to the swift establishment of American institutions—political, social, and cultural. By 1860, San Francisco, with 57,000 people, was the country's fifteenth largest city and the largest west of the Mississippi River. A large number of white men joined the search for gold, but the race for the riches had been a global attraction. Forty percent of the state's population was foreign-born with significant numbers from England, Germany, France, Mexico, Peru, Ireland, Belgium, and in the largest concentration, China. Already, California was a unique and cosmopolitan land. The rich variety of people that California displays today was amply evident during the gold rush.

In a practical sense, the gold that came from the rush had an enormous global economic impact. By the end of the 1850s, the worldwide supply of gold had increased by six-fold. It has been estimated that the gold that was extracted during this decade was greater than all the gold that had been mined throughout the world during the previous 150 years. And because people in California needed to import nearly everything they needed and were willing to pay outrageous prices for their needs, California gold quickly made its way around the globe. Gold soon replaced silver as the standard metal for world currencies and the minting of gold coins increased by 700 percent.

Bayard Taylor remained a strong proponent of the gold rush. More than a decade after the publication of *El Dorado,* he returned to writing about California with an updated assessment in *New Pictures from California,* published in 1862. In the book, Taylor extended the largely favorable impressions he had formed in 1850. He interpreted events that one might well consider to be harmful and bad to be otherwise. Taylor argued that the five significant fires which swept through San Francisco during the 1850s, each consuming large portions of the mostly wooden buildings, allowed the city the chance for a Phoenix-like rebirth as an even greater city with better built structures. He saw "grandeur" in the technology of hydraulic mining. Taylor wrote, "Like a giant bleeding to death from a single vein—the mountain washed itself away."

Most importantly, Taylor saw in the gold rush a vindication of Manifest Destiny. Here, free Americans, working in harmony with one another, reaped the riches of the land which no other people or nation had taken before. If nothing else, the gold dug out of the steams and hillsides fed into, and helped enlarge, the mythification of California and the West as a land of unique and endless possibilities.

Popular fiction set in the era of the gold rush contributed to the myth-making of California as well. Led by Bret Harte and Mark Twain, western writers of the 1860s and early 1870s transformed the gold rush into tall tales that blended optimism and faith in the essential goodness of man, with nostalgic sentimentality for the unfettered freedom found in the early days of the experience. This mythic history was easy to accept as it ignored unpleasant and sometimes brutal realities while supporting a concept of America as "right."

In the late 1800s, historian Frederick Jackson Turner added academic gravity to the stories of the fiction writers. Turner argued that the discovery of gold in California, with its ensuing flood of people west, was part of the central story of American history. The people who hurried into the region quickly transformed a "wilderness" into the "civilization" of the United States. The "out of darkness" theme, the taming and improving of the rugged frontier and all of its "wild" people, was a central theme to a great many historical interpretations well into the twentieth century.

Certainly, there can be little argument that the gold rush first defined the state of California and the character of its people. The pursuit of gold attracted bold adventurers and risk-takers who sought to "strike-it-rich," not by the slow and careful accumulation of wealth over time, but now. California was not a place for the timid, the conservative, or the traditional. The rush was populated with people who were vigorous and energetic. When it came to making money, it encouraged entrepreneurialism and often rewarded innovation and creativity. Just as important, since most people did not "pan-out" as miners, there was not much of a social stigma attached to failing. This would stimulate even more daring business ventures. In short, the "California dream" was born.

The Case Against the Gold Rush

It can be argued that the state might have been better off if it contained no gold. Critics can point to the plain fact that the rush was all about money, and a mass hysteria for getting it brought out brutal passions of greed. Ironically, most miners were unsuccessful. Obviously, the excessively high prices charged them countered much of what they made. And though there was a great deal of gold found and money made, the economic boom was quickly taken over by large companies, and only a relatively small number of people truly became rich.

Freedom, economic or otherwise, is a double-edged sword. In the rush, the line between being an enterprising person of business and an exploitive profiteer was blurred to the point of being indistinguishable. Everything seemed to have a price on it, and there appeared to be no limits on what people would do for money. Whether it was pushing young girls into prostitution, or placing discriminating taxes on anyone not from the United States, one can argue that there was a general attitude of selfishness.

The speed of the rush gave birth to a multitude of negative effects. The lack of government authority resulted in spikes in violence in what was essentially a lawless land in 1849. In this vacuum there arose vigilantism in which the innocent were sometimes swept up with the guilty. By 1855, it was estimated that Californians had purchased $6 million in bowie-knives and pistols, and that 1,700 people had been murdered over the previous five years.

Natives suffered intensely as those living in the gold country were brutally pushed off their ancestral lands. By 1870, a native population that had been 150,000 the year of Marshall's find, had been reduced to 31,000; an estimated 4,000 Indians had been sold into the slave trade, and the state government had paid out $1 million in bounties for the scalps and heads of murdered natives.

The attitude of "get in, get rich, get out" had allowed the environment to be devastated. An estimated twelve billion tons of earth had been displaced and more than seven thousand tons of toxic chemicals had been introduced to the land, rivers, and lakes. A gradual development of agriculture and industry by people who viewed the land as a long-term investment might have been more orderly and considerate of nature.

The rush created and accelerated racial tensions in a turbulent time in the nation's history. The admission of California as a state had little order and rational planning and this was only because of the desire to secure the rights to the gold fields. It took nine months of divisive debate in the federal government over the question of whether to have slavery, or not, in California. The compromise that allowed its admission as a free state did nothing resolve the debate. If anything, it widened the split between the pro- and anti-slavery sides and hardened their positions. In retrospect, the granting of statehood for California was a defining moment in the history of the United States as it moved the nation that much closer to secession and civil conflict. It might have lacked the glitter, but a California without the rush would have been better managed, more peaceful, and respectful of others.

Farewell, dear wife, keep up good cheer,
There's glittering scenes before me
You soon with me the wealth shall share
That lays in California.
I'll hunt the mountains, search the sand,
Through weather clear and stormy,
With shovel, spade, and sieve in hand,
Dig Gold in California.

— "*The Gold Hunter's Farewell to his Wife*" written in 1849

Slavery, Statehood and the Civil War

When Major Robert Garnett volunteered to design a state seal at California's constitutional convention in 1849, his inclusion of the Roman goddess Minerva was appropriate for several reasons. In mythology she was born fully grown out the head of her father, Jupiter. California, too, was "fully born," bypassing a period as an official territory of the United States, instead progressing directly into statehood. Also, it was proper that Minerva was a goddess of both wisdom and war because the controversial entry of California into the Union was resolved only by a calibrated political compromise that, for a time, balanced two diametrically opposed forces, one adamantly in favor of and one increasingly against, American slavery. The rapid entry of the 31st state intensified the national debate over slavery's continued future.The awful national divide is epitomized in Garnett himself. He designed the seal for a state whose very creation widened the political wedge and moved the nation one step closer to the precipice of civil war. When that war did begin, California chose to remain inside the Union. Yet, thousands of men in the state, opted to serve for the confederacy. Garnett, a Virginian by birth, was one of those men. Soon, he was a brigadier general and taking order from Robert E. Lee. In July, 1861, in western Virginia, he was shot by pursuing Union troops. Garnett became the first general on either side to die in the Civil War.

Background to the National Fight Over Slavery

California became an important factor in the national debate over slavery that was roiling the nation by the 1850s. While strong moral, religious, and ethical arguments were made against the enslavement of humans, most antebellum white Americans were not among the abolitionists who called for an immediate end to the practice. Morality aside, the thought of ending slavery carried with it many practical concerns to the minds of white Americans. People were uncertain about the legality of forcibly taking what was considered private property. They were unsure, if this did happen, who should pay, and at what cost. By 1855, slavery was, in dollar value, the largest business in the nation. It was more valuable then railroads and manufacturing combined. And sadly, racism did not end as one moved north past the Mason-Dixon line. Far too many northern whites who might have opposed slavery on principle, were unsettled, if not outright hostile, toward the idea of four million blacks suddenly gaining the freedom to move out of the South and become a new population of social and economic competitors. Therefore, a majority of northern whites saw the "solution" to slavery to be its containment in the South. Keep in from expanding west, the notion went, and as the nation grew in size and population, the influences of pro-slave forces would be diluted and weakened. Overtime, the institution might well die out on its own.

This stance was as popular as it was clearly self-serving. It required nothing of northern whites while it gave them years, if not decades, or having to actually deal with the end of the slave system. And should that end come, there would be no obvious obligation on the part of northerners to assume responsibility for the freed slaves. It was self-delusion, however, to believe that slave-holding whites would passively play their role in this chimera. It was all too obvious that for slavery in the United States to continue to flourish, it had to spread to new lands, and that meant it had to move west.

Since the beginning of the Republic, the federal government had kept the country stitched together by developing political compromises on slavery. It was an issue that defied ignoring. In 1790, the first national census revealed that slaves made up 18 percent of the total U.S. population (700,000 out of 3.8 million) Thus, as it was three years earlier, in 1787, at the Constitutional convention in Philadelphia, that bargains were made on this cruel business. The right to own slaves codified as law (the earlier Articles of Confederation, 1781-1787, had been silent on the issue). Yet, even some who supported slavery abhorred the brutal international slave trade across the Atlantic Ocean. Thus, a compromise was born in which after 20 more years of the slave trade, in 1808 it would be outlawed. By this time, there were 1.2 million slaves in the country with a total population of 7.2 million.

As the country expanded west, new compromises came with it. The Missouri Compromise of 1820 had defused the debate over whether to add the territory of pro-slave Missouri to the nation, upsetting opponents of slavery. The compromise was to serve both interests by bringing a free territory of Maine at the same time. The Louisiana Territory was similarly divided, half-free and half-slave. This scenario would be repeated in the next decade. In 1836, Arkansas was admitted as a slave state; in 1837, Michigan was added as a free state. With these trade-offs in hand, the nation plodded on, half-free, half-slave. But in the 1840s, an immense acreage of land was rapidly added to the country's western side. This would prove to be its eventual undoing.

In 1824, the United States was roughly the same size and population as Mexico. The United States had 9.6 million people spread over 1.8 million square miles. Mexico had 6 million people living within 1.7 million square miles. By 1849, much had changed. As a result of the Oregon Treaty signed with Great Britain in 1846, and the Treaty of Guadalupe Hidalgo signed with Mexico in 1848, the United States had gained more than one million square miles of land, including more than half of what had been Mexico. One significance of this massive shift of property is both Great Britain and Mexico had outlawed slavery within their countries. Now, the borders had been extended for the slave-allowing United States and the prospect of slavery existing from Atlantic to the Pacific was very much a possibility. And then the gold rush began and tens of thousands of Americans quickly moved into California.

Slavery in the Gold Rush

There was not a large contingent of slaves in California during the gold rush. Their numbers are estimated somewhere between 2,000 and 4,000 individuals. However, their presence in California and the debate they sparked was considerably large and noisy. A slave who was worth $1,000 in Virginia growing crops, could be worth upwards of $5,000 in California working in gold mining. If California ended up as a slave state, one could expect the demand for slave labor in the West to be great. It might lead to shortages of slaves in the South, which would raise prices there as well. These were all favorable prospects for slave-holders. But as soon as the first white southerners arrived, there were public declarations made against slavery. There were nearly as many pronouncements against blacks as well. In 1848, both *The Californian* and *The California Star* asserted that neither slaves nor free blacks should be allowed to live in California. Public resolutions in Sacramento and San Francisco made similar statements.

White miners also took a strong anti-slavery stance. In July 1849, prospectors on the Yuba River drew up a series of ordinances regarding mining. One rule limited the size of a claim to what a single miner could work by himself. Clearly, the intent was to prevent a miner from taking out a much larger claim of land and then working it with slave labor. As in the cities, this anti-slavery stance was not one based on abolitionist morality or racial tolerance. Whites did not want their work to be equated with slave labor, and they certainly did not want additional competition for the gold. The Yuba miners enforced their rules with threats, violence, and even by hanging violators.

The racism of many white Californians was as marked against blacks as it had been against the natives, and would be towards the Chinese and the Japanese. A steady stream of repugnant slurs would define the debate over slavery in the region. In sum, people of all color save white, were characterized as inferior beings who would be a drag on the development of the key features of society, such as its political system, economy, and cultural life. The very presence of any and every non-white person, it was argued in the newspapers, at public halls, degraded individualism and ideals of the region. Enslaved or free blacks were considered equally a "threat" by white miners who feared southerners would dump their unwanted slaves in California, flooding it with new freemen as economic competitors. There were a few voices of tolerance and reason in this debate. These whites argued that the very principles of individualism and personal rights freedom were endangered by the call to ban all black people from California.

For American slaveholders, however, by the gold rush, moving west was the only direction in which American slavery could grow. To the south, Mexico, which had no significant slave trade for nearly a century, had formally abolished slavery in 1829. To the north, sections of Canada had banned slavery in 1803, and it was outlawed throughout Canada in 1833. Both countries had become safe havens for runaway slaves. Thus, slavers had pushed into Texas, even when it was under the authority of Mexico. They had obtained an exemption that allowed their human chattel, and by 1836 there were 5,000 slaves working there. Now, many set their sights on California.

Statehood and the Compromise of 1850

The stage was set. The Unites States wanted and needed California to enter the Union. There was great agreement it was too valuable not to bring it in, and the surging population in the region would not allow a delay if they attempted to wait. The question was if it would be slave or free. On that issue there was great disagreement. Zachary Taylor was the president at the time. Taylor was from Louisiana. He owned more than one hundred slaves and firmly supported slavery as an institution that had a right to exist. It would seem clear what his opinion would be regarding the "question" over California. But he was also a brigadier general with a long military career serving the interests of the country. He was a nationalist with a pragmatic streak in him. He understood the polarization of the views regarding slavery. Whatever side his administration supported would only inflame the anger and intransigence of the other side.

Therefore, Taylor urged Americans in California to quickly adopt a state constitution that prohibited slavery. Once a state, Taylor asserted, the California legislature could decide whether or not to maintain that status. At the same time, he promoted the same plan for the territory of New Mexico. Taylor believed it best if each state, not the federal government, decided on its own, simply because the slave issue was so explosive and divisive on the federal level. He wanted to avoid a prolonged political fight. Congress, however, balked, thereby assuring the slave question would remain a national topic and, as Taylor feared, one in which there would be no easy answer.

Looking back, one sees the nation moving on its course toward secession and war. For a democracy to function there needs to be a measure of compromise and respect for dissension—two qualities that were in short supply in 1850. Both sides of the slave question bitterly resisted the other. At the time California was on the threshold of statehood, southerners were blocking an effort to abolish slavery in the District of Columbia. They violently opposed, but could not prevent, northern representatives from passing a "personal liberty" law which prevented courts from returning runaway slaves to their owners. For the slave interests to accept the 31st state as "free" was simply, in the minds of many, an intolerable proposition. If nothing else it would end the numerical balance between free and slave states, currently at fifteen to fifteen. That could have significant national ramifications for the future composition of the Congress, as well as who would occupy the White House.

The few moderates on slavery and unionists spent the winter of 1849–1850 trying to craft an agreement. The political debate raged for seven months. During negotiations, remarkable suggestions were made. South Carolina Senator John C. Calhoun suggested dividing California as well as the entire country along the Missouri compromise line parallel 36° 30' north. In other words, the senator proposed slicing the country in half, horizontally. He called for the creation of a dual presidency for the country; one for the free North, the other for the slave South.

Before the audacious proposal could gain serious support, the 68-year-old Calhoun died of tuberculosis in March 1850. His death was followed four months later by the loss of President Taylor as well. In the days following the Fourth of July celebrations in which he sampled many food brought as gifts by ordinary citizens, including a dish of milk and cherries, the president developed a violent stomach disorder and died on July 9th. The official cause of death as gastroenteritis (bacteria from improperly or contaminated prepared food or water) has been upheld by recent

DNA tests and is widely accepted by historians. Nevertheless, a handful continue to theorize Taylor was deliberately poisoned during this tumultuous period. It was left to Taylor's vice-president, the mannered and dignified Millard Fillmore from New York, to shepherd the compromise bill through Congress. Fillmore was considered more flexible and resulting legislation demonstrated that characteristic.

In the end a plan emerged that would have California enter the United States as a free state. In return, the rest of the lands that had recently been taken from Mexico and were currently American territories would have no restrictions on slavery. Additionally, in Washington D.C. there would still be slavery but no slave trade. There would also be a new set of laws regarding fugitive slaves. The Fugitive Slave Act required all U.S. citizens to assist in the return of runaway slaves. Not only would the Act make it easier for slaveholders to capture and regain control of runaways, in their minds it strengthened the belief that slaves were owned property.

The birth of the state of California was anything but idealistic or high-minded. The 31st state was a piece in the complicated puzzle of sectional politics being practiced by a country that was slowing being pulled apart at its seams. And inside the state, the political scene had been just as muddied. During the debate, California had been under federal military control, which was standard for all territories. During this period, there was little semblance of political stability. There had been five governors in ten months of U.S. occupation: Commodore John Sloat, Commodore Robert Stockton, Colonel John Fremont, General Stephen Kearney, and Colonel Richard Mason. Local power was held by an *alcalde*, something akin to a mayor except with ill-defined and much greater authority. It was clear that the governance of California was in need to refinement.

The Legacy of the Statehood Battle on the Civil War

Looking back, the compromise brought California into a union that would only survive for ten more years. There were features in the compromise for every interest to dislike. Slave holders remained unhappy by their exclusion from the rich gold regions in California. The South saw itself losing political power to a North that was also continuing to increase its economic lead over it. For their part, northerners resented being forced into a closer association with the slave system as a result of the enhanced Fugitive Slave Act. Their more intimate experiences with the brutality of slavery turned more of them into abolitionists during the 1850s. The Act outraged one long-time abolitionist, Harriet Beecher Stowe, to write *Uncle Tom's Cabin* (1853), a fictional but emotionally powerful story that focused on the sorrowful plight of a slave family owned by a heartless master, Simon Legree. The book became an international best seller, the most widely read novel in American history up to that time. It was one of many major developments that came from the compromise that stretched the bonds of national unity to their breaking point.

The tipping point came in November 1860 with the election of Abraham Lincoln. Though not an abolitionist, Lincoln clearly disliked slavery, considered it immoral, and wanted to see it contained, if not eventually ended. He was elected with only 40 percent of the national vote as it was a hotly contested four-man race. With Lincoln waiting in the wings, South Carolina became the first state to declare its secession from the United States. It would quickly be joined by six other states, and later an additional four more. The country's remaining twenty-three states had to decide their own destiny as well.

One might think it would be a given that the free state of California would remain in the Union. Certainly, a majority of the citizens at the time felt that way. But a review of the results of the state's voters in the presidential race indicates Californians were just as divided as the nation as to who should lead the country at the most acrimonious and volatile stage in its history.

The 1860 presidential election results in California:

Abraham Lincoln (Republican Party)	38,733	votes 32.3%
Stephen Douglas (Northern Democrat)	37,999	votes 31.7%
John Breckinridge (Southern Democrat)	33,969	votes 28.3%
John Bell (Constitutional Union)	9,111	votes 7.6%

Nationally, Lincoln beat Douglas by 10 percent. In California, the margin of victory was.06 percent, a mere 734 votes. Still, that gave him all four of the state's electoral votes. Lincoln received most of his support from San Francisco and the Bay area, as well in some parts of the southern and eastern portions of the state. He did poorly in northern California, on the central coast, and in the Central Valley.

As the nation split in two, a few people publically advocated the idea that California become a separate republic that would leave the United States but not join the southern Confederate States of America. When the war began, the state's pro-union politicians quickly gained the upper hand. They passed legislation pledging the state's loyalty to the United States. All but five senators and twelve assemblymen voted for it. Legislators moved to create two regiments of cavalry and five regiments of infantry for the Union cause.

However, it was not the state's men that the Lincoln administration most wanted. In 1861, California had more than one-quarter of million combat-age men. (Of these, about 13 percent were men originally from slave states.) Whatever their political sympathies, they were very distant from the battlefields and it would have been prohibitively expensive to transport significant numbers of them. Long-distance travel to the East remained as it had for decades, either by the long overland trails or by ship through Central America. Over the course of the Civil War, 16,000 Californians volunteered to serve for the Union side but few saw battle. Most were assigned to police Indians in the state, serve in western forts and garrisons, or to escort and protect the overland mail delivery—the pony express.

What the Union wanted most from California was its gold supply. Throughout the war, two or three specially-guarded steamships sailed from the port in San Francisco. On average, each ship carried $1 million in gold. A few ships would be loaded with more gold, sometimes $2 million and once $3 million. In 1864 alone, $46 million in gold was sent via Panama to help the Union side. The gold was sold to provide nearly one million Union soldiers with pay, weapons, and food.

The 1864 presidential election results in California:

Abraham Lincoln (Republican Party)	62,053 votes	58.6%
George McClellan (Democrat)	43,837 votes	41.4%

A lot had changed since 1860. By 1864, Lincoln had signed the Morrill Act, the Homestead Act, and the Pacific Railway Act into law. These three laws had monumental impact on the development of California and the western United States as a whole. The rough beginnings of statehood were smoother, though racial troubles and the emergence of a tremendously powerful railroad still awaited California in the next decades.

An Unexpected Challenge

The Shifting State Capital

To see the unsettled and hasty nature of California's statehood, one needs not look further than its capital. It was no simple task to choose and agree upon a capital city. During the Mexican era, the capital was designated by each territorial governor, and it moved a lot. The capital had been in San Diego, Santa Barbara, Los Angeles, and Monterey—its location in 1850. Of course, Monterey was also the gathering site for the forty-eight delegates to the constitutional convention. At that first assembly, San Jose, which had been founded in 1777, was selected as the capital city. As it turned out, this began an almost comic series of events and decisions that would see the capital move eight times in eleven years between five cities. It was yet another example of how the gold rush pushed the region into statehood before it was fully ready for the responsibility.

When the delegates to the first session of the state legislature initially met in San Jose in November 1849, they were confronted by practical problems. They were expected to work in an inadequate building with limited space. Adding to their displeasure was the shortage of housing for themselves. It was also a consensus of opinion that the town was short on other amenities such as restaurants and creature comforts in general. After two sessions, ending May 1, 1851, and upon receiving an offer of improved conditions by General Mariano Guadalupe Vallejo, a vote was taken and they agreed to open the third session in the town of Vallejo.

Though the offer looked good, the town of Vallejo did not when the legislature convened there in January 1852. Not only were the promised buildings incomplete, they also lacked some of the necessary furniture and fixtures. There were no printing materials in town and a docked steamship had to be converted into housing for the representatives. In less than a month, the delegates left, moving to Sacramento and giving General Vallejo one year to complete the work in order for them to return. They did return the next year but found the facilities still woefully lacking and they left again in less than a month.

This time, the legislature moved to Benicia which offered a fine, new two-story brick building. But while the building was the best yet, it quickly proved to be too small for all the reporters, political aides, and visitors who arrived during the fourth and fifth sessions, February 1853 to February 1854. Limited housing and poor weather did not help matters.

Thus, in 1854, the capital was relocated to Sacramento, the largest of the cities so occupied. The city did have good accommodations. It boasted a new courthouse and had dozens of hotels. There was an excellent transportation system that utilized its large waterways and stagecoaches. There was a limited telegraph service. Perhaps as important, there was a "can-do" attitude among its citizenry. After a fire in July 1854 destroyed the courthouse, along with a large section of the city, the response was both dramatic and positive. In less than four months, a new courthouse was completed in time for the next legislative session. Plans for a grand capitol building were soon drawn up.

The capital would have one more move, although it was temporary. In December 1861, much of Sacramento was flooded and the legislature relocated to San

Francisco for the next five-month session. Construction on the new (and current) capitol building had begun in 1860. After the law makers returned to Sacramento, there were proposals at times to move once more but they could not budge the delegates. The new capitol building was fully completed in 1874; in 1879, Sacramento was officially declared to be California's seat of government.

California Agriculture: Real and Imagined

Like so many things in California, its economy is very diverse and very large. It has a huge financial and trade market. Leading industries include aerospace and defense, computer technology and electronic equipment, entertainment and tourism, transportation, light manufacturing, and biotechnology. Principal natural resources include timber, petroleum, cement, and natural gas. Agriculture is another important sector of the economy, yet farming accounts for less than 2 percent of the state's total gross product. Even so, California, by far, leads all other states in total dollar agricultural production and has done so for many decades. By the end of the 1920s, farming was already a $1 billion industry in the state. One key to this dominance has been the diversity within agriculture itself. Whereas many farm states may produce ten to fifteen commodities, and be best known for a single crop—potatoes from Idaho, corn from Iowa—California offers over four hundred farm products and is the leader in dozens of them.

Many farm commodities closely associated with California today originated far away—avocados from Chile, navel oranges from Brazil, Valencia oranges, peaches, and Meyer lemons from China, nectarines from Afghanistan, olives from Spain and Italy, kale from Croatia, pomegranates from Malta, and dates and figs from the Middle East. Through advantageous climate conditions, intensive and often innovative cultivation, the development of massive water transport systems, and a great deal of hard labor, California farming has become an agricultural giant.

Today, the consumer desire for California crops may seem a given, but it was not always that way. For one thing, for a very long time in American history, people had no or limited access to many perishable food commodities. As a result, they often did not include most of these products as part of their normal diet. These people would have to be convinced otherwise. While education of the nutritional merits of some crops would play its role, careful marketing began in earnest in the late nineteenth century. The skillful creation and management of an idealized image of the state helped define an image that endures to the present—California as a land of health.

Early Marketing of California Agriculture

Several iconic agricultural images that today identify California's fruits and vegetables were formed a century or more ago. This was done in concert by the state's principle boosters—land speculators, the railroads and the allied tourism industry, political interest groups, and agri-business itself The press often played a supportive role as well. In the first decades of the twentieth century, the popular depiction of California as a land of rugged, natural beauty was augmented with visions of its agricultural richness. Typically, there was an emphasis on the healthfulness of California products along with the pastoral and charm of the land. Some of the more enduring of these images were widely promoted at two international expositions that occurred in 1915: The Panama Pacific International Exposition in San Francisco, and the Panama California Exposition in San Diego, both of which celebrated the completion of the Panama Canal. Visitors— 19 million to San Francisco's expo alone—saw advertising which showcased farm products on items such as packing crate labels and postcards. One very successful marketing effort was for the raisin industry; a group of Fresno girls dressed in white blouses & blue sunbonnets handed out samples of the fruit. The next year, one of those girls, Lorraine Collett, was chosen to be the face of the Sun-Maid company. More than a century later, she still is.

However, the two readings from Ted Steinberg's Pulitzer-nominated book show that Americans a century ago had a very different diet than today. Their meals relied heavily on meats, animal fats, and starchy food. It was not common to eat fresh produce, and many fruits and nuts were considered "special occasion" fare, limited to times like Christmas. To persuade people to alter what and when they ate, marketers associated the sunny moderate weather of California's Central Valley and southland farms with the notion that, as the state was "good for one's health," therefore, so were the foods that grew from its soil.

Down to Earth: Nature's Role in American History, by Ted Steinberg

Chapter 11: "Movable Feast"

"Land of Sunshine"

In the late nineteenth century, boosters tried to lure people to the Golden State by selling them on the climate. And n one did more to market the image of California as a sun-drenched oasis than the journalist Charles Fletcher Lummis. In 1885, Lummis, recovering from a bout of malaria, decided that the best route to recovery was to journey, by foot, from his home in Cincinnati, Ohio, some 3,000 miles to Los Angeles. After 143 days of walking, Lummis arrived in southern California, tan, fit, and eager to testify to the virtues of the west coast's magnificent climate. In 1895, Lummis became editor of a magazine aptly named *Land of Sunshine*. In it he argued that California's sunny climate made people healthier and fostered intellectual and creative talents. It was no coincidence that some of the world's greatest minds, from Jesus to Plato, to Michelangelo, came from lands blessed with a great deal of sun. In the United States, he deduced, all roads led to Los Angeles.

Much of what Lummis told his reader was hype. But the was little question that California's cloudless skies—putting aside for the moment the agricultural implications of too little rain—gave it an edge over the East when it came to growing food. Indeed, California is one of only five places on the planet blessed with such a sun-rich climate (the others are central Chile, southern Africa, southern Australia, and the Mediterranean basin.) In Fresno, California, the heart of raisin country, for instance, average precipitation in May is just a third of an inch. Barely a tenth of an inch falls in June and essentially none in July and August. Virtually all of the area's 10 inches of precipitation occurs between November and April. The rest of the year is sunny, amazingly so, with sunshine favoring the city an average of more than 90 percent of the time in the summer months.

Californians have something known as the Pacific High to thank for all the sunny weather. This zone of high pressure lies stationed off the coast of the central part of the state, deflecting all precipitation north to the Pacific Northwest. From late March until October the high pressure stands watch over the Golden State's sunny skies, before drifting south to Mexico in the fall and allowing rain to slip in. As regular as clockwork, the Pacific High returns north in the spring, and with it sunshine beats down on the land, creating perfect conditions for photosynthesis. With respect to solar radiation, California has struck it rich. But the state's good fortune does not end there. It extends into the realm of geology as well. One of the largest river valleys on earth, the Central Valley, an area nearly the size of England, stretches more than 400 miles through the center of the state. Drained by the Sacramento River in the north and the San Joaquin in the south, the valley is, in the words on one environmental scientist, "the richest agricultural region in the history of the world."

"Sun Kissed"

California's early dependence on gold and silver mining was overcome through the development of large-scale irrigation projects and the expansion of commercial agriculture. In its early period, 1860s-1870s, wheat was a dominate crop. Much of this is credited to Isaac Friedlander, a native of Germany, who made his way to California, drawn by the Gold Rush. Unsuccessful in the gold fields, Friedlander would strike it rich in the fertile dirt fields of the state's Central Valley. Embracing the new technology of speedy clipper ships and the new trans-Atlantic telegraph cable to Europe, Friedlander became a major supplier of wheat to Great Britain. He purchased thousands of acres of land in the valley, and built grain elevators, grist mills and canals to serve and expand his enterprise. The "Wheat King," as he was called, died when he was only 54, but wheat would remain the major crop of the state until the 1890s, when competition from the Great Plains and Russia prompted more California farmers to shift to specialty crops such as citrus and grapes.

Before the late nineteenth century, few Americans believed, as many commonly do today, in the value of a diet rich in fruits and vegetables. In fact, many urbanites worried that eating fresh produce might actually worsen their health, bringing on dread diseases as cholera or dysentery. Aside from the nuts and raisins consumed once or twice a year at holiday time, the diet of most Americans centered on foods full of fat, starch, and salt.

Although truck farms had sprung up outside of major cities, introducing residents to a variety of fresh produce, it took a self-conscious effort on the part of California orchards to sell consumers on the idea that fruits and vegetables ought to play a part in everyone's daily fare. By the turn of the century, the campaign appeared to be paying off. "The old prejudice against fruit are fast passing away." Observed one grower in 1893. "Fruit has become a necessity rather than a luxury." In 1910, a housewife put it this way: "When I first began to keep house, ten years ago, we ate cereal, eggs, coffee for breakfast, with fruit occasionally instead of cereal; but now we must have grapefruit every morning... {T}hen, when I go to the market and see fresh beans, cucumbers and spinach, I buy them without really stopping to think, so easily tempted are we." As the reference to fresh produce suggests, marketing on the part of California growers initially helped to increase the demand for locally grown produce.

At one time, fruit passed into eastern markets with little concern for quality. But in an effort to stimulate national demand, California orchards set out to standardize their products. Growers and shippers joined in establishing formal sets of rules for packing fruit, specifying uniform box sizes and shapes. The fruit itself was classified into various grades—fancy, choice, and standard. "We must be guided by the experience and adopt the practices of other successful manufacturers, and so arrange and classify our products that each purchaser may secure the *identical commodity* he orders in the most convenient form," explained one grower. The state government in California, spurred on by a freeze in 1912 that left many growers with little choice but to ship damaged fruit east, also stepped in and passed the Fresh Fruit, Nut, and Vegetable Standardization Act of 1917 to regulate quality.

Growers themselves chose to specialize in those species of fruit that best met market imperatives. Some 60 different varieties of pears—Bose, Giffard, Joan of Arc, Vicar, Wilder Early, among others—once grew on this continent. But California farmers eventually zeroed in on one main variety, the Bartlett, a pear that was easy to grow, can and ship, and thus suitable for commercial harvesting. By the early twentieth century, Bartletts made up roughly 80 to 90 percent of the pears raised in California.

Standardization helped orchards sell fruit in eastern markets, but to transform crops such as raisins and oranges into year-round staples, growers had to become more aggressive. New marketing organizations formed to oversee the harvesting, processing, and shipping of fruit, while engaging in brand name advertising. California raisin growers, centered in sunny Fresno County, produced record-setting yields in the 1890s, but found that demand did not keep up with supply, forcing down prices. To solve the problem of under consumption, the growers founded a cooperative organization, but it soon failed. Then, in 1912, the California Associated Raisin Company was formed, a group uniting over 1,000 orchards. In one of the new company's very first moves, it created the "Sun-Maid" brand name to market its product. Using one part feminine mystique and one part raw natural power, the company tried to sell Americans on the idea that they could get back in touch with nature and improve their health by buying the product. The Sun-Maid label, showing a girl in a red bonnet with the sun in the background, became one of the most successful trademarks in food history. Then the growers launched an advertising campaign, pitching the raisins in newspapers and women's magazines. Sales agents went from grocer to grocer in major cities hawking the product. In the 1920s, the growers marketed raisins in little nickel packages, the perfect size to fit into a school lunch sack. In six months' time, the company sold 17,000 tons of five-cent boxes valued at 18 million dollars. As consumption boomed, raisins went from being a luxury item eaten only on holidays to an expected and ordinary part of daily fare.

As late as the early 1880s, oranges too remained a luxury item, more a Christmas stocking stuffer than a dietary staple. Since the end of the Civil War, growers in Florida had shipped oranges north by boat during the holiday season. By the mid-1880s, improved railroad transportation allowed Florida orchards to out compete their counterparts in California for the eastern market. One New Jersey vegetable farmer marveled at the way farmers in Florida "with their evergreen productiveness, have been able to revolutionize the old conditions, by sending to northern cities, even when snow clad and ice bound, the fruits of balmy summer." Then, in 1895, a freeze pummeled the Sunshine State. The year before the cold, Florida outstripped California by roughly one million boxes. The onset of the freeze, however, caused Florida production to plummet. By 1909, nearly three-quarters of all citrus consumed in the United States came from California.

But more than a cold spell accounted for California's lock on the national orange market. In 1885, Americans consumed almost no citrus fruit; in 1914, they were eating roughly 40 oranges per year. Credit for that change must go to the California Fruit Growers Exchange, founded in 1893 (eight years after Florida established a similar organization). The exchange united some 15,000 growers and 200 packing associations around the processing and marketing of citrus. At one time some 200 different brand name oranges existed. The fruit exchange, however, sought to streamline marketing by creating the Sunkist (originally Sun Kissed) trademark and stamping it on each and every orange grown. During the early decades of the twentieth century, Sunkist's marketers blanketed the nation with images of its product. It created picturesque labels for use on the tens of millions of citrus crates it shipped every year. It advertised in newspapers and magazines, set up billboards, helped grocers and especially chain stores to create elaborate window displays, and ran promotional spots on the radio. By the early 1930s, the organization had over 1,000 billboards in 11 metropolitan markets, including one in New York's Times Square, that reached, it is estimated, one million people each day.

The Human Element in the Fields

The success of California's agricultural industry is a favorable combination of several natural and human-created factors. Yet, in an industry with such variety of crops with their many planting and harvesting schedules, there will always be periods of an intensive need for a large labor supply, often with diverse sets of skills. Coupled with the sheer scale and geographic size of the industry, California field labor has a long history of innovation, contention, and a sometimes violent struggle between farm employers and their employees.

Timeline for California Agricultural Labor

1769—Franciscan priests and Spanish soldiers bring Native people living near missions in Baja north to work in Alta California. They help build missions at San Diego and Monterey, and develop the settlements' first farming fields and orchards.

1848—Gold is discovered on the American River. In fewer than two years, California's non-Native population quadruples. Farming rapidly expands in response to the increased demand for food.

1852—A bill to import Chinese contract agricultural workers fails in the state legislature, but thousands of Chinese immigrants begin arriving on their own.

1870—Chinese immigrants are 15 percent of California's farm labor force. In Sacramento, San Mateo & Alameda counties, they make-up between 25 and 50 percent of farm labor.

1877—Anti-Chinese protests and attacks on Chinese spread throughout California.

1882—Congress passes Chinese Exclusion Act, suspending Chinese immigration into the U.S.

1891—Japanese immigrants arrive in California primarily as agricultural laborers.

1894—A district court rule that Japanese immigrants cannot become U.S. citizens because they are not "a free white person" as required under the Naturalization Act of 1790.

1903—Immigrant sugar beet workers in Oxnard form the Japanese-Mexican Labor Association and strike over low wages, the state's first organized farm labor action. Growers negotiate a settlement, raising wages.

1905—The Asiatic Exclusion League is formed in San Francisco by 67 labor unions.

1907—Sikh laborers from northern India begin working on California farms.

1908—Japan and the United States, to reduce tensions between the two nations, form the "Gentlemen's Agreement" which halts the Japanese immigration to the U.S.

1909—An estimated 30,000 Japanese work on California farms, or 42 percent of the labor force.

1913—California passes the Alien Land Act, prohibiting noncitizens from owning land.

1930s—In response to the economic collapse of the Great Depression, more than 500,000 Mexican Americans are deported nation-wide under the Mexican Repatriation Act, resulting in a decrease of Hispanic workers on California farms.

1939—*Factories in the Field* by Carey McWilliams & *The Grapes of Wrath* by John Steinbeck are published, focusing national attention on the poor conditions of migrant farm workers.

1942—Following the United States' entry into World War II, President Franklin D. Roosevelt signs Executive Order 9066 authorizing the exclusion of civilians from any area without due process. More than 110,000 California residents of Japanese ancestry are forced into internment camps. At the same time, the U.S. and Mexico create the *Bracero* program, which allows for the importation of temporary contract agricultural workers from Mexico into the U.S. to alleviate the wartime farm labor shortage.

1943—Congress repeals Chinese Exclusion Act.

1948—U.S. Supreme Court rules California's Alien Land Act is unconstitutional.

1960—*Harvest of Shame* is broadcast on Thanksgiving by CBS. The documentary focuses on the poor working and living conditions of farm laborers.

1962—National Farm Workers Association (NFWA) is created by Cesar Chavez.

1964—The Bracero program ends, having brought 4.6 million Mexicans temporarily into the U.S.

1965—Filipino members of the Agricultural Workers Organizing Committee (AWOC) strike against Central Valley grape growers. They are joined by the largely Mexican members of NFWA. Both unions call for a consumer boycott of table grapes.

1966—AWOC and NFWA merge, forming the United Farm Workers Union.

1970—Central Valley grape growers sign UFW contracts, ending strike and boycott.

1975—California passes the Agricultural Labor Relations Act, the first law recognizing the rights of farmworkers to organize and bargain collectively.

1986—Congress passes the Immigration Reform and Control Act, which grants amnesty to illegal immigrants who have resided in the United States since 1982, and imposes sanctions on employers who knowingly hire illegal immigrants.

1994—California voters pass Proposition 187, denying undocumented immigrants access to public schools, medical care, and other social services, and requiring public employees and law enforcement officials to report undocumented immigrants to the Immigration and Naturalization Service. Federal courts later strike down nearly all its provisions.

2006—An estimated 750,000 farmworkers are employed in California; 80 percent are Mexican immigrant males.

2010—Undocumented workers in California are five times more likely to lack health insurance.

2014—An estimated 829,000 farmworkers are employed in California, including 30,200 in Santa Barbara county

2016—In California, 90 percent of migrant agricultural workers are foreign-born and an estimated 60 percent are in the United States illegally; the median age is 38; the average annual earnings are $15,000-$17,000.

Status of California Agriculture Today

Today, the statistics of California's agriculture reveal its immense value and sheer dominance in producing many farm products as compared to other states. Southern California soon was producing more than two-thirds of the nation's orange crop, and more than 90 percent of its lemons.

California agriculture is large, diverse, and complex. In many ways, it is the most important industry in the state. In 2015, it generated $47 billion in cash receipts (Iowa was second with $27 billion.) California has led the nation's states in agricultural revenue every year since 1948. Exports to other countries accounted for $14.7 billion of sales, with Canada, the European Union, China, Japan, and Mexico being the top five export markets. Although only 4 percent of the nation's farms are found within its borders, California produced 13 percent of the nation's total farm output. Twenty-seven percent of the state's 77,500 farms generated $100,000 or more in total sales. The average California farm is 441 acres, compared to 418 acres nationally. An estimated 18,100 jobs are created for every $1 billion in farm sales in California. Today, one out if every ten jobs in the state is related to agriculture. In 2018, the year-round labor force was 388,100 employees, a number that balloons to nearly 750,000 during the summer. Labor contractors estimate that 65 to 80 percent of the agricultural labor force consists of illegal aliens.

Approximately 25.4 million acres of land in the state is used for farms or ranches. Perhaps its single defining feature is the diversity of the crops. There is large-scale production of seventy to eighty major commodities: thirty-one vegetables, twenty fruits and nuts, seventeen field crops, and ten livestock and poultry products. In total, more than 400 agricultural products come from the state.

California produces more than one-half of the nation's fruits, nuts, and vegetables. It is the nation's sole producer (99 percent or more) of 15 commodities: almonds, artichokes, dates, dried plums, figs, garlic, kiwifruit, olives/olive oil, peaches (clingstone), pistachios, pomegranates, raisins, rice (sweet), table grapes, and walnuts.

California produces more than 90 percent of the nation's processed tomatoes, wine, plums, and broccoli. In addition, the state is the nation's largest producer of more than 80 other crop and livestock commodities. These include alfalfa seed, apricots, asparagus, avocados, beans (black-eyed, lima, garbanzo), bell peppers, brussel sprouts, carrots, cauliflower, celery, chili peppers, cotton, cut flowers, dairy (milk and cream), eggplant, eggs, hay, honey, honeydew melons, lemons, lettuce (head, leaf; romaine), melons (cantaloupe, casaba, crenshaw, honeydew, persian), nectarines, nursery stock, onions, pears (bartlett), rabbits, raspberries, safflower, spinach, strawberries, turnips, and wild rice. In 2016, the leading commodity by dollar was milk, followed by almonds, and grapes.

Of the 3,133 counties in the nation, nine of the top ten counties for farm produce sales are in California. Fresno County, in the heart of the Central Valley, leads in agricultural production. Of its 3.84 million acres, 1.88 million is devoted to farming which, in 2016, produced $6.61 billion in crops from 5,600 farms. Tulare, Monterey, Kern, and Merced round out the top five counties. Together, these five counties alone exceed the farm production of forty-three of the states in the nation. (source: Fresno County Farm Bureau, 2016)

Projections for Tomorrow

When it comes to California farms, the past is not necessarily a prologue for the future. The population of farmers is aging and it is uncertain who will take their place. In 2014, the average age of the primary operator of a California farm was 58 and one out of five were over the age of 70. The number of farmers who are older than 65 years outnumber those who are under 25 years by more than sixty-to-one. Farm labor in California has other concerns. One is that the large percentage of the state's agricultural workforce consists of illegal immigrants. This workforce that is unstable given the popular and political pressures, both in state and nationally, to clamp down on people living illegally in the country.

In 2012, President Barack Obama tightened controls on the flow of people crossing illegally from Mexico to the United States. This has been followed by President Donald Trump's call to deport undocumented people, raid more companies in search of undocumented workers, and to build an enhanced wall on the U.S.-Mexico border. As a result, California farms have experienced significant difficulty in meeting its labor needs. The Trump administration's theory that cutting off the flow of illegal immigrants will free up jobs for American-born workers has proven flawed as few have shown a desire to do such physically demanding labor. Even higher pay has not paid off, at least for the growers. Growers who can afford it have raised wages well beyond minimum wage. According to data from the Bureau of Labor Statistics pay for California's agricultural workers increased 13% between 2010 to 2015, twice as fast as average pay across the state.

Without a change, several radical consequences are possible. California farmers could simply decide to give up on growing some of the state's hallmark fruits and vegetables. Or, they could move some production out of the state. Or, in a throw-back to the *bracero* program, they could see the revival of a "guest workers" program. Lastly, growers could devote more funding to developing automated technology which could replace workers altogether with machines.

Another trend has been the loss of agricultural land. Between 1988 and 1998, California lost 497,000 acres of farmland to urban development. On average, 82,000 acres are converted from agricultural to urban use each year. The Central Valley, which produces 230 farm products, may be one of the world's most important farming regions. If population projections hold true, urbanization presents a serious threat to its agricultural future. Case in point Fresno, the nation's top agricultural county. In 1990, the population of Fresno County was 672,000. In 2000, it was 800,000. In 2017, it had surpassed 989,000. By 2040 it is projected to be 2.4 million. If housing and population densities do not change, the county will need approximately one million acres of new urban development to support this increase. The same is true for the entire valley. The population of the entire Central Valley was 5.0 million in 1990. In 2010, the population was 6.5 million and is the fastest growing region in the state for the last twenty years. The population is projected to rise to 12 million by 2040, and 25.4 million in 2080. That would be a 500 percent increase from 1990.

Even more important is what may happen to the crucial farmland on the valley floor. The floor of the Central Valley is 42,000 square miles, or, 10.2 million acres, of which 9.2 million acres are suitable for agricultural use. In 1990, 3.6 million people lived on 740,000 urbanized acres, a little more than 7 percent of the valley floor. The trend between 1990 and 2050 projects the population to increase at about 1.25 percent each year. Therefore, the population of the valley floor is projected to increase to 10.9 million in 2040, and may be 19.2 million in 2080. By that time, it is estimated that four million acres, or 40 percent of the valley floor, would be urbanized. As a consequence, there would be a 52 percent loss of the farmland that existed in 1990.

The decision over whether to use land for farms or for buildings is not all pro-development. The success of the California Land and Conservation (Williamson)

Act attests to that. This landmark 1965 legislation was designed to maintain agricultural land through tax breaks to farmers and ranchers who entered into long-term contracts with their county government. In return for agreeing to keep their land in use for agriculture or grazing for at least ten years, the land was taxed at a preferred, lower rate. The law was enhanced in 1998 with an additional tax reduction going to a farmer or rancher who agreed to a twenty-year contract. All contracts are automatically renewed in one-year periods until the landowner opts out.

In 2009, fifty-four of California's fifty-eight counties had Williamson Act contracts covering more than sixteen million acres, more than half of the total in the state. The agreements save landowners approximately $150 million on their property taxes. This loss of county revenue is offset by reimbursement from the state. For the state, the bottom line is measured in acres, not dollars. And by that measurement, the land conservation effort has been successful. Of all the land entered in contract since the Williamson Act began, 89 percent has remained rural and for agricultural use. In 2011, Governor Jerry Brown signed into law a five-year extension of the Act. It remains in effect today, with no termination date.

California's intensive agriculture also has positive and negative environmental consequences. There are problems with how to deal with high concentrations of salinity in land that is continuously irrigated. Also on the negative side, there are problems with the types, volume, and application methods of certain pesticides which can be harmful to both humans and the ecosystem. One trend has been for farming operations to move away from older, more broad-based pesticides (in general, the broader the application's use, the more complex and lethal the product) toward newer, more environmentally friendly methods.

There is other good news. Proponents of maintaining agricultural land point out that farmland takes carbon dioxide (CO2) out of the air, helping reduce global warming. It is estimated that the acres under the Williamson Act alone eliminated 3.5 billion pounds of CO2. This does not account for the additional emissions which would have resulted had the land been urbanized.

As problematic as the conversion of farmland into urban use is, analysts believe that biggest struggle in the twentieth-first century for California agriculture will be over water. In a typical year, agriculture uses 40 percent of all the water used in the state. In 2014, that amounted to 1.05 trillion gallons of water. That year, the state endured its fourth year of sub-normal rainfall, and 58 percent of the state was classified as being in "exceptional drought." In these conditions, water-needy crops did not escape attention. For example, a single almond requires one gallon of water to produce, or a pair of blue jeans made from pima cotton takes 2,800 gallons of water to make.

In 2015, the state delivered water to 25 million Californians and 750,000 acres of farmland. The total population of the state is projected to be 58.7 million in 2040 and possibly 76 million in 2080 with the corresponding increase in industry and services. And competition for water is not limited to in-state interests. In 2000, California and six other states reached a historic agreement in which Southern California officials agreed to a fifteen-year deadline to cut its use of the Colorado River, freeing up water for other states.

There are many ways to address the water needs of agriculture and for the state as a whole. Research into converting wastewater into drinking water is ongoing. Investing in water restoration projects and increasing water storage capacity is being studied. One of the quickest and least expensive ways to manage water supplies can come by improving efficiency and teaching conservation of water. Better water recycling projects, improving water supply reliability, and developing new water transfer programs may very well be part of the solutions.

John Muir and the Sierra Nevada Mountains

The unique nature of California's wildlife, topography, and botany was recognized early on by some Americans who saw a need to protect and preserve the land, not just exploit its resources. It was no accident that California became one of the birthplaces of the conservation movement. It was recognized that the state's natural wonders needed protection, even from their admirers who flocked to see them. As early as the Lincoln administration, a group of influential Californians had seen to it that the Federal government put the Yosemite Valley and nearby giant sequoia groves under California's protection as a park.

John Muir was one of California's earliest conservationists and remains one its best known. Born in Scotland in 1838, he immigrated to the United States with his family when he was eleven and grew up on a farm in Wisconsin. Muir developed an appreciation for nature as a child, As a young man, he became enthralled with the study botany. In 1867, after nearly losing his sight in an accident on the job, he decided to leave factory work and focus on his passion for nature. That fall, he started what became a thousand mile walk that took him from Indianapolis, Indiana, to the Gulf of Mexico. In 1868, he crossed the Isthmus of Panama, and sailed up the California coast, landing in San Francisco. That same year he walked across the San Joaquin Valley into the Sierra Nevada Mountains for the first time, where he made his home in Yosemite.

In 1876, at age 38, he gave his first public lecture in Sacramento. The topic was glaciers in California. As it turned out, Muir was exactly half-way through his life. He spent his second 38 years as an educator of the public on the natural world. His devotion to the conservation of nature led him to publish more than 300 articles and ten books. Although he would travel throughout many parts of the world, his heart belonged to California and the Sierras. His relationship with Yosemite reminded people then and now of the powerful connections humans have to the wild, and how beautiful places can inspire us.

In addition, he emphasized how interconnected was the world. He sought to remind people that everything that lived depended on other living things for their existence. Therefore, people should be fully invested in valuing, enjoying, and maintaining the ecological system. To try and live apart from nature—to only see it through a window or from a distance, was both a spiritual loss and practical folly. Muir was a strong believer in collective activism. In 1892, he founded the Sierra Club to promote the responsible use of the earth and its resources and to protect nature from wanton abuse or destruction. Muir remained its president until his death in 1914.

In 1916, one of Muir's long-time dreams was fulfilled as Congress established the United States National Park Service, a new federal bureau within the Department of the Interior. The Park Service was responsible for protecting what was at the time 35 national parks and monuments across the country; today, there are more than 400 such areas.

Another glorious day, the air as delicious to the lungs as nectar to the tongue.

—Muir, *My First Summer in the Sierra,* 1911

Keep close to Nature's heart . . . and break clear away, once in awhile, and climb a mountain or spend a week in the woods. Wash your spirit clean.

Wilderness is not only a haven for native plants and animals but it is also a refuge from society. Its a place to go to hear the wind and little else, see the stars and the galaxies, smell the pine trees, feel the cold water, touch the sky and the ground at the same time, listen to coyotes, eat the fresh snow, walk across the desert sands, and realize why its good to go outside of the city and the suburbs. Fortunately, there is wilderness just outside the limits of the cities and the suburbs in most of the United States, especially in the West.

—Muir, *Our National Parks*, 1901

It took more than three thousand years to make some of the trees in these Western woods - trees that are still standing in perfect strength and beauty, waving and singing in the mighty forests of the Sierra. Through all the wonderful, eventful centuries God has cared for these trees, saved them from drought, disease, avalanches, and a thousand straining, leveling tempests and floods; but he cannot save them from fools - only Uncle Sam can do that.

—Muir, *The American Forests*, 1897

This reading is from *The American Reader,* Diane Ravitch, editor, 1990.

The Mountains of California by John Muir, 1894

Making your way through the mazes of the Coastal Range to the summit of any of the inner peaks or passes opposite san Francisco, in the clear springtime, the grandest and most telling of all California landscapes is outspread before you. At your feet lies the great Central Valley glowing golden in the sunshine, extending north and south farther than the eye can reach, one smooth, flowery, lake-like bed of fertile soil. Along its eastern margin rises the mighty Sierra, miles in height, reposing like a smooth, cumulous cloud in the sunny sky, and so gloriously colored, and so luminous, it seems to be not clothes with light, but wholly composed of it, like the wall of some celestial city. Along the top, and extending a good way down, you see a pale, pearl-gray belt of snow; and below it a belt of blue and dark purple, marking the extension of the forests; and along the base of the range a broad belt of rose-purple and yellow, where lie the miner's goldfields and the foot-hill gardens. All these colored belts blending smoothly make a wall of light ineffably fine, and as beautiful as a rainbow, yet firm as adamant.

When I first enjoyed this superb view, one glowing April day, from the summit of the Pacheco Pass, the Central Valley, but little trampled of plowed as yet, was the one furred, rich sheet of golden compositae, and the luminous wall of the mountain shone in all its glory. Then it seemed to me the Sierra should be called not the Nevada, or Snowy Range, but the Range of Light. And after ten years spent in the heart of it, rejoicing and wandering, bathing in its glorious floods of light, seeing the sunbursts of morning among the icy peaks, the noonday radiance on the trees and rocks and snow, the flush of the alpenglow, and a thousand dashing waterfalls with their marvelous abundance of irised spray, it still seems to me above all others the Range of Light, the most divinely beautiful of all the mountain-chains I have ever seen. The Sierra is about 500 miles long, 70 miles wide, and from 7000 to nearly 15,000 feet high. In general views no mark of man is visible on it, nor anything to suggest the richness of the life it cherishes, or the depth and grandeur of its sculpture. None of its magnificent forest-crowned ridges rises much above the general level to publish its wealth. No great valley or lake is seen, or river, or group of well-marked features of any kind, standing out in distinct pictures. Even the summit-peaks, so clear and high in the sky, seem comparably smooth and featureless. Nevertheless, the glaciers are still at work in the shadows of the peaks, and thousands of lakes and meadows shine and bloom beneath them, and the whole range is furrowed with canyons to depth of from 2000 to 5000 feet, in which once flowed majestic glaciers, and in which now flow and sing a band of beautiful rivers.

Though of such stupendous depth, these famous canyons are not raw, gloomy, jagged-walled gorges, savage and inaccessible. With rough passages here and there they still make delightful pathways for the mountaineer, conducting from the fertile lowlands to the highest icy fountains, as a kind of mountain streets full of charming life and light, graded and sculptured by the ancient glaciers, and presenting, throughout all their courses, a rich variety of novel and attractive scenery, the most attractive that has yet been discovered in the mountain-ranges of the world.

In many places, especially in the middle region of the western flank of the range, the main canyons widen into spacious valleys or parks, diversified like artificial landscape-gardens, with charming groves and meadows, and thickets of blooming bushes, while the lofty, retiring walls, infinitely varied in form and sculpture, are fringed with ferns, flowering-plants of many species, oaks, and evergreens, which find anchorage on a thousand narrow steps and benches; while the whole is enlivened and made glorious with rejoicing streams that come dancing and foaming over the sunny brows of the cliffs to join the shining river that flows in tranquil beauty down the middle of each one of them.

The walls of these park valleys of the Yosemite kind are made up of rocks mountains in size, partly separated from each other by narrow gorges and side-canyons; and they are so sheer in front, and so compactly built together on a level floor, that, comprehensively seen, the parks they enclose look like immense halls or temples lighted from above. Every rock seems to glow with life. Some lean back in majestic repose; others, absolutely sheer, or nearly so, for thousands of feet, advance their brows in thoughtful attitudes beyond their companions, giving welcome to storms and calm alike, seemingly conscious yet heedless of everything going on about them, awful in stern majesty, types of permanence, yet associated with beauty of the frailest and most fleeting forms; their feet set in pine-groves and gay emerald meadows, their brows in the sky; bathed in light, bathed in floods of singing water, while snow-clouds, avalanches, and the wind shine and surge arid wreathe about them as the years go by, as if into these mountains mansions Nature had taken pains to gather their choicest treasures to draw her lovers into close and confiding communion with her . . .

In every walk with nature one receives far more than he seeks.

—John Muir

"White Gold:"
The Los Angeles Aqueduct

California, like a lot of the West, was settled without much planning or practical thinking. People settled where they wanted, whether or not the surrounding natural resources had the capacity to sustain them. The city of Los Angeles is outstanding example of the development of a small settlement that became a large metropolis existing in a region clearly lacking in one of the key ingredients necessary for life—fresh water. The fact that the city did grow and thrive reveals the desire and persistence of its people to adjust and survive. This accomplishment came from a combination of municipal ingenuity, costly and risky investments in engineering, and an audacious attitude by civic leaders who proved to be as innovative as they were brazen. There were also significant negative environmental and human consequences in order to sustain a city that, logically, had no business being where it was.

The facts regarding water and California are simple, but the solution is complex. Today, the majority of the people live far from where most of the fresh water is found. About three-fourths of California's annual precipitation occurs in the mountainous northern region of the state, whereas about 80 percent of the water demand (much of it for agriculture) exists in the southern half of the state. To put another way, today, 45 percent of California's population lives in the Los Angeles Basin, an area that contains just.06 percent of the state's water stream flow. Thus, while the image of Los Angeles as a land of perpetual sunshine—"It Never Rains in Southern California," as the song goes—is real and has an obvious appeal, it presents a monumental practical problem. Moving water from where it naturally exists to where people want it has been created has been one of the greatest challenges, and accomplishments, in the history of California.

Early Los Angeles

Because the land was dry, water was scarce and no gold was to be found, Los Angeles in the mid-nineteenth century was still a small town. Founded by Spain as a pueblo town in 1781, *El Pueblo de Nuestra Senora la Reyna de Los Angeles del Rio de la Porciuncula*, ("town of our lady the Queen of Angels of the River Porciúncula"), grew slowly. In 1850, after California became part of the United States, the U.S. Census recorded the population of Los Angeles at 1,610. Twenty years later it was 5,728, four percent of the size of San Francisco.

The main source of fresh water for drinking and irrigation came from the Los Angeles River, sometimes called the *Zanja Madre,* or "Mother Ditch." It originated in the foothills of the San Fernando Valley, some forty miles away from downtown LA. The river itself was of modest size and flow. It had nine tributary offshoots as it meandered through the basin and valleys on its way to the Pacific Ocean. The *zanjas* were gradually channeled into an underground piped system, with most water being sold by private companies, In 1874, Benjamin Eaton, a Los Angeles lawyer and engineer, oversaw the building of the first iron-pipe water system to serve the arid and nearly empty Pasadena area.

Significant growth did not begin until after 1876 when the Southern Pacific built a direct line connecting the town to the statewide railroad system. In that age of unbridled business corruption, that access came at the cost of a $600,000 paid by city officials. By 1880, the population had nearly doubled during the decade to 11,183. Already, water and the means required to move it was becoming an issue for the community. Fires in town often burned longer and created greater destruction because water supplies were either not adequate or available to fire crews. Unbeknown to nearly everyone, Los Angeles was on the cusp of an explosion.

In the 1880s, a real estate boom emerged in Los Angeles. It was partly triggered by a railroad rate war between the Southern Pacific and the competing Santa Fe, which had recently entered the market. The price of a one-way passenger ticket from a Midwest town such as Kansas City dropped to a little as $1. Soon, over 100,000 people a year traveled to Los Angeles. Spurred on by zealous land speculators, many of them decided to stay permanently. Quickly large tracts of agricultural and grazing land was sold and converted to commercial and residential use. Land that sold for $100 an acre one year, was being resold for fifteen times that the next.

The frenzy to get rich took over. In the 1880s, more than 100 new towns were being planned in the greater Los Angeles area. Orange County was founded, and in 1897 a major port was built in San Pedro, twenty miles from downtown Los

Angeles. By 1890, the population of Los Angeles had soared to 50,395. A decade later, it had doubled to 102,479. Just five years after that, the population passed 200,000 and showed no sign of slowing. The Census recorded 319,198 residents, an astonishing tripling of people in ten years.

Throughout this period of spectacular change, one constant was the water of the city; people hated it. There was no comprehensive water treatment or sewer system. Public complaints about the quality of the water were widespread. Its foul smell, poor taste, and frequent warmth were all cited as concerns. The water was described as being anything from a serious nuisance to a deadly health risk. There were reports of animals that had fallen into reservoirs and drowned but their remains were not removed before the water was piped into people's homes. On occasion, small fish came through home water taps. As bad as the water quality was at times, far worse was when there was not enough of it.

Owens Valley

In the late 1870s, during one of the periodic droughts that gripped Southern California, Los Angeles city officials began looking for a new supply of water. They began to focus on the Owens Valley, 250 miles to the north. The Owens Valley, in Inyo County, runs more than 100 miles in a north to south direction. It is bound by the Sierra Nevada range on its west and the Inyo Range on its east. The valley is an example of the enormous geographic variety of California. At its northern end towers Mount Whitney, the highest peak in the continental United States. At its southern end lies Death Valley, in which is found the lowest elevation in the United States. Running through the valley, and what really attracted Los Angeles, was the Owens River, a large river fed by the melting snow of the Sierras. At the time it drained into Owens Lake. The valley, river, and lake were all named in 1845 by John C. Fremont for Richard Owens, one of Fremont's guides. The distance between Los Angeles and Owens seemed too great to overcome and the river was left to itself.

Owens Valley did not experience the extraordinary changes that the gold rush brought to other parts of California. In 1865, a small-scale rush began when gold was discovered north of Owens Lake, but it did not last long. In 1872, a large earthquake again captured some attention for the area when most of the town of Lone Pine was destroyed and twenty-seven people, ten percent of the population, perished.

Aside from these events, the valley was primarily home to a collection of small farms and ranches. When it flooded, the Owens River turned the valley lowlands into swamps, but as there was no money for dams or other irrigation projects, much of the valley didn't have enough water to allow for commercial development. Then, in 1902, with the passage of the National Reclamation Act, hopes ran high in the valley that the government would help develop its water resources and open a new era of prosperity for the region.

Water Crisis in Los Angeles

In order to have legal access to Los Angeles water, one had to live within the city limits. To accomplish this, there were large annexations to the city and Los Angeles became a vast, sprawling municipality. By the close of the nineteenth-century, more than 20 million gallons of water a day were being used. One-quarter of this total was used to water lawns and plants, while another two and a half million gallons was sprinkled daily on dirt streets to reduce dust. It was clear that new water sources were urgently needed to support just the existing population, let allow more growth.

After more than a century of use, the Los Angeles River was proving unequal to the demands being made on it. In 1903 and again in 1904, the river was 30 percent below its historic average level. If the city was to sustain itself, it was evident that the Los Angeles River could no longer be relied on. The problem was there were no other significant local water sources.

Also proving inadequate was the privately held Los Angeles City Water Company. Water, specifically, the control of it, became a major political issue and source of contention. After several years of political maneuvering, more than thirty lawsuits, and intense bargaining, in 1902 control of the city's water was turned over to a newly created municipal organization, The Water Department, which was overseen by a seven-member Board of Water Commissioners. William Mulholland was named the first superintendent of the newly formed department.

Mulholland favored conservation—he successfully lobbied for the installation of water meters in 1902—but he also knew the city needed new water sources. A study of the existing supply had concluded the city would run short of meeting the expected demand in fewer than five years. In 1904, Fred Eaton, a former mayor of Los Angeles, and an engineer, brought the Owens Valley to Mulholland's attention. The Owens River drains along the eastern slope of the Sierras for more than 150 miles. In so doing, the natural course of the river points it south toward Los Angeles.

The two men made several trips to Owens Valley, being discreet about who they were and what was the purpose of their visits. Mulholland was impressed both by the river's purity and its flow, which he measured to be 20,000 miner's inches. (A miner's inch is an archaic and somewhat arbitrary measurement. The term refers to a device with a square inch opening that was used by early miners to determine the flow of water. In 1905, in southern California, water companies considered a miner's inch to be equal to 0.020 cfs (or 1/50th of a cubic foot per second. Thus, according the Mulholland's measurement, the Owens River flowed at 400 cfs. If all that water was captured it would be more than 258 million gallons per day).

The Federal Bureau of Reclamation also had its eye on Owens Valley as a possible candidate for an irrigation project. The Reclamation Act authorized the federal government to commission water diversion, retention and transmission projects in arid lands, particularly in the west. Seeing the threat, Eaton led a group of southern California officials to Washington and lobbied that water projects be steered to Los Angeles with the argument that it would serve a much greater number of people than in Owens Valley. J.B. Lippincott, supervising engineer for the Bureau of Reclamation, was the man in charge of putting together recommendations for the government. He also worked as a consulting engineer with Mulholland and the L.A. Water Department.

Lippincott's efforts for the Reclamation Service resulted only in the valley's public lands being set aside for future development; no rights to the land were secured. It was around this time that Eaton quietly set about buying up options on strategic land in the valley—land that would be needed for construction of an aqueduct. To curious valley residents Eaton implied that he was affiliated with the Reclamation Service, not the city of Los Angeles, as was actually the case. This deception would lead to a long bitter relationship between Owens Valley residents and Los Angeles.

Finally, in July 1905, after months of mapping dam sites and a route for a possible aqueduct, the Owens River Project was announced in Los Angeles. The project was not only expensive, it was very ambitious. At 233 miles, when completed it would be the longest aqueduct in the world and part of the largest single water project as well. Mulholland wryly encouraged the project with such statements as, "If Los Angeles does not secure the Owens Valley water supply, and she will never need it."

President Theodore Roosevelt's Position

Another major proponent of the aqueduct was President Theodore Roosevelt. Deciding that "infinitely greater interests" of the nation would be met by having a large city on the west coast of the country, Roosevelt wrote in favor of Los Angeles and, perhaps more decisively, against the opposing interests in Owens Valley. In 1907, the president clearly articulated his position on water projects when he said, in an address to Congress "The constant purpose of the government in connection with the Reclamation Service has been to use the water resources of the public lands for the ultimate greatest good of the greatest number."

On the heels of this success in the national political arena, there followed a series of large bond issues that were overwhelmingly approved by voters. By a greater than ten to one margin, citizens passed the largest bond measure in the history of the United States, $23 million. As the *Los Angeles Daily Times* trumpeted on July 29, 1905, "Titanic Project to Give City a River." City officials had enough money to buy the land and water rights from Eaton and to start construction on an aqueduct. Thus, the residents of Owens Valley, who had 50,000 acres under cultivation and had expected to be the beneficiaries of a federal irrigation project, found themselves out of luck, and water, as construction began on the great Los Angeles aqueduct.

Building the Aqueduct

Planning for the Los Angeles aqueduct began in 1904, the same year the United States started construction on the Panama Canal. Both projects placed extreme challenges on their builders. While the canal would be carved out of dense tropical jungle-covered mountains, much of the aqueduct would be constructed across the blazing hot and extremely dry Mojave Desert.

Actual construction started in 1907. Numbers only begin to tell the story. An estimated 350,000 tons of materials had to be transported to the work sites. Forty-three miles of tunnels were blasted through mountains in which five million pounds of dynamite was used, and two hundred miles of roads were built. After sand destroyed dozens of caterpillar tractors, more than 1,500 mules were brought into service. One thousand tons of hay was purchased to feed the animals.

Vast amounts of concrete were needed to line portions of the aqueduct's massive ditch. To transport the tremendous volume of material would have been prohibitively expensive and extremely difficult. To resolve the issue, Los Angeles purchased the Cuddleback Ranch, five miles east of Tehachapi. On its 4,300 acres were limestone quarries, clay deposits, and deposits of tufa, all used for making concrete. The ranch offered the added advantage of being on the main line of the Southern Pacific Railroad. Eventually, the Monolith Mill built at Cuddleback produced more than 1,000 barrels of Portland cement daily. An additional 200,000 barrels of cement were shipped in from other locations.

As many as four thousand men worked at once; they needed to be fed and housed in the desert during the six years of construction. Fifty-seven camps were established

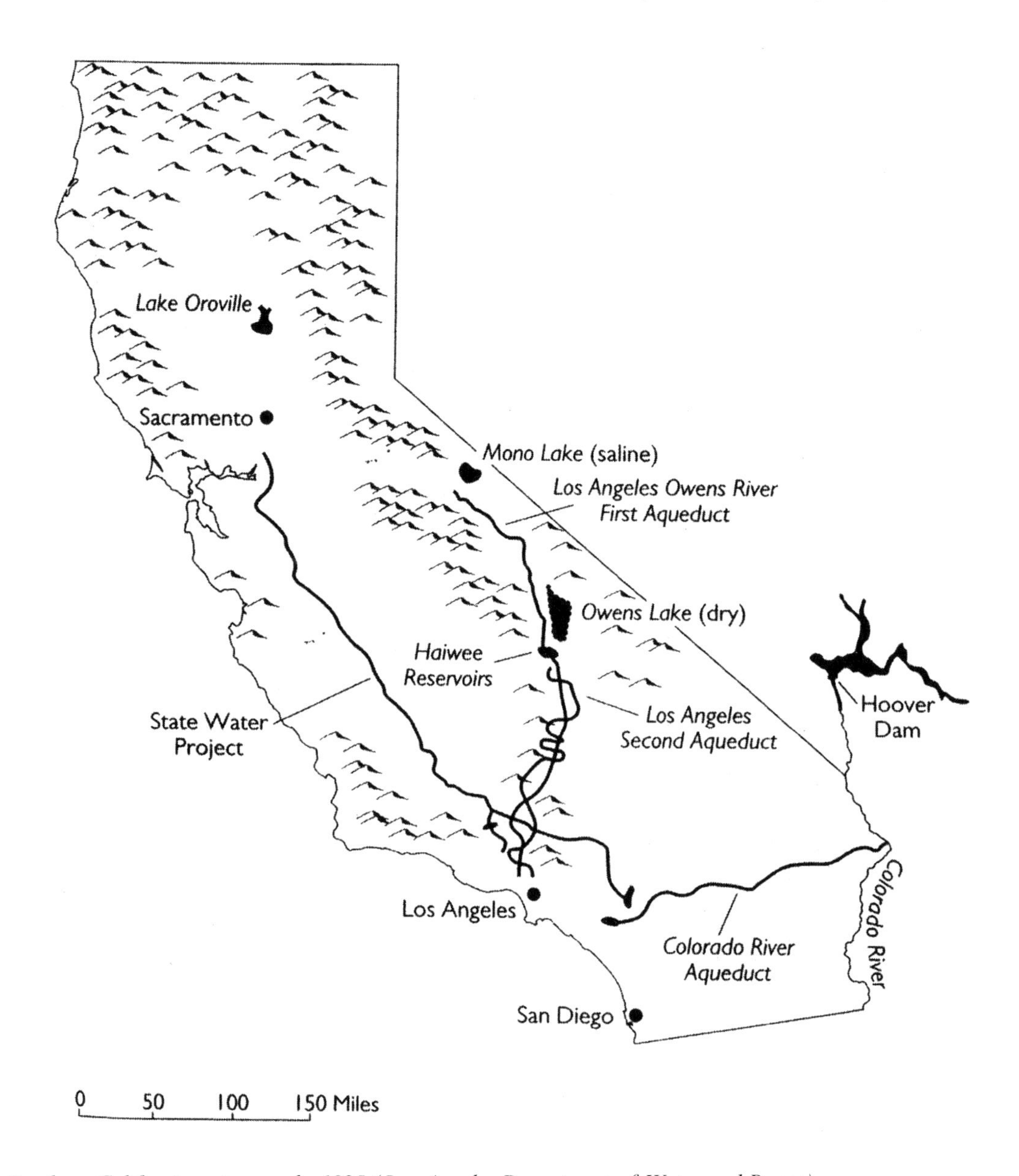

Southern California water supply, 1925 (Los Angeles Department of Water and Power).

along the line of work, most of them in the mountains, and roads were needed to reach them. Post offices were built to mitigate the isolation workers faced. In 1912, the average pay was $2.25 a day, high wages for the time. Forty-three workers would be killed over the course of construction.

The desert created many of the miserable conditions. In the winter months, the weather was windy with bitter cold. In the summer months, the temperature in the bottom of the aqueduct ditch in which workers toiled could reach 120 degrees.

Challenges were everywhere. Some sections of pipe weighed twenty-six tons. To haul them across the sandy ground, huge wagons were assembled with steel wheels and tires that were two feet wide. Teams of fifty-two mules pulled the massive transports. Tunneling was another monumental task. Daily work schedules were set with defined expectations. For example, a tunnel that required wood to shore up its walls was expected to advance at the rate of six feet a day. Systems of bonuses were also offered. Tunnel crews were paid forty cents extra to each man for every foot completed that exceeded the expected six feet. This system would be credited with keeping the project largely on schedule and under budget.

When it was completed, there 230 miles of pipeline, including 12 miles of steel pipes, 24 miles of unlined channel, 37 miles of concrete lined channel, 52 miles of tunnels, and 98 miles of concrete conduit (troughs). In addition, the operation required 218 miles of power transmission line, and 377 miles of telegraph and telephone line. There was no railroad service that connected Owens Valley to the southland so 120 miles of railroad track had been constructed as well.

One of the remarkable features of the aqueduct is that water is moved entirely by gravity flow. No pumps or any energy is used to transport the water up and over a series of mountains. Instead, twelve miles of steel siphons were created. The longest siphon crossed Antelope Valley and was just over four miles in length.

Engineers designed a series of penstocks that sent the water to power plants located at the bottom of drop offs. The force of the water was used to move turbines and create electricity and two hydroelectric plants were built. In 1908, Cottonwood Hydroelectric Power Station began to produce power that was used for the construction of the aqueduct. Cottonwood remains in operation today as the oldest Department of Water and Power station in service. The 1200 kilowatts it produces is used throughout Owens Valley.

The Aqueduct Opens

On November 5, 1913, the aqueduct was officially opened. It had cost $24.6 million dollars, within budgeted expectations. The timing was appropriate. Earlier that summer the city had set a new record for daily water usage when more than 69 million gallons were consumed each day over a ten-day period.

Opening ceremonies were attended by 40,000 people. After a band played "*I Love You, California,*" Mulholland was introduced as "the man who built the aqueduct." Mulholland who once claimed "there was never much sentiment about the aqueduct, it has been a plain business proposition from start to finish," made a short speech in which he dedicated the aqueduct "to you and your children and your children's children, for all time." As the last gates holding back the water were opened, and the first of what would be trillions of gallons began to pour down a cement cascade, Mulholland turned to gathered representatives of the city and stated succinctly "There it is gentlemen, take it."

The headline in the Los Angeles *Times* the next day read, "Silver Torrent Crowns the City's Mighty Achievement." With its water supply assured, the city continued expanding. In 1915, major sections of the San Fernando Valley were annexed and, with it, the city doubled in size. Los Angeles soon would surpass San Francisco as the largest and most influential city in California. Between 1909 and 1928, Los Angeles grew from 61 square miles to 440 square miles and, in 1930, had a population of 1,238,048. Owens Valley never recovered. The diversion of the river resulted in the Owens Lake drying up and disappearing, along with most of the farms and homes in the valley.

Lingering Anger

Even before construction on the aqueduct began, critics were suspicious that officials involved with the project were acting out of self-interest. The advance purchase of land, especially in the nearly empty San Fernando Valley by Fred Eaton and other city officials has long been viewed akin to "insider trading" in the stock market. In 1912, a pamphlet by W. T. Stilman, a long-time critic of the city's water division, circulated around Los Angeles. Its title, "The Conspiracy: An Exposure of the Owens River Water and San Fernando Valley Land Frauds" set the table for what followed. Stilman claimed Los Angeles had plenty of water and officials who stood to gain personally if the aqueduct was built had manipulated supplies to create artificial shortages. No legal judgment on the various charges was ever made. To the present, however, the charges linger, resurfacing in many water histories of Southern California.

The aqueduct itself came under violent attack. In 1924, it was damaged by vandals who used dynamite in an attempt to sabotage it. The actual damage was not significant, though it led to considerable vilification of the opposing sides by people from both Owens and Los Angeles. Several months later, a group of about one hundred residents in Inyo County seized a part of the aqueduct and opened gates to let the water pour into the surrounding land. A five-day standoff ensued before the protesters relinquished their temporary control of the water.

The aqueduct was hit by dynamite attacks multiple times in 1925, causing a quarter of a million dollars in damage to the aqueduct, siphon, and two powerhouses. Eventually, two men were convicted though it was widely believed many more people were involved.

Added to the unhappiness in Owens Valley was that Los Angeles continued to buy land until it owned nearly the entire valley. By 1928, Los Angeles owned 90 percent of the water rights. And it is still owns it today. Los Angeles controls 350,000 acres in Inyo and Mono counties. The four principal valley towns—Bishop, Big Pine, Independence, and Lone Pine—are hemmed in by this and can expand if only Los Angeles gives up some of its claims, something it has long been reluctant to do as to desire to control water rights has not diminished.

The 1972 film, *Chinatown,* is a highly fictionalized story that supports the perspective of a grand conspiracy perpetrated by intensely corrupt Los Angeles officials to enrich themselves through covert land purchases, and by deliberately creating water shortages to ensure the creation of new water transport systems into those lands.

One consequence of Owen Valley's inability to grow is that it remains lightly populated, with just 25,000 residents in the entire valley in 2018. In a bit of irony, today, some residents are pleased the area did not experience the massive development, with its attendant traffic and air pollution problems, that characterize Los Angeles today.

The Legacy

The "David vs. Goliath" battle between the Owens Valley and Los Angeles, in which Goliath had emerged the decided victor, led to decades of bitterness. Residents in Owens Valley were furious with the aqueduct. It ended most of forty years of farming in the valley and prevented what might have been a period of significant growth for the area had the Bureau of Reclamation built a water project for the valley, as initially hoped. Instead, the region would have to deal with a severe environmental problem.

In 1997, Los Angeles ended a twenty-year legal dispute with Inyo County which had sued the city because of the negative environmental effects caused by the aqueduct. With the diversion of the Owens River, the lake it previously fed dried up. Starting in the 1970s, the city pumped groundwater to feed a second aqueduct. Most vegetation died as a result. In a small version of the Dust Bowl of the 1930s, great quantities of dust from the lake bed was scattered by the strong valley winds. The particulates were toxic, containing naturally occurring amounts of alkali, a caustic and corrosive substance. Los Angeles officials agreed to stop taking the groundwater, to make plantings, and establish a vast sprinkling system over much of the dry lake to tamp down the dust.

The legal fight was far from over. At the start of the dust mitigation project in 2001, the Owens Lake was the largest single source of man-made particulate matter air pollution in the United States. Since 2010, the City of Los Angeles used 95,000 acre-feet of water annually for shallow flooding and managed vegetation on more than forty square miles of the Owens Lake bed. The level of air particulates were reduced by 75 percent, though it still exceeds allowable federal standards. It has been an expensive task, taking longer and costing more (even adjusted for inflation) than the building of the aqueduct. In its first decade, more than $500 million was spent digging hundreds of miles of trenches and installing pipelines and drains in mostly open desert. Thirty water treatment and pumping stations were constructed to feed 3,500 miles of drip irrigation. In another irony, the project to return water to Owens Valley created scores of new jobs in what became the largest public works project in the history of Inyo County.

Finally, in 2014, after spending more than $1.5 billion over several decades, Los Angeles concluded litigation in the Owens Valley over the aqueduct. The entire mitigation project was completed in 2017. And Los Angeles, the once small pueblo town, is now the second-largest city in the United States.

The Battle Over Mono Lake

For thousands of years, Mono Lake existed in relative solitude, high in the remote Eastern Sierras. Even today, few people live near the lake and there is minimal significant commercial activity associated with it apart of environmental tourism. Yet, after long serving as a vital breeding area for a wide array of bird species, and helping to support small bands of native peoples, just forty years ago Mono's continued viability was threatened, its very survival uncertain. Today, the lake's ecological health is improving and its future appears to be favorable. It was the human altering of the lake's ecosystem that caused harm to it, and it was human activism that helped save it. The story of the success in restoring and preserving the lake is as unusual as many other characteristics of the lake itself.

The Lake

Mono Lake is ancient. It is somewhere between 760,000 and one million years old, making it one of the oldest continuously existing lakes on the North American continent. Located just east of the Sierra Nevada, at an elevation of 6,400 feet, it sits in the Mono Basin, seven hundred square miles of arid land ringed by inactive volcanoes. The lake was fed by huge glaciers during the last Ice Age 15,000 years ago. The average depth of the lake is sixty feet, one-sixth of what it once was, although in a few spots it still reaches one hundred and fifty feet in depth. Although, today it covers only one-fifth of its former area, it holds a greater volume of water than any other natural lake in California. Within its 66 square miles there are two major islands, the *Negit* and *Paoha*. These were the result of a volcanic eruption three hundred years ago and were named by the Paiute Indians who lived in the surrounding area for more than 5,000 years.

It is a lake with several unique features that play an important part in the natural history of the state. But to many people, Mono Lake is simply an oddity, with little to no use in terms of the activities commonly associated with lakes. It will

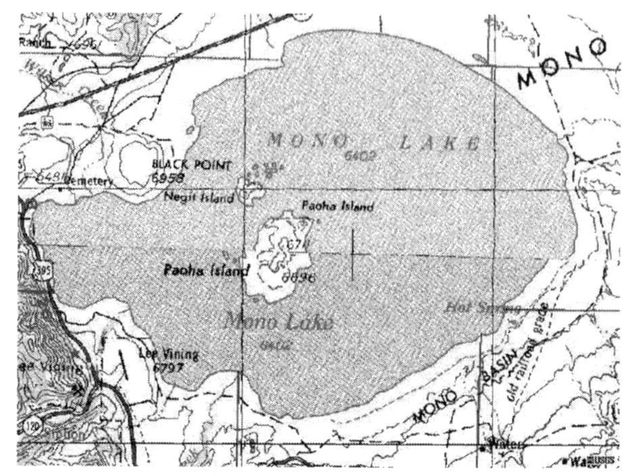

U.S. Geological Survey.

not figure in the minds of most recreational users. There are no fish to catch. It has few species of amphibious life. It has no commercially viable resources. A person who swims in its waters will emerge with a covering of uncomfortable salt residue. It is the home to millions of flies. Today, motorized boats are not allowed. There is some tourism development in Lee Vining, population 222 (in 2018), located two miles away but at the lake there prevails an atmosphere of tranquil calm, in keeping with its low-key and remote location.

Mono is a terminal lake, meaning it has no natural outlet. No streams or river leave from it. The only way water leaves is by evaporation. The lake loses about 45 vertical inches of water through evaporation annually, while it only gains seven inches in precipitation. All the rest of its water flows in from tributaries. Five major Sierra streams (Lee Vining, Parker, Walker, Rush, and Mill) flow into Mono. These stream waters travel over rock and soil picking up trace amounts of minerals and salts. Over the centuries, those minerals and salts stayed in the lake as the water regularly evaporated and was replenished and their concentrations multiplied. Thus Mono today is very salty and alkaline. In its natural condition it is two to three times more salty and eighty times more alkaline than ocean water. By volume, the lake is 10 percent salt. No lake in the world is as alkaline as is Mono.

An initial impression may be that Mono Lake has little life. That is far from the truth. The basin in which it sits contains more than 1,100 species of plants. And while there are no fish, the lake supports a simple but amazingly productive food chain. At the bottom of that chain are microscopic, single-celled planktonic algae. The algae serve as food for one of the major inhabitants of the lake, brine shrimp. These aquatic crustaceans, little changed over the past 50 million years, are small, less than one-half an inch, but can reach maturity in a week and, therefore, breed in enormous numbers.

One cubic yard of lake water can contain more than 50,000 brine shrimp. In total, it is estimated that during the hot summer months, Mono is home to between four to six trillion shrimp that, collectively weigh six million pounds.

The brine shrimp offer a huge food source for the alkali flies which exist at Mono in equally impressive numbers. In the summer, the lake's many miles of shoreline are crowded with flies. Researchers have counted as many as 4,000 flies per square foot. However, they spend most of their lives underwater. That is where they hatch from eggs and feed on algae until they reach adulthood. As adults, a two-week lifespan, they live on the shore, the females eventually returning to the water to lay eggs. Tiny hairs on their bodies trap thin layers of air, creating an air pocket that allows them to stay underwater for as long as 15 minutes.

The food chain from algae, to shrimp to flies continues as the flies, in turn, serve as the major food source for birds that nest at the lake each year. Birds are the flies primary predators and untold numbers of them are eaten. In their pupae stage, they offer their highest level of calories. Many larvae are dislodged by lake currents and rise to the surface making them easily available and rather helpless. An estimated metric ton (2,200 pounds) of larvae and pupae can be found on the lake's surface each summer day. The Paiutes also used the flies as a food source, harvesting and drying the pupae as winter food.

The lake itself is a major nesting area for more than two million for birds each year. An estimated 50,000 Western Gulls breed at Mono each summer (85 percent of California's population, and the second-largest gull colony in the world.) There are least 80 species of shorebirds. Most common is the Eared Grebes (1.5 million, 30 percent of the North American population). These birds live only on water and migrate between Mexico and Canada. During their time at Mono they can double their body weight, feasting on flies. Other birds include several species of Killdeer, Sandpipers, Loons, Osprey, Eagles, Hawks, and Plovers, such as 400 endangered Snowy Plovers (11 percent of the state population.)

The Mono Basin Extension of the Los Angeles Aqueduct

For thousands of years, Mono Lake experienced change on a glacial scale. But eighty years ago, change came sudden, dramatic, and potentially perilous. In 1941, the City of Los Angeles began to divert water from the Mono Basin into the Owens River. There it flowed into the Los Angeles Aqueduct which had opened in 1913. When the aqueduct was being built, the city's 1910 population was 319,000. But by 1940, its population had soared to 1,504,000. City water officials looked far and wide for new sources and Basin water was taken to try and quench the southland's unending thirst. In 1963, a second diversion was built taking most of the water from four of the five tributaries that fed the Mono Basin. Stream waters were instead carried by an eleven-mile tunnel to the upper Owens River and Lake Crowley, and then into the aqueduct that ultimately traveled the nearly 400 miles to Los Angeles, whose population had increased by another million people since 1940.

The amount of water taken annually from the Mono Basin was approximately 100,000 acre feet (acre foot = one acre/4,840 square yards of water, twelve inches deep.) In the early 1980s, this represented 15 percent of the entire water supply for Los Angeles and met the needs of 500,000 residents.

The diversions created tremendous change to Mono. With only a comparative trickle of stream water still allowed in, the elevation of the lake began dropping 18 inches a year; forty-five feet in thirty years. In 1941, the lake held 4.3 million acre feet of water; by 1982, water volume had been cut in half, to 2.1 million acre feet, and the surface area was reduced by a third. The lake's elevation had declined to 6,372 feet. Winds blew on the exposed portions of the dry lakebed, picking up hazardous toxic alkali dust. The declining water level created a land bridge between *Negit* Island and the shoreline. This allowed coyotes and other predators to plunder the eggs from gull and other bird nests. At the same time, the alkalinity of the water more than doubled. Its salinity, naturally fifty parts per thousand of salt, was measured at ninety-two parts per thousand. The reproductive ability of the brine shrimp was lessened and the numbers of both shrimp and flies were reduced, further threatening the birds that used the lake.

Perhaps the most visual feature of the declining lake level were the emergence of the Lake's most physically intriguing feature, the tufa (pronounced "toofah") towers. Seen along much of the shoreline, particularly on its southern end, Tufas are formed underwater from calcium carbonate which makes its way into the lake from underground freshwater springs. The calcium and carbonate combine to form limestone that builds up over time around spring openings found on the lake bottom. As the lake level began its dramatic drop after 1941, the tufa towers were increasingly revealed. Today, some of these towers rise up as much as thirty feet on portions of the 17,000 acres of now exposed dry lake bottom.

The Mono Lake Committee

In 1976, a group of a dozen graduate science students from Stanford, University of California, Davis, Santa Cruz, and elsewhere, conducted a two-month ecological survey of Mono. They grew alarmed at environmental changes that were affecting the lake. At the current rate of diversion, their studies predicted that by the year 2000, the level of the lake would drop another 50 feet. It would lose another one-third of its surface and 80 percent of its volume. The receding water would turn *Paoha* Island into a peninsula. The algae, shrimp and fly populations would collapse, devastating the bird population.

As with the drying of the Owens River lake bed when its river was diverted to Los Angeles by way of the aqueduct, dust from the uncovered Mono Lake bed contained alkali, sulfates and other elements that were harmful to plants, animals, and humans. In short, the water diversions were threatening an entire ecosystem while simultaneously creating long-term health hazards.

In 1978, David Gaines, who earned his master's degree studying the ecosystem of Mono, founded the non-profit citizens Mono Lake Committee. The group began to explore ways to promote and protect the lake. A key goal was to raise and then stabilize the water level of the lake to ensure a healthy ecosystem. Joined the next year by the National Audubon Society, Friends of the Earth, and later by Cal-Trout, and other individuals, they began a public relations and legal battle over the future of Mono Lake. The committee opened an office and storefront in Lee Vining. There they offered slide shows, gave lake tours, and sold guidebooks. Blue and white bumper stickers proclaiming "Save Mono Lake" brought the lake, and its plight, to the attention of the public, many for the first time. Over the next several years, the grass root efforts resulted in thousands of memberships in the Mono Lake Committee.

The Mono Committee and the other environmental groups filed lawsuits against Los Angeles, charging that the water diversions violated the intent of public trust in the use of public resources. In 1983, the California Supreme Court ruled the public trust must be protected "as far as feasible" at the Mono and throughout the state. Of critical importance, the ruling broadened the scope of who in the state might have an interest in the future of the lake. It also underscored the laws which required the protection of wildlife and stream tributaries. The meaning was clear; Los Angeles could not continue to divert water as it had been doing for four decades if those actions significantly harmed the land, air, or wildlife around Mono Lake. In the mid-1980s, Judge Terrance Finney, ruled that the flow of water in streams feeding the lake be increased to raise the lake eighteen vertical feet, and, in 1989, set a minimum level for the entire lake.

In 1993, the State Water Resources Control Board held forty-three days of public hearings where both the Mono Lake Committee and the Los Angeles

Department of Water and Power presented legal and scientific evidence. In September 1994, both sides agreed to the Water Board decision to reduce the diversion of streams and return and maintain the lake at its 1984 elevation of 6,392 feet. This is approximately twenty-five feet below its level in 1941 when the water diversions began. The Los Angeles Department of Water and Power was initially allowed to continue to divert 31,000 acre-feet of water per year, or about one-third of the city's previous diversion from the Mono Basin. Later, that was reduced to 16,500 acre-feet per year. Improved conservation and water recycling were anticipated to make up for the reductions in the diversion. Mono Lake is once again growing—although slowly. In 2018, the elevation of the lake had risen to 6,382 feet, ten feet below its target level. It is expected to reach that level around 2038.

Already, improvements in the environment are evident. The land bridges that extended to *Negrit* Island have been covered once more by water, keeping the coyotes away from nests of eggs. The alkali dust, left as the lake receded, has been reduced, improving the air quality of the entire basin. More than four dozen species of birds have been recorded along the now-restored tributaries. As their waters have returned, so has the vegetation and wild grasses, ponds, lagoons and wetlands. Also returning are some birds that disappeared over the years, including the yellow warbler, and the rare songbird, the willow flycatcher.

In 2018, the Mono Lake Committee had 16,000 members. Its mission is to continue to restore the natural habitat, some of it eradicated by the decades of water diversions, to the land surrounding the lake. It also provides public education, such as through seminars and guided field trips. And, course, it continues efforts to maintain political and legal protection for the lake itself.

"Roughing It" at Mono Lake

Introduction

Published in early 1872, Roughing It *was Mark Twain's follow-up to his highly successful* Innocents Abroad *(1869). It was another travelogue and was based on his extensive travelling through California and Nevada over a five-year period in the 1860s. Twain had to cope with several personal losses during the writing of the book, and he considered it "pretty poor stuff" when it was completed. Nevertheless, the book was a critical and commercial success. With Twain's combination of trademark wit and wisdom, it remains one of his most popular collections of travel writing. This selection, chapter 38 from the book, describes his visit to Mono Lake in the early 1860s. His descriptions and experiences there are clearly aimed more at entertaining the reader than educating him or her, but much of the humor is rooted, at least loosely, in factual realities of this unusual—what Twain considered alien—lake.*

Roughing It by Mark Twain

We held a council and decided to make the best of our misfortune and enjoy a week's holiday on the borders of the curious Lake. Mono it is sometimes called, and sometimes the "Dead Sea of California." It is one of the strangest freaks of Nature to be found in any land, but it is hardly ever mentioned in print and very seldom visited, because it lies away off the usual routes of travel and besides is so difficult to get at that only men content to endure the roughest life will consent to take upon themselves the discomforts of such a trip. On the morning of our second day, we traveled around to a remote and particularly wild spot on the borders of the Lake, where a stream of fresh, ice-cold water entered it from the mountain side, and then we went regularly into camp. We hired a large boat and two shot-guns from a lonely ranchman who lived some ten miles further on, and made ready for comfort and recreation. We soon got thoroughly acquainted with the Lake and all its peculiarities.

Mono Lake lies in a lifeless, treeless, hideous desert, eight thousand feet above the level of the sea, and is guarded by mountains two thousand feet higher, whose summits are always clothed in clouds. This solemn, silent, sail-less sea—this lonely tenant of the loneliest spot on earth—is little graced with the picturesque. It is an unpretending expanse of grayish water, about a hundred miles in circumference, with two islands in its centre, mere upheavals of rent and scorched and blistered lava, snowed over with gray banks and drifts of pumice-stone and ashes, the winding sheet of the dead volcano, whose vast crater the lake has seized upon and occupied. The lake is two hundred feet deep, and its sluggish waters are so strong with alkali that if you only dip the most hopelessly soiled garment into them once or twice, and wring it out, it will be found as clean as if it had been through the ablest of washerwomen's hands. While we camped there our laundry work was easy. We tied the week's washing astern of our boat, and sailed a quarter of a mile, and the job was complete, all to the wringing out. If we threw the water on our heads and gave them a rub or so, the white lather would pile up three inches high. This water is not good for bruised places and abrasions of the skin. We had a valuable dog. He had raw places on him. He had more raw places on him than sound ones. He was the rawest dog I almost ever saw. He jumped overboard one day to get away from the flies. But it was bad judgment. In his condition, it would have been just as comfortable to jump into the fire. The alkali water nipped him in all the raw places simultaneously, and he struck out for the shore with considerable interest. He yelped and barked and howled as he wen—and by the time he got to the shore there was no bark to him—for he had barked the bark all out of his inside, and the alkali water had cleaned the bark all off his outside, and he probably wished he had never embarked in any such enterprise. He ran round and round in a circle, and pawed the earth and clawed the air, and threw double somersaults, sometimes backward and sometimes forward, in the most extraordinary manner. He was not a demonstrative dog, as a general thing, but rather of a grave and serious turn of mind, and I never saw him take so much interest in anything before. He finally struck out over the mountains, at a gait which we estimated at about two hundred and fifty miles an hour, and he is going yet. This was about nine years ago. We look for what is left of him along here every day.

A white man cannot drink the water of Mono Lake, for it is nearly pure lye. It is said that the Indians in the vicinity drink it sometimes, though. It is not improbable, for they are among the purest liars I ever saw. [There will be no additional charge for this joke, except to parties requiring an explanation of it. This joke has received high commendation from some of the ablest minds of the age.]

There are no fish in Mono Lake—no frogs, no snakes, no polliwogs— nothing, in fact, that goes to make life desirable. Millions of wild ducks and sea-gulls swim about the surface, but no living thing exists under the surface, except a white feathery sort of worm, one half an inch long, which looks like a bit of white thread frayed out at the sides. If you dip up a gallon of water, you will get about fifteen thousand of these. They give to the water a sort of grayish-white appearance. Then there is a fly, which looks something like our house fly. These settle on the beach to eat the worms that wash ashore—and any time, you can see there a belt of flies an inch deep and six feet wide, and this belt extends clear around the lake—a belt of flies one hundred miles long. If you throw a stone among them, they swarm up so thick that they look dense, like a cloud. You can hold them under water as long as you please—they do not mind it—they are only proud of it. When you let them go, they pop up to the surface as dry as a patent office report, and walk off as unconcernedly as if they had been educated especially with a view to affording instructive entertainment to man in that particular way. Providence leaves nothing to go by chance. All things have their uses and their part and proper place in Nature's economy: the ducks eat the flies—the flies eat the worms—the Indians eat all three—the wild cats eat the Indians—the white folks eat the wild cats—and thus all things are lovely.

Mono Lake is a hundred miles in a straight line from the ocean—and between it and the ocean are one or two ranges of mountains—yet thousands of sea-gulls go there every season to lay their eggs and rear their young. One would as soon expect to find sea-gulls in Kansas. And in this connection let us observe another instance of Nature's wisdom. The islands in the lake being merely huge masses of lava, coated over with ashes and pumice-stone, and utterly innocent of vegetation or anything that would burn; and sea-gull's eggs being entirely useless to anybody unless they be cooked, Nature has provided an unfailing spring of boiling water on the largest island, and you can put your eggs in there, and in four minutes you can boil them as hard as any statement I have made during the past fifteen years. Within ten feet of the boiling spring is a spring of pure cold water, sweet and wholesome. So, in that island you get your board and washing free of charge—and if nature had gone further and furnished a nice American hotel clerk who was crusty and disobliging, and didn't know anything about the time tables, or the railroad routes—or—anything—and was proud of it—I would not wish for a more desirable boarding-house. Half a dozen little mountain brooks flow into Mono Lake, but not a stream of any kind flows out of it. It neither rises nor falls, apparently, and what it does with its surplus water is a dark and bloody mystery. There are only two seasons in the region round about Mono Lake—and these are, the breaking up of one Winter and the beginning of the next. More than once (in Esmeralda) I have seen a perfectly blistering morning open up with the thermometer at ninety degrees at eight o'clock, and seen the snow fall fourteen inches deep and that same identical thermometer go down to forty-four degrees under shelter, before nine o'clock at night. Under favorable circumstances it snows at least once in every single month in the year, in the little town of Mono. So uncertain is the climate in Summer that a lady who goes out visiting cannot hope to be prepared for all emergencies unless she takes her fan under one arm and her snow shoes under the other. When they have a Fourth of July procession it generally snows on them, and they do say that as a general thing when a man calls for a brandy toddy there, the bar keeper chops it off with a hatchet and wraps it up in a paper, like maple sugar. And it is further reported that the old soakers haven't any teeth—wore them out eating gin cocktails and brandy punches. I do not endorse that statement—I simply give it for what it is worth—and it is worth—well, I should say, millions, to any man who can believe it without straining himself. But I do endorse the snow on the Fourth of July—because I know that to be true.

Upton Sinclair and the 1934 Governors Race

It is a safe bet that few political campaigns for governor hold much space in the collective public memory. Even less remembered would be the candidate who lost a race. Yet, occasionally, the importance of a campaign transcends the time in which it took place. Never before, or since, has the nation endured an economic crisis anywhere approaching the situation that existed in the 1930s. The extent of the deprivation and suffering experienced by millions of people was both board and deep. Like all national events, the impact of the Depression was not uniform and the hard times made those inequities more plain to see. In 1932, when New York City had eighty-two soup kitchens serving 85,000 hungry people each day, Charles Revson and his brother founded the Revlon cosmetic company. In Detroit, as unemployment topped 60 percent, Henry Ford reportedly earned $14 million in a year. Other individuals did not appear to suffer at all and even prospered throughout the crisis. A few had so much while so many had so little. It looked to a growing number of Americans that the time had come for significant, even radical changes to the country's economic structure. The traditional practice of having no federal public economic welfare—no financial safety net—appeared to be outmoded, counter-productive, and even cruel. The response by states was limited and aid did not reach most. Private charities were overwhelmed. What to do about all of this was the question of the day. As California and the nation endured the fifth year of the Depression, Upton Sinclair thought he had the answer.

In 1934, Sinclair was an internationally-known novelist. But he had long been interested in politics and public affairs, particularly regarding the struggle between the working class and the leaders of capitalism. Much of his written work, although fiction, had been to publicize the politics and causes he believed in. Sensing the unique opportunity in the midst of the economic calamity, he seized the moment. The legacy of his run to be California's governor was the emergence of a new style of political advertising that was extremely vitriolic and negative. It also helped change the political order of California. Perhaps Sinclair was the target of this brand of campaigning because, as he later said, "We threw an all-mighty scare" into the people who held the power in California at that time.

The Context of 1934

The Great Depression, 1929-1941, was by far the worst economic crisis in American history. Even a cursory study of statistics for 1934 sheds light on the hard times—fourteen million people (25 percent of all workers) were unemployed. Counting all the people supported by these former jobholders, and there were forty million people, 32 percent of the nation's total population, without a steady source of income in that year. For those who were employed, median weekly wages had declined by one-third since 1929. Work hours had been slashed as well. The nation's economy had been convulsed by four straight years of unprecedented decline, each year being worse than the previous one. By 1933, the stock market had lost 80 percent of its value, 4,300 banks, one-quarter of the nation's total, had gone out of business, and the national Gross Domestic Product had dropped 53 percent. And there were other numbers, more personal and chilling. The national suicide rate jumped 18 percent, while the birthrate in 1933 dropped to its lowest point in a generation. The number of people graduating from high school declined as did the number of new marriages. Tremendous worry, stress, and apprehension for the future seemed to be a part of the daily lives for millions.

Given these conditions, the overwhelming defeat of President Herbert Hoover in 1932 and the election of Franklin Roosevelt surprised few (Hoover himself being one of the exceptions.) Under Roosevelt, there had been some changes for the better. Unlike the conservative and personally dour Hoover, the charismatic Roosevelt had taken unprecedented and dramatic steps to stabilize the banking industry and create hundreds of thousands of publicly-financed jobs. It had helped and spirits rose.

But even if the bottom of the Depression had been reached, conditions remained miserable for millions. What historians now recognize with the clarity of time is that Roosevelt's New Deal, although a groundbreaking experimental mixture of reformist measures, would only be a "holding action" against the Depression. The 60 billion dollars that the federal government poured into relief and recovery, it was later realized, were much too little given the magnitude of the crisis. It would take the 380 billion dollars spent during World War II to end the Depression. In 1934, of course, no one knew that.

The Depression was so broad, deep, and persistent that more than a few Americans began to lose their faith in capitalism as the economic basis for the nation. Some people openly wondered if the free market had run its course and now was the time for wholesale change. In California, wages for what jobs there were remained low. One out of every four workers in the state was without a job. State relief paid only $4.50 a *month* and most of the unemployed did not even receive that. Farm prices had all but collapsed. Business remained nearly at a standstill. People were being evicted from their homes and apartments. Some took to living in their automobiles or on the street. Others took off and throngs of hobos rode in freight trains in search of something better. Conditions only worsened with the arrival of tens of thousands of poor tenant farmers from the drought-stricken Midwest. Other unemployed people from all over the country migrated to California as well. Many found that the only employment available was in the fields, where pay averaged ten to fifteen cents an hour.

The Life and Work of Sinclair

Californians knew more about the work of Upton Sinclair than about his life. He was born in Baltimore in 1878. His grandfather had been an admiral in the United States Navy. However, his father was an alcoholic who frequently changed jobs and his family was extremely poor. Upton was withdrawn and thoughtful child who learned to read at age five. When he was ten, the family moved to New York City. There he lived for short periods with his wealthy grandparents. He later claimed that witnessing these extremes in economic disparity is what later prompted him to become a socialist.

Early on, Sinclair showed an early talent for writing. He published his first story in a magazine when he was fourteen and enrolled at New York City College. By seventeen, he was supporting himself through writing for newspapers and other periodicals. Two years after that, he entered Columbia University. He dropped his plan to study law after he became even more interested in literature and later, politics.

After getting married in 1902, he published a string of critically well-reviewed, but poor-selling novels. Then, in 1906, he published *The Jungle,* and it was an immediate and massive success, selling 150,000 copies in its first months. The work was a biting exposure of the realities of the filthy, unsanitary conditions in the meatpacking industry. Sinclair had worked for seven weeks in a slaughter house as research for his book. The novel inspired President Theodore Roosevelt to successfully press for the nation's first federal meat inspection laws. Congress would establish the Pure Food and Drug Act in June, 1906. That, however, was only one aspect of the book, which was a fundamental indictment of capitalism as a whole. Readers, though appalled by the circumstances in which their meat was prepared, were mostly indifferent to the exploitive qualities of capitalism. Later, Sinclair famously commented, "*I aimed at the public's heart, and by accident I hit it in the stomach.*"

Four years before publishing *The Jungle*, Sinclair had joined the Socialist Party. Like many American socialist intellectuals, Sinclair was not a Marxist. His political beliefs combined European radicalism with American populism. He desired to see profound changes in the American political system, but sought to bring about those changes by activating people as voters, not bomb-throwers. In 1906, with the support of the Socialist Party, he ran in New Jersey for a seat Congress in which he earned only 750 of 24,000 votes (3 percent.) In 1915, he moved to Pasadena where he continued to write searing attacks on capitalism. He and other social critics were labeled muckrakers, a term coined by President Theodore Roosevelt. By 1934, he had written forty-seven books, taking on many mainstays of society, corporations, the oil industry, organized religion and the academic establishment. By this time, the Socialist Party of America promoted a political platform that called for national unemployment and health insurance and old-age pensions. The Party believed the prolonged depression was evidence that the capitalist system had collapsed and the time had come for a government take-over of private industry.

Sinclair Enters the Race

It was under these worst of economic conditions that Sinclair announced he was running to be the next governor of California. Although he promised radical changes to the economy very much in line with his views of socialism, views that would have been untenable to most voters just a few years earlier. For tactical reasons, he ran for the nomination as a Democrat. To his own surprise, his ideas quickly found a large and receptive audience, desperate for help and willing to follow anyone who had a plan.

In 1934, high unemployment was certainly not the only problem confronting people. Unlike all other western, industrialized nations at that time, in the United States there was no federal welfare system. For the jobless, the poor, retired elderly, and the disabled, survival depended on family support and private charity, if any was available. The Social-Darwinist philosophy of rugged individualism put the onus on the individual to financially succeed or fail. "Poverty is the breeding grounds for success," Henry Ford, the automaker once said. Early in the Depression he also asserted the economic collapse was a "good thing" as it strengthened the initiative of labor. Now, no one was buying Ford's cars and he had completely closed his plant, putting 50,000 employees out of work. People were expected to cope without help from the federal government. As the private sector had largely stopped functioning, there was little security. Fear was one of the few commodities in abundance.

Sinclair had other factors favorable to his unlikely campaign. In California, Republicans had held the governorship for the last thirty-five years. The current governor was the notably conservative Frank Merriam. He called himself the "behind-the-scenes" governor, while others nicknamed the bald-headed politician "Marbletop." He had been governor only a short time, assuming the office the death of Governor James Rolph on June 2nd. The lackluster Merriam did not generate much personal enthusiasm among his party, but he would receive praise for his handling of labor turmoil in San Francisco. He also enjoyed the traditional support given to Republicans from the state's major industries of oil, agriculture, and the movies. Conversely, the state Democratic Party was weak and divided. The energetic Sinclair, already world famous through his books, certainly brought a fresh new direction to the party.

The desire for change seemed to be everywhere 1934. It was a violent year for labor as workers, reeling from the Depression, but encouraged by President Franklin Roosevelt's support of unions, staged a series of major strikes in a number of important industrial cities, several of which were guided by socialist or radical leadership. Unlike past attempts, several of these strikes achieved important gains for the working class, raising hopes and expectations among broad layers of the population. In Minneapolis, truck drivers, organized by members of the Communist League of America, initiated a series of successful strikes that led to union recognition and laid the basis for the transformation of the Teamsters from a relatively small craft union into a mass organization based on the industrial union model. Autoworkers in Toledo fought with police and National Guard troops to win a union contract that led to the organization of dozens of auto plants.

Working class militancy was in California as well. In San Francisco, longshoremen, seeking the right to organize, went on strike in May, closing the city's port for two months. Violence erupted on July 5th, when police broke through strikers' picket lines and a fight ensued. Police shot at the protesters, and two workers were killed with more than seventy wounded. Dozens were arrested. Hours later, Governor Merriam, stated the strike defied "common sense and good citizenship" and declared a state of emergency for San Francisco. The California National Guard, who had already been called up, was ordered into San Francisco. Soon, 1,500 guardsmen, carrying machine guns and rifles with fixed bayonets, were patrolling the waterfront. Believing the governor was attempting to break the strike, more than 100,000 sympathetic union workers walked off their jobs, creating a citywide general strike. For four days, nearly all city services shut down. People began to hoard food. Newsreels shown across the country blamed "radical agitators" and Communists for the strike. With all of this going on, the Democratic primary was just five weeks away.

The EPIC Plan

> *"The "EPIC" (End Poverty in California) movement proposes that our unemployed shall be put at productive labor, producing everything which they themselves consume and exchanging those goods among themselves by a method of barter. . ."*
>
> —Upton Sinclair, October 13, 1934

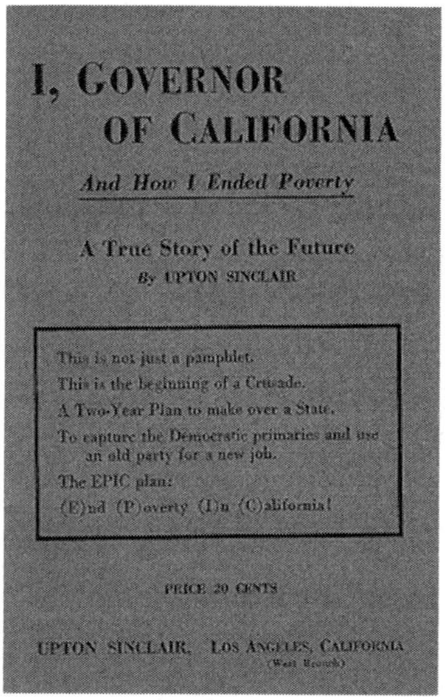

I, GOVERNOR
OF CALIFORNIA
And How I Ended Poverty
A True Story of the Future
By UPTON SINCLAIR
This is not just a pamphlet.
This is the beginning of a Crusade.
A Two-Year Plan to make over a State.
To capture the Democratic primaries and use an old party for a new job.
The EPIC plan:
(E)nd (P)overty (I)n (C)alifornia!
PRICE 20 CENTS
UPTON SINCLAIR, LOS ANGELES, CALIFORNIA

Upon announcing his candidacy, Sinclair published a sixty-page pamphlet that predicted his own election: *I, Governor of California, and How I Ended Poverty—a True Story of the Future.* In it, he advanced what he described as a two-year plan to "End Poverty in California," soon popularly known as EPIC. There were twelve principles set out for the plan. Principle #6 may have been drawn from his own experience as a poor youth who visited his wealthy grandparents: "The existence of luxury in the presence of poverty and destitution is contrary to good morals and sound public policy." The key principle, however, was #11: "The remedy is to give the workers access to the means of production and let them produce for themselves, not for others."

Sinclair envisioned a "people's crusade" of change in which the state would take over idle farms and factories. These resources would be turned over to the unemployed who would operate them as worker cooperatives. People would barter, trade goods, and use scrip in place of national currency. In Sinclair's vision, these cooperatives would compete with privately owned businesses and corporations and eventually would prove their economic superiority.

"Production for use" would triumph over "production for profit" and would ultimately bring an end to for-profit businesses and capitalism.

Part of the EPIC plan was inspired by the existence of 176 cooperatives that already dotted the state in 1934. Here, the poor and unemployed bartered among themselves for goods and services. Other planks in the EPIC plan included other major changes—the repeal of the sales tax, an increase on corporate tax and a graduated individual income tax which would place a larger tax burden on the wealthy. There was to be an inheritance tax on the rich but a property tax exemption for small homeowners. On the spending side, were a series of public works programs, as well as monthly pensions for widows, the elderly, and the disabled.

A 1934 film, *Our Daily Bread,* directed by King Vidor, offered a highly favorable portrayal of what could be accomplished through cooperatives. In the film, a young city couple, hit hard by the Depression, move to a farm where, with the eventual coming together of a string of down-on-their-luck people, a cooperative is born and a successful farm arises. Movie studio chiefs blocked the planned summer release of the film in California, concerned it would inspire public support for Sinclair and his EPIC plan. It would not be shown in wide release until late that year. Although in the film a character explicitly criticized communism, the Hearst newspapers called it "pinko" due to its Socialist themes.

Sinclair's ideas initially evoked an enthusiastic public response. To many, his EPIC plan was just common sense. California had an abundance of good farmland—it had not been hit by the drought that was ravaging the sections of the Midwest at that time. And while there were numerous closed businesses, there was also an army of ready-to-work unemployed. In their minds, it was the capitalist system, with its need for profits, which prevented economic improvement. If the profit motive was removed as a factor for production, people could return to work and begin to provide for themselves.

Within a few weeks, *I, Governor. . .* was the fastest selling book in the state. The bumblebee became the symbol of the campaign and Sinclair was now known. as "the man with the plan." Sinclair later expanded on the twelve principles with *Immediate EPIC,* which detailed his proposals. Reflective of its grass roots appeal, more than 2,000 EPIC clubs were established. The movement published a weekly newspaper, *EPIC News,* which at one point boasted a circulation of 500,000 at a time when the state population was about six million. In the final weeks of the campaign, the circulation rose to two million.

Sinclair's supporters organized rallies, sang songs, signed-up new voters, put out newsletters, led parades, rodeos, and more. By the primary day, August 28, there were 350,000 newly registered Democrats. In a state that had been solidly Republican for decades, with Republican registration normally surpassing Democratic by a three to one margin, for the first time in state history, there were more registered Democrats than Republicans. Sinclair won the primary with 436,000 votes, more than all the other candidates combined. Sinclair's vote total was also larger than the primary vote received by Governor Merriam. It appeared likely that a Democrat could win the governor's office for the first time since 1899.

Traditional Democrats were not happy with Sinclair's victory in the primary. The party establishment considered him too radical and, rightly, not a true member of their party, but an interloper and opportunist. Sinclair knew an endorsement by President Roosevelt was imperative if he were to hold on to the party base. He asked for, and received an invitation to travel east to meet with the president. One year into his own administration and with the New Deal well underway, Roosevelt, however, had already begun work on the new social security system. His secretary of labor, Francis Perkins, was crafting legislation that would establish a federal insurance program for old age, health care, and unemployment. Aware that the administration's plan would inevitably be attacked by critics as government intervention as a disguised form of socialism, the president's meeting with Sinclair took on a heightened meaning. Roosevelt, who as president-elect, had refused to meet with out-going President Herbert Hoover, understood the need to keep his distance from unpopular or controversial politicians.

The president and the Sinclair had a two-hour private meeting at Roosevelt's home in Hyde Park, New York. Characteristically, in private, Roosevelt was full of charm and sought to disarm Sinclair while committing himself to nothing officially. Sinclair left the meeting with a wave and smile for photographers, but kept to an agreement he accepted from the president to make no public statement regarding the details of their discussions. Privately, Sinclair was thrilled, convinced that he had secured a vital political endorsement of his candidacy and it was only a matter of time before Roosevelt would make a public announcement. Sinclair next traveled to Washington where he met Harry Hopkins, Director of the Federal Emergency Relief Administration, who did offer a public endorsement. Ultimately, the endorsement from Roosevelt never came. He kept his distance and his silence, and let events in California play themselves out.

The Plan to Defeat Sinclair

Without a doubt, the monied establishment in California wanted nothing to do with Sinclair or EPIC. Of the 700 newspapers in the state, not one endorsed Sinclair. Just about every institutional force feared and loathed Sinclair's candidacy. Following Sinclair's success in the primary, their frenzied opposition bordered on hysteria. In September, Louis B. Mayer, the studio chief of Metro Goldwyn Mayer, C. C. Teague, president of California Fruit Growers Exchange (better known as the "Sunkist" orange growers), and Harry Chandler, publisher of the *Los Angeles Times,* met for three days with other prominent Republicans to plan a strategy to defeat Sinclair. They formed the group, United for California.

In a first for American politics, they hired an advertising agency and Campaigns, Inc., a political consulting firm founded by Clem Whitaker and Leone Baxter, to direct a statewide campaign, more to defeat Sinclair, than to re-elect Merriam. For his part, Merriam's strategy was to largely stay out of the public eye, so all attention could be turned on Sinclair. The modern media campaign was being born. What followed in California made political history as the greatest negative campaign in American campaigning. What followed in the next few months in California made political history as the greatest negative campaign in American politics.

Anti-Sinclair cartoons were mailed free of charge to newspapers across the state. The *Los Angeles Times* printed a series of front-page boxed features all designed to condemn Sinclair and what Chandler once described as his "maggot-like horde" of supporters. One technique, repeated numerous times, was to publish quotes attributed to Sinclair which criticized traditional social institutions such as organized religion, the family, and marriage. What was not made clear to readers was that the quotes actually were lines "spoken" by characters in various novels he had written, some decades ago. Whether or not they reflected the author's true beliefs was never made clear as the quotes were taken out of context with only the purpose to smear Sinclair's image.

Kenneth Kingsbury, President of Standard Oil of California, mailed to his thousands of stockholders a pamphlet entitled, "Sinclairism means the destruction of all business and property in California." He suggested that the election of Sinclair would imperil "the business of this company and the value of your stock."

Joseph Knowland, publisher of the *Oakland Tribune,* father of William Knowland, who later became a Republican senator and an early supporter of Joseph

McCarthy, ordered his attorneys to research the question of how boldly his paper could lie about Sinclair and legally avoid libel suits.

A United for California radio campaign included a soap opera in which members of a middle-class family chatted around the dinner table. "Sis," coming home from school, worried she wouldn't be allowed to graduate from high school if Sinclair took over because he was opposed to education. "Dad" told his wife he was afraid his factory would close down if EPIC took effect. "Junior" urged everyone to hurry up and eat so he could go to the movies—something he might not be able to do for long because Sinclair promised to put Hollywood out of business. And Sis was further anxious to leave for choir practice at church, something that surely would be suspended under the atheistic EPIC plan.

The scare tactics were as pervasive as they were over-the-top. This excerpt is from an advertisement published shortly before the election by a San Francisco based organization called the California League Against Sinclairism. In it, voters were told the election was about much more than selecting a governor:

> *"If it (Sinclairism) is successful, it will destroy California's business structure, bankrupt our families, overthrow out organized labor, confiscate our homes, wreck our industries, and rob our employed workers of their employment. Your personal security is at issue – the welfare of your home and family; your American citizenship, your rights of self-rule and freedom of worship – your job and your independence."*

Perhaps the most deceptive—and effective—effort were three short films titled *California Election News*, in which the "inquiring cameraman" conducted "man on the street" interviews. This were shown as newsreels in movie theaters around the state in the last weeks before the November election. Studio chief Mayer put MGM's most important producer, Irving Thalberg, in charge of overseeing production of these newsreels, in which Merriam supporters—in reality, Hollywood actors posing as ordinary voters—were presented as sober and well spoken working people and businessmen. Sinclair supporters were shown as shifty-eyed vagrants, some speaking in thick foreign accents; others identified themselves in the films as socialists or believers in communism. Other newsreels showed hobos, again played by actors, riding freight trains headed for California in anticipation of a Sinclair victory. Some of the footage used was taken from recent feature films. Nevertheless, it was said that the state would soon be overrun by poor people and radicals.

These "red scare" films were presented as genuine news stories and distributed free to movie theaters across the state. Audiences had never been shown such cleverly faked presentations of "news." Up to that time, newsreels in theaters were just that, actual news, not political ploys. Although the Hollywood trade publication *Variety*, as well as the *New York Times*, reported the interviews and films were staged, and members in some audience allegedly shouted and booed in the theaters, the historical consensus is that the films significantly hurt Sinclair at the ballot box.

Along those lines, representatives of a non-existent New Citizen Cooperatives Relief Committee passed out pamphlets soliciting donations of clothing, food, money, and living space for the 1.5 million indigents they claimed would arrive in Los Angeles within days of a Sinclair victory. Don Belding, an advertising agent who managed some of the activities against Sinclair, said after the campaign, "We hired the scum of the streets to carry placards saying, 'Vote for Sinclair."

Anti-Sinclair forces spent up to $10 million, a very considerable figure. In 2018 dollars, that would be equal to $186 million. Major contributors included Southern California Edison, Southern Pacific Railroad, Standard Oil, and Pacific Mutual, a life insurance company. Mayer solicited donations from the other studio heads and imposed a levy on his own employees of one day's pay from each of them through the election.

Sinclair and his followers expected a battle with those who they attacked, particularly the leaders of business and industry. Still, they were likely less prepared for the extent of those attacks. The drive to stop Sinclair had united virtually the entire big business establishment in the state and had the support of all major press outlets. The effort was described by historian Arthur Schlesinger Jr. as the "first all-out public relations blitzkrieg in American politics." It was as one-sided as it was dirty. Ninety-two percent of media outlets endorsed Governor Merriam, and five percent endorsed Progressive Party candidate Raymond Haight. The others remained neutral. Not one newspaper endorsed Sinclair, aside from his own

Many efforts were made to link the EPIC plan with Communism. Sinclair's name was advertised as SincLIAR and EPIC as Endure Poverty In California. The press vilified Sinclair as a "Bolshevik." He was falsely called an atheist, a Communist, and a believer in "free love" without marriage. Typical was an October 5, 1934 column in the *Los Angeles Times* that declared the EPIC movement represented "a threat to sovietize California." In fact, many American Communist newspapers had sharply criticized Sinclair themselves, claiming he was willing to co-exist with capitalism, rather than seeking its outright destruction.

Several newspapers predicted a rush of unemployed to California if Sinclair were elected. William Hearst's *San Francisco Examiner* ran a cartoon showing Stalin,

Hitler, and Mussolini on horseback with Sinclair riding a hobbyhorse, rushing to catch up. "Wait for me boys," Sinclair shouts. The California Real Estate Association announced its backing for Merriam with the slogan, "It's Merriam or Moscow" The *Hollywood Reporter* reported that at least four and possibly six of the major movie studios would shut down and move all productions to Florida if Sinclair was elected.

Merriam supporters flooded the mail with anti-Sinclair tracts. In one of the first uses of direct mail, they tailored their message to target audiences. Everyone from university professors to Christians—even the Boy Scouts—received specialized anti-EPIC propaganda pieces.

As the election neared, *Literary Digest* published results of a voter survey purporting to show Sinclair's campaign collapsing, with the candidate garnering the support of just 25 percent of voters. The wide publication of the survey helped demoralize the Sinclair forces. It was later revealed that the magazine had not polled voters in the areas of the state in which the largest concentrations of Sinclair's support existed.

The day before the election, the *Los Angeles Times* devoted half of its front page to a blistering attack on Sinclair. It called him a "literary dynamiter," "apostle of hatred," "collaborator of radicals," "admirer, defender, and instructor of Communist Russia."

Merriam supporters challenged the registration of thousands of Democratic voters in Los Angeles. The California Supreme Court threw out the challenge a few days before the election, calling it a "sham proceeding and a perversion of the court process." Despite this, Republican officials threatened to personally challenge the registration of voters on Election Day.

The Aftermath

On Election Day, Sinclair made a relatively strong showing considering what his campaign had endured. But it wasn't nearly enough. He polled 37.8 percent, receiving 879,537 votes, as compared to 1,138,620 for Merriam and 302,519 for Haight. On the other hand, many progressive candidates did win office, in both state and national positions. Of the eighty California state legislators elected, twenty-seven came from the EPIC organization. Nationally, Democrats won at historic levels, capturing more than 70 percent of the seats in the house, senate, and governor races. It was the worst election for Republicans since its formation as a party seventy-four years before.

The EPIC movement, however, soon dissolved. Sinclair wrote again on the 1934 race: *I, Candidate for Governor and How I Got Licked.* He withdrew from active politics and returned to his prodigious writing. Sinclair could routinely write eight-thousand words a day and between 1934 and 1940 he published fourteen works of fiction infused with strong political opinions. His 1942 book *Dragon's Teeth*, which dealt with the Nazi takeover of Germany during the early 1930s, won the 1943 Pulitzer Prize for the Novel. In the mid-1960s, after living nearly forty years in California, Sinclair moved to Bound Brook, New Jersey, where on December 18, 1968, he died in his sleep. He had written a total of ninety books.

After 1934, the Democratic Party became a potent force in California politics, in part due to the efforts of Sinclair and the EPIC movement. In 1936, President Roosevelt and the Democrats swept the state. In 1938, one of the new state senators, Culbert Olson, from Los Angeles country would be elected to the office that Sinclair had failed to gain. Olson became the first Democrat elected governor since 1894, soundly defeating Frank Merriam.

Since Merriam's defeat, the two major parties have largely split control of the governor's office with five Democrats and six Republicans holding the office. A similar split was found in presidential elections. Between 1936–2016, the Democratic presidential candidates carried California twelve times, while the Republican presidential candidates won the state nine times. However, beginning in 1992, California voters have leaned decidedly left, with the Democratic presidential candidate carrying the state in seven consecutive contests. In 2016, Democratic candidate, Hillary Clinton, won 17 of the 20 largest counties, earning 2.5 million more votes in the state then her opponent.

It was in the state legislature that the Democrats would come to dominate. Between 1970–2018, Democrats continuously controlled Senate, as well as the Assembly, except for two years 1995–1996. In 2018, Democrats held 27 of 40 seats in the Senate seats, and 53 of 80 seats in the Assembly.

As for Sinclair and his EPIC proposals, in the final analysis the creation of cooperatives as a solution to the mass unemployment caused by the Depression ignored basic social and political realities. For one, it assumed without reason that it was possible to end poverty and unemployment in California, separate from the rest of the nation, not to mention the world. The national economy was far too interconnected for California to move away from paper money and private property. In addition, the EPIC supporters assumed that the Roosevelt administration could be convinced of the reasonableness of the plan to the point he would support it.

While, it may have influenced the New Deal, Roosevelt steered clear from any endorsement of it. At the same time, it was naive to put faith in the notion that wealthy capitalists would peacefully acquiesce to it, even though the EPIC movement stated its intention of challenging "production for profit," the cornerstone of the capitalist system.

It was not the merits (or lack) of Sinclair's plan which make the 1934 election significant. That election perhaps holds the distinction of being the dirtiest one of the century. The attack on Sinclair and EPIC were so elaborate and intensive, so blatant for their lies and deceptions, it marked the beginning of a new era in the history of American political campaigning. Although personal attacks and other forms of negative campaigning date back to the earliest period of American politics, it can not be ignored that the tremendous ridicule and lies heaped on Sinclair had reached new lows, yet were effective. Voters responded to them as Sinclair's opponents had hoped. Another lesson appeared to be that if enough money were poured into a race even if based on lies, it might be enough to help swing the outcome.

The Internment of Japanese in California: Manzanar Camp, 1942–1945

Introduction

"The camp was surrounded by barbed wire. Guards with machine guns were posted at watchtowers, with orders to shoot anyone who tried to escape. Our own government put a yoke of disloyalty around our shoulders. But throughout our ordeal, we cooperated with the government because we felt that in the long run, we could prove our citizenship."

—Isamu Horino, gardener at Manzanar

"A Jap's a Jap. It makes no difference whether he is an American citizen or not. There is no way to determine their loyalty."

—General John DeWitt

The issue of individual liberty and collective security is a significant and relevant public concern today. In a free society, of course, it has always been a concern. Building a society in which personal safety does not come at the expense of personal freedoms is problematic. Defining the proper balance between the two may be difficult, if not possible at times. Although they are not in total disparity to each other, ensuring individual rights can make the goal of mutual safety more problematic.

Historically, in a period of heightened concern for public security, particularly during war, the divide between the two concerns widens. And often it is individual rights that are diminished. During the American Civil War, President Abraham Lincoln authorized the suspension of habeas corpus (the right of a person arrested to be brought before a judge) and allowed the arrest and imprisonment of suspected Confederate sympathizers without charge or trial. Under the Woodrow Wilson administration, the Alien and Sedition Acts of 1917-1918 were passed during World War I. These two federal laws made it illegal under the threat of imprisonment or deportment to publicly criticize any aspect of the American government, its leaders, or their conduct of the war. The Acts effectively denied the Constitution's First Amendment right to freedom of speech, yet they were not repealed until 1921, three years after the end of the war.

During World War II, in 1942, under the claim of enhancing public safety and protecting military resources, President Franklin Roosevelt authorized the detainment of any persons deemed a threat to the internal security of the nation by the U.S. military. As his executive order was applied, the result was the arrest and removal of entire populations of persons of Japanese ancestry from urban areas, mostly in California, to rural camps where they were confined, without charge, for up to three years. Although since that time, the federal government has made a judgment as to whether or not that order and the actions it sparked were just, the public discussion on the issue continues. In the continued aftermath of the attacks on the United States on September 11, 2001, and the focus on fighting terrorism around the world, that debate has only intensified.

For many American citizens, there were compelling reasons in 1942 to have the internment camps. The federal government, the military, the courts, and most of the public either actively supported it or did not openly oppose it. It is worth remembering however, that most of the people sent to the camps were also American citizens. Today, a majority of people view the internment camps as a symbol of war hysteria and hatred. But, one still finds considerable support for the use of the camps, even by some who argue that the camps were "unfair but still necessary." It appears the nation's referendum over individual rights and collective security remains ongoing.

Background to Executive Order 9066

On September 1, 1939, Germany, under the control of Adolf Hitler and the Nazis, invaded Poland, setting off the Second World War. In the United States, President Franklin Roosevelt declared the nation to be officially neutral. As the months progressed, and one country after another fell to Germany, it became increasingly evident to President Roosevelt that American intervention was going to be necessary if Hitler was to be stopped. But Roosevelt's desire to engage in the war faced strong and organized opposition at home. Partly as a result of the vengeful Treaty of Versailles that closed World War I, and inadvertently set the basis for World War II, many Americans did not want to become involved in another "European war." Organizations such as "America First" opposed the nation's entry into the war and attracted prominent supporters and widespread public attention.

The illusion that the United States could remain out of a global war was shattered on the morning of December 7, 1941 when Japan attacked the center of the American Pacific fleet at Pearl Harbor, Hawaii. The assault, without a formal declaration of war, was intended to give Japan, an ally of Germany with its own aspiration of military hemispheric dominance, control over the Pacific Ocean and access to much needed raw materials essential for its war machines. History has shown that Japan's decision to attack a nation with ten times the industrial capacity of its own was an enormous miscalculation that resulted in dire consequences for their nation. But on the morning of the December 7th, the attack appeared to be a great success. Although the next day, President Roosevelt asked for, and quickly got, a declaration of war against Japan, it was clear that the United States was not truly ready to go to war and needed time to assemble both the people and production in order to fight.

It did not matter that the full extent of the damage inflicted by Japan at Pearl Harbor was withheld from the public. It was clear to everyone that the losses were unprecedented to that time. With more than 2,100 Americans killed by the "sneak" attack and many ships damaged or destroyed, public anger at Japan's "treachery" was palpable. On December 8, the FBI arrested 2,000 Japanese men considered "security risks." Despite this, in the weeks after, Roosevelt came under increasing pressure from within the military and other areas of the administration to do something more substantial to reassure the public the government was committed to improving national security. Opinion polls in California indicated strong public support to arrest or otherwise control all the Japanese living in the state. Only 20 percent of the general public favored treating at each of them on a case-by-case basis.

On February 19, 1942, President Roosevelt signed Executive Order No. 9066. This authorized the Secretary of War to designate areas of the country that had importance to the military and to protect those areas from espionage and sabotage by excluding from those areas "any and all persons" at the discretion of the secretary or "appropriate military commander." The order did not specify any persons or groups, nor did there have to be any reason given for who was detained. Additionally, while the military was responsible for the transportation and care of those excluded, the order did not specify where they were to be taken or for how long they would be kept there. The only notable public opposition to the order came from the Society of Friends (Quakers) and the American Civil Liberties Union.

Although the executive order was nationwide in scope and a few thousand German Americans and Italian Americans (Italy being an ally of Germany) would be detained and relocated in several states, by far, the primary group affected were Japanese civilians living in California. A significant supporter and proponent of the order was Lieutenant General John L. DeWitt (1880–1962), head of the Fourth Army and Western Defense Command. General DeWitt had called for the evacuation of the Japanese on December 9th, two days after the attack on Pearl Harbor. He considered an attack on California, either from Japan or by Japanese living in the state, to be inevitable. With Roosevelt's order in hand, and $5 million in funding from the federal government, the decision was made by DeWitt to relocate all persons of Japanese ancestry, citizen or not, from the designated military areas under his control.

In this tense and uncertain time, the federal government was acting out of simple fear of the Japanese Americans. It was a fear unsupported by evidence. On the contrary, the government had collected information that undercut the sweeping nature of Order No. 9066. In early 1941, the U.S. Office of Navel Intelligence investigated the Japanese community to assess the probability of disloyalty toward the country. A report prepared by Lieutenant Commander Kenneth Ringle stated the number of potentially disloyal Japanese to be under 3,500 people. At the time, he noted most of these persons were already being held in detention or were under surveillance. Ringle estimated that more than 90 percent of second-generation Japanese immigrants were "completely loyal." Another report from the U.S. State Department offered stronger numbers, concluding that "90 to 98 percent of Japanese American citizens were loyal to the United States." The War Relocation Authority itself noted in a 1943 report that all its evidences indicated that the great majority of internees "are completely loyal to the United States." However, individual loyalty hearings were not held, partly from the concern they would undermine the entire rationale for the internment system. As it turned out, throughout the entire war, there was not a single recorded case of sabotage, subversion, or espionage by any Japanese American.

Seventeen assembly centers were created to collect and process the internees. Thirteen of these were in California: Fresno, Manzanar, Marysville, Merced, Pinedale, Pomona, Sacramento, Salinas, Santa Anita, Stockton, Tanforan, Tulare, and Turlock. Identification cards were issued to the internees. For the majority, these cards included the phrase "citizen's indefinite leave" above a photograph and name of

WESTERN DEFENSE COMMAND AND FOURTH ARMY
WARTIME CIVIL CONTROL ADMINISTRATION

Presidio of San Francisco, California

May 3, 1942

INSTRUCTIONS TO ALL PERSONS OF JAPANESE ANCESTRY

Living in the Following Area:

All of that portion of the City of Los Angeles, State of California, within that boundary beginning at the point at which North Figueroa Street meets a line following the middle of the Los Angeles River; thence southerly and following the said line to East First Street; thence westerly on East First Street to Alameda Street; thence southerly on Alameda Street to East Third Street; thence northwesterly on East Third Street to Main Street; thence northerly on Main Street to First Street; thence northwesterly on First Street to Figueroa Street; thence northeasterly on Figueroa Street to the point of beginning.

Pursuant to the provisions of Civilian Exclusion Order No. 33, this Headquarters, dated May 3, 1942, all persons of Japanese ancestry, both alien and non-alien, will be evacuated from the above area by 12 o'clock noon, P. W. T., Saturday, May 9, 1942.

No Japanese person living in the above area will be permitted to change residence after 12 o'clock noon, P. W. T., Sunday, May 3, 1942, without obtaining special permission from the representative of the Commanding General, Southern California Sector, at the Civil Control Station located at:

Japanese Union Church,
120 North San Pedro Street,
Los Angeles, California.

Such permits will only be granted for the purpose of uniting members of a family, or in cases of grave emergency.

The Civil Control Station is equipped to assist the Japanese population affected by this evacuation in the following ways:

1. Give advice and instructions on the evacuation.
2. Provide services with respect to the management, leasing, sale, storage or other disposition of most kinds of property, such as real estate, business and professional equipment, household goods, boats, automobiles and livestock.
3. Provide temporary residence elsewhere for all Japanese in family groups.
4. Transport persons and a limited amount of clothing and equipment to their new residence.

The Following Instructions Must Be Observed:

1. A responsible member of each family, preferably the head of the family, or the person in whose name most of the property is held, and each individual living alone, will report to the Civil Control Station to receive further instructions. This must be done between 8:00 A. M. and 5:00 P. M. on Monday, May 4, 1942, or between 8:00 A. M. and 5:00 P. M. on Tuesday, May 5, 1942.
2. Evacuees must carry with them on departure for the Assembly Center, the following property:
   (a) Bedding and linens (no mattress) for each member of the family;
   (b) Toilet articles for each member of the family;
   (c) Extra clothing for each member of the family;
   (d) Sufficient knives, forks, spoons, plates, bowls and cups for each member of the family;
   (e) Essential personal effects for each member of the family.

All items carried will be securely packaged, tied and plainly marked with the name of the owner and numbered in accordance with instructions obtained at the Civil Control Station. The size and number of packages is limited to that which can be carried by the individual or family group.

3. No pets of any kind will be permitted.
4. No personal items and no household goods will be shipped to the Assembly Center.
5. The United States Government through its agencies will provide for the storage, at the sole risk of the owner, of the more substantial household items, such as iceboxes, washing machines, pianos and other heavy furniture. Cooking utensils and other small items will be accepted for storage if crated, packed and plainly marked with the name and address of the owner. Only one name and address will be used by a given family.
6. Each family, and individual living alone, will be furnished transportation to the Assembly Center or will be authorized to travel by private automobile in a supervised group. All instructions pertaining to the movement will be obtained at the Civil Control Station.

Go to the Civil Control Station between the hours of 8:00 A. M. and 5:00 P. M., Monday, May 4, 1942, or between the hours of 8:00 A. M. and 5:00 P. M., Tuesday, May 5, 1942, to receive further instructions.

J. L. DeWITT
Lieutenant General, U. S. Army
Commanding

000

SEE CIVILIAN EXCLUSION ORDER NO. 33.

the individual. In total, 120,000 people were moved, sent to one of ten relocation centers. These centers were scattered about in Topaz, Utah; Minidoka, Idaho; Gila River and Poston, Arizona; Granda, Colorado; Rohwer and Jerome, Arkansas; Heart Mountain, Wyoming; Manzanar and Tule Lake, California. Manzanar was the first assembly and relocation center to open.

Manzanar War Relocation Center

Manzanar has a history that, ironically, involved the forced relocation of people on more than one occasion. At 4,000' elevation, it is located at the foot of the Sierra Nevada in eastern California's Owens Valley. Because of the Sierra rain-shadow, there is little precipitation, about 4" a year. The land is open with scrub bush and low trees. Daytime temperatures range from the 40s in the winter to 100 in the summer. Nighttime lows are in the 30s and 40s year-round. High winds are common. There is evidence of human presence by Native Americans dating back 10,000 years. About 1,500 years ago Numu (now called Owens Valley Paiute) Indians established settlements in the area where they hunted, fished, collected pine nuts. In the early 1860s, American miners and ranchers moved into the region and began to homestead on the Native lands, raising cattle, sheep, fruit, wheat, and other crops. In 1863, the U.S. military was used to forcibly relocate nearly 1,000 Owens Valley Paiute 225 miles away to Fort Tejon (near Bakersfield).

In 1910, the actual town of Manzanar—the Spanish word for "apple orchard"—was founded. A small community of farmers and ranchers, more than 500 acres of apples, pears, peaches, corn, potatoes, and alfalfa were developed in the surrounding area.

Beginning in 1905, the Los Angeles Department of Water and Power was buying land and water rights in valley so it could build the Los Angeles Aqueduct, which was completed in 1913. The aqueduct would pass just a mile from the town. The buyouts continued and in 1924 the city of Los Angeles had purchased 5,000 acres on which the town of Manzanar sat, giving it control of all of its land and water rights. Without water to farm, most people were forced to leave. Within five years, the town was largely abandoned. In the 1930s, those few local residents who remained hoped that tourism could sustain their economy, but the start of World War II undermined their plans as gas rationing and other war conditions resulted in a dwindling of visitors.

In 1942, the U.S. Army leased 6,200 acres from Los Angeles to establish the Manzanar Relocation Center to hold the Japanese Americans they planned on moving.

It was initially operated by the Army's Wartime Civilian Control Administration. Later it became the first of ten relocation centers overseen by the War Relocation Authority. Though some valley residents opposed the construction of the internment camp, others helped build it and worked there. Among these were a few Owens Valley Paiute whose own families had been exiled from the area eighty years before.

The Manzanar Relocation Center was built by Los Angeles contractor Griffith and Company. Working ten hours a day, seven days a week, major construction was completed in six weeks. Tar paper barracks, which were 2,400 square feet each, were divided into six one-room apartments. Blocks of fifteen barracks shared common bath, toilet, and kitchen facilities. The entire perimeter of the camp was surrounded by barbed wire fences that was patrolled by armed guards, some with dogs. Eight tall guard towers ringed the camp. Guards were authorized to use deadly force if necessary. To be clear, this was not a forced labor camp. Rather, its purpose was to isolate the internees from the general population. In March, the first few dozen Japanese Americans made a 220-mile journey by bus from Los Angeles. Over the next few days, 146 more Japanese Americans arrived in cars and trucks under military escort. Soon another 500 arrived by train, mostly older men, from Los Angeles. Throughout April as many as 1,000 a day arrived, and by mid-May the camp's population had passed 7,000. At its peak, there were 10,046 people. More than 90 percent of the evacuees were from the Los Angeles area, particularly the San Fernando Valley, San Joaquin County, Stockton, and Bainbridge Island, Washington.

Evacuees, many of whom were given three days notice prior to being relocated, could only bring essential personal effects; bedding and linens, toiletries, clothing, and eating utensils. No pets, personal items, household goods, vehicles, or any furniture were allowed. All excluded possessions had to be stored, sold, or entrusted to others. For those who owned a business with its inventory and equipment, the challenge was even more daunting. In some instances, friends and neighbors did help in arranging to care for possessions. For most, however, given the short time between the announcement and the actual internment, it was simply not possible to make adequate long-term arrangements. Many things were sold at great loss or were simply forfeited. For many, upon eventual release, there was little or nothing to return to.

When looking at the total population of those who were sent to the camps, the sweeping nature of the internment becomes evident. Anyone with as little as one-sixteenth Japanese blood was included. Seventy-thousand were either "Nisei," U.S. citizens by birth or "Issei," first-generation immigrants. More than half of all the internees were children, with nearly 2,000 under the age of five. Another 2,000 people were over sixty-five years old. Over 1,000 individuals had serious physical disabilities. More than six out of every ten internees were citizens of the United States. Ironically, there would was no general internment of Japanese Americans living in Hawaii where the attacks had taken place. Only 1,200 of the 150,000 Japanese Americans there were interned. This may be due, in part, to the impractical idea of arresting one-third of the islands' population.

There was very little public outcry over internment. There were no organized protests, even from within the Japanese American community. Twice, however, while the camps were in operation, legal cases were brought against the United States government over the internment. In the cases of *Hirabayashi v. United States* (1943) and *Korematsu v. United States* (1944), defendants argued their Fifth Amendment rights were violated by the U.S. government solely because of their ancestry. In other words, the actions taken by the government were racially-motivated, nothing more. In particular, attention was called to the last part of the Fifth Amendment which reads "[no person shall be] deprived of life, liberty, or property, without due process of law; nor shall private property be taken for public use without just compensation." Also noted was the petition clause of the First Amendment. This express right entitles citizens to argue against government misconduct in matters of poor policy, waste, corruption, and incompetence without endangering public order. In both cases, the Supreme Court ruled in favor of the federal government and allowed the internees to be held without legal charges.

In January 1945, nearly three years after signing Order No. 9066, President Roosevelt rescinded it and a general release of internees began. Although the war against Japan would continue until August with some heavy fighting in the Pacific, by that time, Japan was severely on the defensive as the Americans relentlessly advanced toward the island nation. By the end of the year, all of the internees had left the ten camps. At Manzanar, most of the buildings were quickly dismantled and the materials were sold to the public. Released internees were given $25 and a bus ticket to the community they had been taken from.

Legacy and an Apology

Forced into the camps, ultimately more than 5,700 Japanese Americans renounced their American citizenship. Some moved to Japan. Most, however, were returned to where they had been taken and attempted to pick up the pieces of their lives. There was an initial effort to redress the economic losses. In 1948, President Harry Truman signed the Evacuation Claims Act into law. It authorized payments to

Japanese Americans who could document economic loss as a result of their being placed in the internment camps. In reality, it did little. One stipulation of the allowed only ten cents to be paid for every one dollar of provable loss. The Justice Department took 17 years to review 23,689 claims. By 1965, it had awarded a total of $38 million, an average of $1,600 per claim. The true financial losses suffered by those relocated have been conservatively estimated at $400 million. The half-hearted effort of the Evacuation Claims Act reflected the broader general public sentiment that, on the whole, paid little attention to the entire relocation occurrence, especially after the war was over.

However, the historical disregard of the internment events began to change in the early 1970s. In 1972, California designated the Manzanar site a state historic landmark. In 1976, it was placed on the National Register of Historic Places. It was declared a National Historic Landmark in 1985.

The first important public remembrance of the camps came in 1972. J. S. Holliday, historian and executive director of the California Historical Society, organized an exhibition of the internment system called "Executive Order 9066." The exhibit featured the photographs by Dorothea Lange and others and proved to be an important milestone in the internment story. It was controversial as it challenged the public to recall what was now an uncomfortable, even painful chapter of the war. Initially, several museums rejected the exhibit. Finally, the De Young Museum in San Francisco accepted it, and it opened in February 1972. Over 100,000 people viewed the artifacts and photographs during a six-week run. Many thousands more saw it during a national tour that included stops at the Utah Museum of Fine Arts and the Corcoran Gallery of Art in Washington, D.C. California state historian Kevin Starr stated that Holliday had "helped break the silence" surrounding the internment.

Another important contributor in raising attention to the camps was the publication of *Farewell to Manzanar* by Jeanne Wakatsuki (Houston) in 1973. Her memoir told of her family's experience of being one of the first to be brought to Manzanar from their home in Santa Monica and being one of the last to leave. Seven years old when she arrived, Wakatsuki, felt the experience dramatically changed her life as she struggled for years to find peace within her own identity. Since its publication, *Farewell to Manzanar* has sold more than one million copies and is now a standard work adopted by many schools and colleges throughout the country.

In 1982, a U.S. congressional investigative commission concluded there had been no military justification for the internment and that the execution of Order 9066 had run counter to the basic premise that an immigrant's loyalty to the United States was in question simply because of his or her country of origin. The commission concluded that racial prejudice was a major cause for the internment.

Forty-six years and eight presidents after the Order No. 9066 was issued, Congress passed the Civil Liberties Act of 1988. In signing the bill into law, President Ronald Reagan said that the relocation had been based on "race prejudice, war hysteria, and a failure of political leadership." In 1990, additional legislation authorized a payment of $20,000 to each surviving Nisei and Issei internee. As the reparation program began, President George H. Bush wrote, "A monetary sum and words alone cannot restore lost years or erase painful memories; neither can they fully convey our nation's resolve to rectify injustice and uphold the rights of individuals." Offering "a sincere apology," President Bush noted, "that serious injustices were done to Japanese Americans during World War II." Ultimately, $1.2 billion was paid to more than 60,000 former internees still living.

In 1992, Congress established the Manzanar National Historic Site to preserve and interpret the "historic, cultural, and natural resources associated with the relocation." The 550 acres of the former camp would now be administered by the National Park Service, under the U.S. Department of Interior. By the early 1990s, all that remained from the 1940s on the site of the camp was a guard post at the entrance, the remains of unpaved roads, and one large building—a high school auditorium/community center built by the internees in 1944.

Today, the Manzanar site is the best restored of the camps. In 2004, the Manzanar National Historic Site Interpretive Center opened. The $5 million interactive museum is housed in the former auditorium. Notable features of the camp are being restored. A barrack for families, a community kitchen, latrine, guard tower, and other structures have been reconstructed. Located on Highway 395, five miles south of the town of Independence, the center presents the opportunity for the current generation to understand the insecurity, fear, and racism that led to the establishment of Manzanar and the other relocation camps, and allows one to assess the question of how best to balance collective security with individual liberty.

Fast Living in California

In 1960, 20 percent of mothers in United States held paying jobs outside the home. In 2017, 65 percent of mothers were employed, In the same year, the number of children who lived in homes where all adults were employed was 62 percent. For all of those homes, 85 percent of all men and 66 percent of all women who held paying jobs worked more than forty hours a week. Americans today work an average of 34.4 hours a week, more than their counterparts in European nations and in Japan. And for those U.S. workers who are full time, the average work week is 47 hours. The average American spends 499 more hours a year on the job than do workers in France. When one adds in general cultural changes of the last few decades in which parents today often take far more active roles in the social and recreational activities of their children, and a time crunch emerges.

Increasingly busy lives are just one component of the tremendous changes to ordinary living conditions in the state and the nation. The creation of the modern, fast-paced society was partly the result of a series of simultaneous innovations in housing, road construction, and the food industry. Overlaying all of this was a post-World War II spike in population, plus a surge in discretionary consumer spending. These changes, although national in scope, had notable effects on California.

Post-War America

California, like the rest of the United States, underwent rapid and profound changes in the aftermath of the Great Depression and World War II. For the U.S., the worst economic period in its history, 1929–1943, was followed by fighting in the deadliest war ever, 1941–1945. For the generation that endured the twin calamities, it was a time of want and an absence of stability. Traditional plans like getting married, having children, building a career, and buying a house and simply enjoying life, were denied, deferred or never to be. And suddenly, the war ended in emphatic victory; peace and prosperity were at hand. Although, the country just entered both the computer and the atomic age, that was not the focus of most people. For millions, hopes ran high that the pent-up desires that were close and immediate would now be available. There was a saying in this time, "After total war can come total living."

Surging Populations

Sixteen million Americans had joined in military service. More than 400,000 had died (including 6,700 Californians.) For the rest, it was a return to their homes to try and pick up the pieces of their lives. One of the initial goals was to marry and start a family. The statistics are telling. In 1946, two million couples nationwide got married. Over the next several years the average age of a person entering into a first marriage dropped by more than two years.

For many, children soon followed. In 1942, there were twenty-one births per 1000 people. Five years later, this figure had risen to twenty-seven births per 1,000. Between 1946 and 1950, there were 21 million births in the United States. The so-called "baby boom" was underway. In the 1950s, the size of the average American family expanded from 3.09 to 3.77 persons. By the time the boom ended, generally agreed to be 1964, more than 76 million children had been added to the national population.

For California, first the wartime economy, and then the general prosperity, swelled the state population. Between 1940 and 1950, it rose a staggering 53 percent, to more than 10.5 million. By 1960, it increased by another 5.2 million, a 48 percent gain. Now there were 15.7 million Californians and the state was on the verge of becoming the most populous in the country (in 1962 it would surpass New York state.)

A Nation of Plenty

In this same period, the end of the war had created an unusual set of global circumstances that heavily favored the United States. It had created a superpower. In 1946, the U.S. was the only nation in the work with the atomic bomb. War devastation abroad would take years to recover from. For the U.S. it meant the nation produced 75 percent of the world's electricity, 80 percent of all the automobiles; in fact, half of all goods sold in the world were American made. The average income of an American worker was fifteen times larger than European workers. Americans had a diet that contained eight times the calories of people in Asia. It was a temporary time, to be sure, but it lasted for years, and had a profound impact on the material and psychological outlook of Americans. It seemed the nation was awash in prosperity.

New Suburbs

Still there were shortages. In 1946, the United States was in great need of new homes. Since the Great Depression began in 1929, the housing market had sputtered and withered. Construction had essentially stopped during the war. Now, in 1946, the nation was five million houses short of demand. William Levitt, a Navy veteran, would transform the housing industry much the way Henry Ford had done in automobile production and what the McDonald brothers were about to do in the restaurant business (see below.) His 17,500 house "Levittown," built on Long Island between 1947–1951, was the beginning of mass-production housing.

A suburb is an outlying residential community within commuting distance of a city. Sometimes referred to as "bedroom communities," suburbs have been around since the late 1800s (East Los Angeles, now called Lincoln Heights, became L.A.'s first suburb in 1873.) So Levitt did not invent suburbs; he innovated the scale and speed of their construction. His goal was to build low-cost houses quickly. To achieve this he bought large tracts of open land, used uniform and interchangeable parts—like Ford—and would offer just a few standard designs. Prefabricated sections were brought to the worksite where they were more assembled on concrete foundations. By 1948, workers at Levitt own were constructing thirty houses a day; they would be sold at an even faster rate.

Soon the Levittown model was being replicated across the nation; since 1950, 75 percent of all new houses have been built in that style. By 1970, the county's suburban population doubled from 36 million to 74 million people. California's abundant land, large labor force, many sunny days, and mild climate combined to put it in the forefront of the migration to suburbs.

Note: Sprawl

Today, there is the question of whether California can continue afford to support the pattern of suburban development, often referred to as "sprawl," that has characterized its growth since World War II. There is no doubt that relatively affordable and massive housing projects enabled millions of people to enjoy homeownership while helping to drive the state's economic boom for decades. But it has become equally clear that sprawl has created enormous environmental, social, and economic problems that, ironically, now threaten to degrade the quality of life.

For example, although in 2010, the city of Los Angeles was the second largest city in the United States in total population, its population density of 7,000 people per square mile was much lower than many other urban centers (New York City, 26,000; San Francisco, 18,600; Boston, 13,300; Chicago, 11,800; Philadelphia, 11,200; Miami, 11,100.) In sum, a continuous expansion of suburbs allowed millions of southern Californians to live in near a large urban city while owning "space," a detached house with a garage, and patch of grass.

With one of every three Californians living in Los Angeles County, the spread of houses has led to some extraordinarily long commutes, greater congestion of roads, more air pollution, and lower worker productivity as people spend more time get to and from work, rather than being at work. In 2005, the South Coast Air Quality Management District, estimated that air pollution in the Los Angeles area cost $7.4 billion, or $600 per resident. It also lowered agricultural crop production in the region by $200 million.

Since that time, congestion has worsened. In 2017, U.S. drivers averaged 42 hours per year driving in congested traffic. But in the southern California drivers spent 104 hours each driving in congestion. That made Los Angeles home to the most gridlocked and congested roads in the world. That total easily topped the second most congested city—Moscow—at 91 hours, and third-place New York City which came in with 89 hours. This data was compiled by Inrix, a transportation analytics firm which studied driving in more than 1,000 cities worldwide. Being stuck in traffic cost the average Los Angeles driver more than $2,800 last year and nearly $300 billion for all U.S. drivers nationwide.

Fast Food's "Fertile Crescent:" San Bernardino

In the history of eating, restaurants, which have been around for thousands of years, traditionally catered on travelers. Taverns and inns offered food to people who were away from home. The idea of eating in a restaurant near to one's home was a foreign concept until the late 1700s and even then, it wasn't something most people ever did. Not until a century later, with a steady rise in urban populations, did the custom of visiting a local restaurant become common. So the combination of eating out for fun without traveling is a somewhat recent development in civilization. Along with this trend came fast food, simply defined as food that is quickly prepared and served, usually by means of standardization and simplicity of the food.

While "fast food" was developed in several places, the heart of the modern industry was located in the greater Los Angeles region. In 1940, two brothers, Richard and

Maurice, opened a restaurant in San Bernardino, an hour east of Los Angeles. They called it *McDonalds Bar-B-Que* and offered a menu with more than forty barbecued items. Customers sat in their parked cars as a wait staff of "carhops" came and took orders and than delivered trays of food through their windows. The business was a strong success, notably among young people, and it joined the many new casual eateries that incorporated automobiles into their operation.

The McDonald's timing was good. Between 1930 and 1940 the population of Los Angeles had increased nearly 275,000 to more than 1.5 million people. The entry of the United States in World War II, added to that boom. In 1939, the United States spent $190 million in California on defense contracts. By 1945, that figure had soared to $8 billion and a good portion of that came to the Los Angeles region, with major funding for aviation and ship construction. San Bernardino was a microcosm of what was happening across the southland. A former pueblo founded by a Spanish priest in 1810, in 1940, its population had edged over 43,000. In the next decade it surpassed 73,000, a 41 percent gain.

Not surprising, other restaurants similar to *McDonalds Bar-B-Que* soon opened in the region. In 1941, in Anaheim, forty miles away, Carl Karcher opened a hot dog stand *Carls Chili Dogs*. A few years later, he moved into a full-service, sit down restaurant and named it *Carl's Drive-in Barbecue*. In 1947, *Mr. Fatburger* was founded in Los Angeles by Lovie Yancey. It was a success and Yancey became an industry rarity, a female African American restauranter. The next year, 1948, Harry and Esther Synder opened their first drive-in restaurant, *In-N-Out*. It was in Baldwin Park and, like *Carls*, it was about forty miles from San Bernardino. As the name implied, speed of service was a fundamental element of the business. The Snyder's added the innovation of a two-way speaker system so drivers could order from their cars and pull up to the building to receive the orders.

Back in San Bernardino, the success of the McDonald brothers attracted another food entrepreneur, Glen Bell. In 1946, he opened *Bell's Drive-in*, a hot dog stand. Across the street was *Mitla Café*, which sold California-Mexican food; enchiladas with mole, but also grilled cheese sandwiches and fries. Bell became intrigued with the idea of selling Mexican food in the style of the hamburger drive-ins; that is, fast and inexpensive. A speciality at *Mitla's* was a hard shell taco with the meat and other stuffings added after the shell was cooked. In 1951, Bell started selling his own tacos. The next year, he changed the name of his business to *Taco Tia* and, later, *El Taco,* and finally, Taco Bell.

Looking back, one sees all the ingredients were in order. A youthful, growing population living in post-war prosperity. Increasing wedded to their automobiles, they were willing to trade some of the comfort and decorum of full restaurant service for speed, low-prices, and convenience. It was the McDonald brothers who took the next great leap forward in bring fast food to southern Californians. In 1948, the brothers closed their $200,000 a year business and retooled. They reduced the menu to nine items, all of which could be prepped in advance of their being ordered. They eliminated utensils and would bag all food for take-out. Every item was disposable, including the drink cups. The carhops were let go; customers would line up at a single counter to place and receive their orders. Food was made in the style of an assembly-line. Large grills were installed for cooking many burgers simultaneously (and flipped by custom-sized spatulas.) A "dressing station" was created to garnish each burger with the same condiments. A large fryer was to quickly cook batches of uniform sized-french fries. Heat lamps and timers helped employees keep track of the process. A soda fountain & milkshake machine completed the kitchen.

In opening their renamed *McDonalds*, the brothers were betting that customers would accept fewer choices and options for their food in return for greater efficiency. They reduced the average wait by a customer from twenty minutes to under one minute. To promote their vision, the brothers created an animated advertising character, Speedee. The response to the changes was overwhelmingly positive. Soon the business was characterized by the crowds of people who lined up for the quick-served hamburgers.

The success of the McDonalds example influenced all the competitors. Company menus, kitchen design, and even the names of the restaurants were altered in the ensuing years. What remained was the fundamental goal of placing a premium on convenient and inexpensive food, rapidly served.

There are, of course, other large food chains, but those founded in San Bernardino and other southern California locales have done remarkably well. In 2016, the numbers for McDonalds were staggering. It had 36,600 restaurants staffed by 1.7 million employees who served 68 million customers (1 percent of the world's population) in 120 countries each day. The company is the nation's largest private purchaser of beef, pork, potatoes & apples. It is estimated McDonalds sells 75 hamburgers every second of every day. This volume generated revenue in excess of $25 billion a year.

While McDonalds was the acknowledged leader, the fast food industry remained intensively competitive. Taco Bell had 7,000 locations serving 40 million customers a week. Carl's Jr. had more than 1,400 restaurants which placed it as the nation's fifth largest chain. In-N-Out and Fatburger were comparably small, with 329 and 200 locations respectively.

In changing the eating habits of so many people, the fast food industry has altered much more of society. It has significantly impacted the global environment, health and medical conditions, and the economies of many allied industries. Whether the net sum of these changes are more positive or negative is an argument that has been playing out for many years, with no end in sight.

Interstate Highway System

The lynchpin to the success of suburbs and fast food was, of course, the automobile. Post-war suburbs, as they were constructed, made owning a car essential as developers and elected civic leaders neglected, if not completely ignored, making public transportation an integral part of suburban development. Most Americans were content to go along with this as the country resumed its love affair with the automobile after 1945. Owning a car was preferred to riding a trolley, or later, a bus. Large cars were desired for their style, social status, and comfort.

Early Influences

As car ownership increased, so did the desire for high-speed roads. A national road was not a new idea. What is recognized as the first transcontinental roadway was the Lincoln Highway. Opened in 1913, it was 3,389 miles of a patchwork of roads affectionately called the "main street across America." It traveled through fourteen states with its official terminals were Lincoln Park in San Francisco in the west, and Times Square in New York City in the east. But good portions of the road were not paved and travel facilities such as service stations, hotels, and restaurants were inconsistently located and often sparse.

In 1926, two more highways involving California were put into use. The more famous one was Route 66. While not as long as the Lincoln, it consisted of 2,347 miles of paved roads from Chicago through Missouri, Kansas, Oklahoma, Texas, New Mexico, and Arizona before ending in California, officially, at the pier in Santa Monica. The other was Route 101. At 1,540 miles, it follows much of the course of El Camino Real, the "royal road" of the Spanish mission era, from Los Angeles north to Olympia, Washington. Today, part of the road north of San Francisco has become the Redwood Highway, as it passes through the great trees.

Another influence on highways came in 1939, when New York City hosted a World's Fair. The Fair's theme was "The World of Tomorrow" and its most popular exhibit was *Futurama*, designed by General Motors. *Futurama* imagined what a city of 1960 could look like. Perhaps not surprisingly, it was a place built around the automobile, as well as a national highway system that was much more connected and faster than anything that existed in the United States at the time. *Futurama* included a full-scale model of a city block so the 30,000 daily visitors to the exhibit could better imagine modern buildings linked by high speed roads.

There were real life examples of such a road system too. In Germany, the construction of the autobahn, a true integrated road system, had been a major focus of Adolf Hitler since he and Nazi party seized control in 1933. By the time the detailed models of *Futurama* opened in New York, 2,050 miles of the autobahn had been opened. Its value to business, military interests, and personal travel were all too clear.

Closer to home, the Pennsylvania Turnpike also began operating in 1940. It was the first of its kind in the United States—a 160-miles road with no stop signs, no intersections, and initially—like the autobahn—no speed limit. It was a great success as people were more than willing to pay the penny per mile toll in return for speed or movement.

Eisenhower's Role

Following World War II, with the development of Levittown and its imitators, the return to automobile production, and the emergence of fast food, car-friendly shopping malls, and alike, the pressure was on the federal government to respond. The idea of a highway system was not new. It had been under study for years and short sections of turnpikes, many of them with tolls, had been built. It would fall to Dwight Eisenhower to oversee the creation of the interstate system. Eisenhower, as a young man in the military, had driven across the country in 1919 on the Lincoln Highway and he was aware of its shortcomings. As Allied Commander during World War II, he had personally seen the autobahn, both flying over and driving on it. He admired it and understood its many uses. As President, Eisenhower signed the Federal-Aid Highway Act of 1956, legislation creating the interstate highway system. At $25 billion it was the costliest federal project to date. In return the plan was to construct 41,000 miles of highways that criss-crossed the nation in uniform design and function (ultimately, the system would be 46,800 miles.)

Legacy

The impact of the highway system can be summed up by Eisenhower himself who, in his 1963 memoir, *Mandate for Change 1953–1956*, wrote, "More than any single action by the government since the end of the war, this one would change the face of America. . . . Its impact on the American economy—the jobs it would produce in manufacturing and construction, the rural areas it would open up—was beyond calculation."

The interstate system is a marvel in engineering and construction: 14,700 interchanges, 55,500 bridges, and 82 tunnels. In California, three of the four longest sections of the highway system run through the state: I10, I40, and I80. A total of 2,455 miles of interstate roads are in the state, second only to Texas. Its creation was a boon to the construction industry and a multitude of businesses. It brought the state and country closer together in time, if not space.

But it created problems too. If divided towns, took out neighborhoods, demolishing tens of thousands homes, farms, businesses, and community sites. It took a lot of land and removed it from having any other purpose. And, by making driving so much quicker, it encouraged urban sprawl, "white flight" from city centers to new suburbs, and contributed heavily to air pollution, global warming, and other costs associated with driving automobiles.

Many elements of the modern California were begun in the post-war era. It is an open question whether the fast living most people have become accustomed to has been a worthy bargain.

The Chinese in California: Perseverance in the Face of Prejudice

Introduction

The history of American freedom is, in no small measure, the history of procedure.

—Felix Frankfurter, Justice of the U.S. Supreme Court, 1945

Injustice anywhere is a threat to justice everywhere.

—Martin Luther King, Jr., 1963

When the rights of any individual or group are chipped away, the freedom of all erodes.

—Earl Warren, Chief Justice of the U.S. Supreme Court, 1959

No Californian gentleman or lady ever abuses or oppresses a Chinaman, under any circumstances.... only the scum of the population do it—they and their children; they, and, naturally and consistently, the policemen and politicians...

—Mark Twain, 1872

In 1846, after the long period of Spanish--and the shorter era of Mexican--rule, California was occupied by forces from the United States. In February, 1848, under the terms of the Treaty of Guadalupe-Hidalgo, which formally concluded the Mexican War, California was included in the vast transfer of lands ceded by Mexico to the United States. In September of 1849, four dozen men met in Monterey as delegates tasked with writing a state constitution as part of the preparation for admission into the United States. Before the year was over, their work was completed and the first state Legislature was seated. In December, that new Legislature elected three justices to the State Supreme Court. Nine month later, on September 9, 1850, California became the 31st state and was now subject to the terms of the U.S. Constitution.

Also beginning in 1850, the U.S. Census began to require from its citizens more information then it previously had collected. Now, the name of every free person was to be listed, not just the head of the household. Census takers also recorded including information from individuals regarding their education, wages earned and taxes paid, the value of their total assets, and other information such as mortality. This more detailed body of data allowed historians to more accurately compare and assess the political, economic, and social status of various racial and ethnic groups living the country.

Today, the California State Supreme Court has seven justices and more than 160 years of history in judicial law-making. The people of California are no different from all Americans in that the society they live in is, to a degree, a product of its laws. A historical examination of those laws and court decisions, coupled with demographic data, reveals California's legal relationship with Chinese immigrants began with a long, dark period of unyielding and calculating racial and ethnic intolerance.

The legal prejudice was so blatant that during the mid-1800s, the U.S. Supreme Court, itself far from an institution promoting equality, would invalidate some of the state's most egregious laws. Still, some incredibly biased laws remained. Undoubtedly, these laws were encouraged and were encouraged by the deep, sometimes violent antipathy toward the Chinese held by many in the general public. But the Chinese were not passive victims and resisted as they could against the waves of discrimination. They not only stayed in California, at times they even thrived. Finally, after nearly a century of statehood, the quest for equality under the law finally began to take hold. And with this came improvements in the societal attitudes towards the Chinese. This reading looks at some of the key highlights of this progression.

Background to the Chinese in California

Following the American Revolution, in 1783 Britain closed off most trade with the United States, or offered it at an egregious disadvantage to the new country. As a result, American trade across the Pacific, into Asia, grew in importance to the early generations of American merchants. From China came increasingly larger quantities of tea, porcelain, lacquer-wood furniture, and silk.

It was during this time that traders from Great Britain became to encourage a great increase in the importation of opium into China. By the 1830s, an estimated as many as twelve million Chinese had become became addicts; when thousands of Chinese eventually left their country, the addictive drug trade would follow them.

By the middle of the 18th century, significant regions of China faced towering challenges. A prolonged drought had created famine conditions for the large class of impoverished rural people. Political rule was unstable as the Qing Dynasty, ruling since 1644, had entered a long period toward eventual collapse. Helping its downward spiral was a direct assault on its power by an opposition state known as the Taiping Heavenly Kingdom. The result of this clash was the Taiping Rebellion (1850–1865) a massive civil war in which at least 30 million people were killed.

As the combined turmoil of these horrific events made life for millions perilous, the discovery of gold in California seemed to offer a beacon of hope. There nearly no Chinese in America previous to this event. The 1840 U.S. Census showed that out of a national population of more than 17 million people, only four were Chinese.

The 14th Amendment

In the first five years following the conclusion of the American Civil War, three major Amendments were made to the U.S. Constitution, the most legal alternations it ever experienced from its creation or since. The 13th Amendment banned slavery (1865), and the 15th Amendment granted voting rights to all men (1879.) While both were monumental legal changes (though, in practice, voting rights would be denied to millions for another century), it would be the 14th Amendment that would eventually emerge as the cornerstone for many progressive legal cases. Ratified in 1868, this Amendment declared all persons born or naturalized in the United States to be citizens and, therefore, entitled to equal protection of the law. Furthermore, no state could make a law which denied this protection. This sweeping new "right," would, like the 15th, be denied as a reality for millions of people until the next century.

The Chinese in California

Immigration to the United States in the 19th century, is very different then it is today. There were no visas, passports, or other official paperwork. For the entering immigrant there were no customs officials, no health inspectors, and no interview. One simply arrived and walked in. In 1850, the U.S. Census showed that 660 persons from China did just that. Two years later, California records showed there were now more than 11,700 Chinese in state. In 1860, there would be nearly 35,000 and, in 1870, more than 48,500. Only the Irish would constitute a larger group of foreign-born people in the gold rush.

Unfortunately, the tremendous numbers and diversity of the people attracted to seeking their fortune in the gold region prompted a near immediate backlash against the immigrants. Seeking to limit the competition for the gold, in 1850, the State Legislature passed what would be the first of many laws aimed at harming either the Chinese in particular, or immigrants in general. Although the courts would curb some of the discriminatory excesses, they would, at the same time, make rulings that were blatantly racist themselves.

Here is a listing of such laws, ordinances, and court rulings with the key features of each:

Foreign Miner's Tax, 1850

A $20-per-month tax on anyone born outside of the U.S. who wanted to mine in California. In 1851, the tax was repealed and replaced with a $4-per-month tax (equal to $120 in 2018.) The tax remained in effect until 1870.

People vs. Hall, 1854

California Supreme Court ruled that no race--other than "Caucasian," could testify against a white person. The ruling effectively excluding non-whites from protection through the judicial system. The ruling remained in effect until 1872.

Chinese Fisherman Tax, 1860

This state legislation required a $4-per-month tax on all Chinese fisherman. The tax was repealed in 1864.

The "Anti-Coolie" Act, 1862

A $2.50-per-month-tax on Chinese workers in California or any Chinese wishing to do business in the state, with a few exceptions, whatever their occupation. The Act was ruled unconstitutional by the State Supreme Court in 1863.

The Cubic Air Ordinance, 1870

This San Francisco ordinance required rental residences to have 500 cubic feet of air per inhabitant. Unequally applied, it was aimed at clearing crowded Chinese housing. The ordinance was voided in County Court in 1873.

The Sidewalk Ordinance or "Pole Law," 1870

This San Francisco ordinance was essentially a form of legal harassment. It prohibited the traditional Chinese method of carrying baskets of vegetables or laundry on long poles. The ordinance was repealed by the city mayor in 1874.

The Laundry Tax, 1873

This short-lived San Francisco ordinance sought to tax laundries using horse-drawn vehicles $4 per year, while those with no vehicles, the vast majority being owned by the Chinese, would be taxed at $60 per year. The ordinance was voided in County Court in 1874.

The "Queue Law," 1875

Another legal harassment, this San Francisco law made it illegal for Chinese men to wear their hair in long braids as was their custom. It called for cutting off queues of all arrested Chinese men. The U.S. Court of Appeals ruled it unconstitutional in 1879.

The Page Law, 1875

This law represented the first federal legislation that restricted immigration to the United States. It barred entry of any Chinese, Japanese, or "oriental" who was a felon, or was suspected of engaging in forced labor, such as prostitution. In practice, it is used to keep out nearly all Chinese women out of the United States. As a result, by 1880, the female population of Chinese women in the U.S. dropped by one-third. The Page Law remained in effect until it was replaced by more expansive exclusion laws.

The Second California State Constitution, 1879

The State Legislature wrote a new state constitution which included many provisions aimed at economically harming the Chinese. Under the constitution, no corporation could employ in "any capacity" any Chinese person. Additionally, no Chinese person could be legally employed for any state, county, municipal, or other public works project, except as punishment for crime. In other words, the only legal occupation for the Chinese was self-employment. The document went on to describe the Chinese as being a "danger to the well-being" of the State and for the Legislature to discourage their immigration and continued presence in California by "all the means within its power." In 1880, the U.S. Circuit Court ruled the employment prohibitions were in violation of the 14th amendment.

The Fishing Act, 1880

This brief San Francisco ordinance prohibited the Chinese from engaging in any commercial fishing activity by denying them licenses to do business. Later that year, the U.S. Circuit Court ruled the ordinance was in violation of the 14th amendment.

The Chinese Exclusion Act, 1882

This law, enacted by the U.S. Congress, represented the zenith of legal discrimination against the Chinese. It is the culmination of three decades of racism and resentment. Although national in application, it was spurred to creation by state representatives from California where its impact would be greatest. In short, the law barred all Chinese immigration to the United States. This was the first time in U.S. history that an entire nation of people were forbidden to immigrate simply because of their race. In 1892, the Act was renewed for another ten years. In 1902 it was renewed on a permanent basis.

Political Codes Amendment, 1885

This alteration to California public laws allowed for the segregation of the Chinese in schools, public facilities, hospitals, and other places.

Scott's Exclusion Act, 1888

This law was essentially an addition to the Exclusion Act. It stated that any Chinese person who temporarily left the United States, could not return. Ultimately, this would prevent the return of about 30,000 Chinese people.

The Geary Act, 1892

This national law, written by a California congressman, required all Chinese residents living the United States to carry photo identification with them at all times. There was vocal criticism within the Chinese community to the law that was unprecedented in the history of the nation. But the U.S. Supreme Court upheld it and it became part of the renewed Exclusory Act.

Anti-Miscegenation Law, 1906

In 1900, it was estimated that 5 percent of the Chinese men living the United States were married to white women. This law now prohibited Chinese from marrying non-Chinese. It would remain in effect until it was legally nullified in 1948.

Angel Island, 1910-1940

Located in San Francisco Bay, this "*Ellis Island of the West*" was the U.S. point of entry for immigrants arriving from the Pacific. As the majority of these immigrants were from Asian nations, Angel Island served as part of the enforcement of the Chinese Exclusionary Act. Whereas at Ellis Island, in New York City's harbor, fewer then 2 percent of its 12 million immigrants were rejected, at Angel Island 18 percent of its 1 million immigrants were turned away.

Alien Land Laws (1913)

This California law prohibited the buying or owning land by "aliens ineligible for citizenship." This applied to the Chinese and other Asian people living in the state. In practice, it meant that all Asian farmers had to rent their land, typically for three-year leases, putting them at an economic disadvantage with other farmers. The laws were ruled unconstitutional by the U.S. Supreme Court in 1948 as in violation the 14th amendment

The Response by the Chinese Communities in California

The cascade of anti-Chinese legal actions no doubt had debilitating impact on the Chinese communities in California, as well as those across the United States. The effect of the many exclusion laws was clear. According to the U.S. Census, in 1880 there were 105,465 Chinese in the United States. A decade later that figure had dropped to 89,863. In 1920, the Chinese were down to 61,639 people.

Within these numbers there was tremendous disparity between the number of men and women. In the gold rush, overall, in the 1850s about 95 percent of the participants were men. For Chinese men, the percent was closer to 99 percent. For the general community, over time, this gender imbalance gradually subsided; by 1900, the two sexes were even. For the Chinese, it was a different story. Exclusionary laws prevented thousands of women from leaving China. As a result, a significant gender imbalance would remain in Chinese American until the middle of the 20th century.

Against the odds, the Chinese who endured in California demonstrated courageous resistance to the discrimination and violence they faced. Lacking formal political authority, they used the power of the pen and wrote. There were Chinese American newspaper which took stands against the battery of unfair laws. Individuals published essays calling for their rights. Posters were produced and shown throughout many Chinese neighborhoods educating and encouraging residents to assert themselves into the struggle.

Because they had no political support or voting rights, many of them turned to the only possible legal recourse available–the court system. It is estimated that 8 percent of all Chinese in California would file suits in courts over many decades. This represents an extraordinarily high percentage of activists within a population.

Yick Wo Court Case

One example of this unlikely activism was the story of Yick Wo, an immigrant to California from China in 1861. For twenty-two years he owned and operated a laundry facility in San Francisco. In 1880, city officials passed an ordinance requiring all laundries that operated in wooden structures to have a permit. At the time, about 70 percent of the city's 320 laundries were run by the Chinese and 95 of them were located in wooden buildings. Permits were granted to nearly all the laundries owned by non-Chinese, while more than 99 percent of the applications by Chinese owners were rejected.

Wo continued to operate his business until he was arrested and imprisoned for failure to pay a $10 fine. He sued the City of San Francisco. In 1886, the U.S. Supreme Court unanimously sided with him and ruled the laundry permits were given out with racial discrimination, in violation of the 14th Amendment. This was the first time the "equal protection" clause of the 14th Amendment was cited by the Court, is requiring states to treat all residents the same legally. This landmark precedent has today been cited in more than 150 civil rights cases, many of considerable magnitude.

There were other legal victories, though it should be noted, it took many decades for these to be achieved and change did not always come through the Chinese community. As previously mentioned, the U.S. Supreme Court invalidated Alien Land Laws in 1948. The case, *Oyama v. California,* was carried forward by a Japanese farmer who sued the state.

In 1947, a naturalized Mexican couple, Felicitas & Gonzalo Mendez sued the state over its school segregation policies. In *Mendez v. Westminster School District*, U.S. Court of Appeals in San Francisco, ruled, in a legal precedent, that segregation, based on race, violated the 14th Amendment. By the end of the year, state school segregation was prohibited by the California Education Code.

In 1948, Sylvester Davis, an African American, and Andrea Perez, a Mexican American, met while working in a defense plant in Los Angeles. Eventually, the couple wanted to marry but were forbidden by law to do so. They sued the state.

In the case of *Perez v. Sharp*, the Supreme Court of California ruled, 4-3, that the state's anti-miscegenation law, in place since 1850, was a violation of the 14th Amendment. With it, California became the first state in the country to allow interracial marriages.

The End of Chinese Exclusion

Global politics would finally bring a close to the era of Chinese exclusion. Once Japan attacked the United States in December, 1941, and the two countries declared war on each other, the U.S. view of China dramatically shifted. China was also under attack by Japan so, unsurprisingly China became an ally of the U.S. As the U.S. ramped up for war, it lashed out at its Japanese residents, leading to their forced removal from the main of society into newly conceived internment camps. The Chinese, however, were now treated as friends.

In 1943, the Magnuson Act fully repealed the Exclusion Act, ending 62 years of one of the most intolerant actions in the history of American immigration. At long last, it permitted the Chinese to be naturalized as citizens as well.

After the war ended, in 1946, the War Brides Act was passed to allow non-citizen spouses and any children of members of the U.S. military to enter the U.S. as non-quota immigrants. More than 100,000 people took advantage of the law, the Chinese being the Asian group that benefitted most.

Later, in 1952, the McCarran-Walter Act of 1952 abolished all racial restrictions in United States immigration and naturalization laws, though it did maintain a quota system, controlling the number of immigrants from each country.

Today, the Chinese are the largest ethnic group of Asian Americans in the United States, at 22 percent. The 2010 U.S. Census recorded more than 3.3 million Chinese living in the country, about 1 percent of the total population. Asians, primarily from China, India, and the Philippines, are the fasted growing populations in both the United States and California.

In the Los Angeles-Long Beach area, in 2016, more than 520,000 residents--4 percent of the population, were Chinese. In San Francisco, once ground zero for anti-Chinese laws and society attitudes, they are more than 21 percent of the population, by far, the highest concentration in any city in the United States.

G. Allan Hancock: A Man on the Go

Ex-Libris bookplates are decorative inside-cover, often either engravings, etchings, or woodcuts, that are used to show the name of the owner of a book. Their use dates back to the middle ages where they became associated with prominent and usually wealthy people. The illustrated images selected to accompany the person's name gave one a chance to define their interests and accomplishments In 1932, the artist James Webb engraved a bookplate for George Allan Hancock. Fifty-seven years old at the time, Hancock had lived much of his life in Los Angeles, where he was one of its more notable and accomplished residents. In Webb's meticulous work, done on hand-made paper, the most prominent figure is a large ship with two smokestacks traveling through the sea. In the sky, flies a fixed wing airplane. Surrounding this scene are illustrations of a family crest, a cello, a spyglass, a globe of the world, a dozen or more books, and an ink well supporting a feather pen. In 1932, Hancock had more then thirty years left to live, during which he would undertake many activities that could have become new features in the bookplate of his life.

Grandfather: Count Agoston Haraszthy

George Allan Hancock was born into a family who had already made important contributions to early California. His grandfather on his mother's side, Count Agoston Haraszthy, (pronounced "hair-is-tee") was a Hungarian noble, born in 1812. He would travel widely in Europe and the United States, and end up in California during the gold rush. Haraszthy was flamboyant and dynamic person. And as his grandson would later also show, he was a man of many interests. Among his activities and occupations was as royal bodyguard and legal magistrate. He learned about wine-making from his family who had cultivated the crop for centuries. In 1833, he married Eleonora Dedinszky. The couple would have six children, including Ida, born third.

In 1840, the Haraszthys left Hungary and traveled across Europe. They were the first Hungarian family to settle in the United States and the first to become citizens. Agoston founded the town of Szepataj (now Sauk City), Wisconsin. While there, he managed a general store, a sawmill, a gristmill and a steamship service. He cultivation of hops was a success but his effort to grow grapes was done in by the harsh upper midwest winters. He continued to travel widely and would later write two books in his native language on his adventures in America.

In 1849, hearing of gold in California, he moved west. He was elected captain of a train of wagons and the family made its way on the Santa Fe Trail. However, Agoston wasn't interested in being a miner; he had other business ideas in mind. Initially, he became an early resident of San Diego. In short order he planted fruit trees he had imported by mail. He opened a butcher shop, helped subdivide an area that became known as "middle San Diego," or "Harszthyville." He became San Diego's first sheriff and town marshal, during which time he oversaw the construction of its first jail in 1851. He planted grapevines (again ordering them by mail) and this time had more success in the moderate southern California climate. Still, the lack of cool evening air discouraged any wine-making aspirations. In yet another turn, he was elected to the new state Assembly and moved north.

Haraszthy relocated near San Francisco where he purchased a 120-acre parcel of land near the Spanish Mission Dolores. In a frenzy of activity, he served in the Assembly where he advocated for lower taxes, aid to the poor, and a failed effort to divide California into two states. He tended his agricultural business and still found time to work at the new U.S. Mint as a metallurgist and smelter, and soon Chief Assayer, taking in gold from the successful miners. In 1855, this position resulted in rumors that he was stealing gold and had embezzled more than $150,000 from the Mint. Although the criminal investigation was dropped and a civil trial declared him innocent on all charges, his distinct name became well-known and linked to scandal.

The notoriety may have been behind yet another relocation, again north. Around 1856, Haraszthy found his way to Sonoma. There he would make his most important mark on the history of California and become best remembered for importing European wine-grape roots and establishing the state's first winery, Buena Vista Winery. He planted his vines on an 800-acre ranch. Although just fifty miles from San Francisco, here, at last, was the land and climate he had been searching for—rich soil, sunny-warm days, cool-breezy nights, the triefecta of wine growing.

His first harvest produced more than 6,000 gallons of wine and he expanded his plantings. Success, as it often does, attracts imitators and soon others arrived in

Sonoma to grow their own wine grapes. One of these would be the Prussian-born Charles Krug, who purchased land directly from Haraszthy and would apprentice under him. Krug would later become one of the founding winemakers of Napa Valley and another important part of the state wine industry.

Haraszthy continued to grow and experiment with methods and materials that proved cutting-edge for wine-making. He dry-farmed and planted on hills for good drainage. He built stone cellars to store his barrels, some of which he had made out of California redwood. He traveled back to Europe and visited numerous wine-producing regions in several countries, returning with hundreds of different grape to try out, including the Zinfandel grape, today the most widely planted grape in the state. He was a vocal booster for the all wine producers and, in 1862, he published, a 400-page volume, *Grape Culture: Wines, and Wine-making, with Notes Upon Agriculture and Horticulture*, the first, and what became essential, book on California wine-making. That same year, in recognition of his efforts, accomplishments, and preeminence, Haraszthy was elected President of the California State Agricultural Society. In 1863, he started the Buena Vista Vinicultural Society, the first large corporation in California expressly for agriculture. He drew investments from across the nation. Yet, at this peak he would soon lose almost everything.

Haraszthy's work and dreams of a wine-making empire were destroyed, unintentionally, by his actions. What he didn't know, what no one knew at the time, was the fertile Sonoma soil he planted in was home to the Grape phylloxera, a microscopic aphid that eats the roots of grape vines. It had not existed in Europe and the hundreds of vines Haraszthy brought back from the continent had no ability to survive attacks by the aphids. His vines browned and withered; he was ruined. By 1867, all of his vines had to be replaced. While the winery would remain, Haraszthy had to declare bankruptcy.

As a side note: It is not certain how and when the Grape Phylloxera came to Europe but it is certainly possible that Haraszthy was one of, if not the first, who accidently introduced the aphids to European vineyards he visited in 1861. He may have left behind the seeds of a catastrophe that would, for a time, destroy much of the European wine industry. It has been estimated that by the early 1900s, France, alone lost 70 percent of its vineyards.

Ever the resilient adventurer, Haraszthy carried on. In 1868, he left the United States and moved to Nicaragua where he founded a sugar and rum plantation near the northwest Pacific coast. It was there that his wife, Eleonora, who had followed him throughout his moves, contracted yellow fever and died. In a final tragedy, Haraszthy died the next year when he was killed while either working near or attempting to cross a river abundant with alligators. His body was never recovered.

Parents: Ida Haraszthy & Henry Hancock

Allan Hancock's mother, Ida Haraszthy, was born 1843 in Imperial (today, Peoria) Illinois. Her mother, Eleonora Dedinsky, was descended from Polish nobility and whose family had long lived in Hungary. Shortly after Ida's birth, the family moved to Wisconsin. When she was six, she traveled with her family in oxen-drawn covered wagons to California, first to San Diego and then to San Francisco and Sonoma.

Because of her father's financial success, in the late 1850s, Ida was able to return to Europe for a period, this time sailing with her mother on a clipper ship around Cape Horn in South America and on to France. There, they resided in Paris where, by all accounts, Ida received an excellent academic education. She and her mother would return to California, having reunited with Argoston in 1862.

1849, was also the year that Allan Hancock's father, Henry Hancock, moved to California. He arrived in San Francisco after sailing from Boston around Cape Horn. Henry had been born in Bath, New Hampshire in 1822 to parents of English ancestry. As a young man, he studied engineering and, at Harvard University, law. He had served as a quartermaster in the United States Army during the Mexican War, 1847–1848. Now, his interest was in the new gold rush. While many miners would fail to strike it rich, Hancock was one of the lucky few. He mined placer gold and in just six short weeks, he made a fortune of $20,000 ($600,000 in today's money.)

In 1852, Henry moved to Los Angeles. He also became that city's second land surveyor, laying out numerous 35-acre lots. He has the distinction of publishing the first map of city. In 1853, he predicted Los Angeles would one day have a population exceeding 300,000 people.

With southern secession and the outbreak of the Civil War, Henry's military service resumed as he served as a major for the Union. He was stationed at Camp Drum, located near the port of Los Angeles. There were many Confederate sympathizers in the city and the camp was to prevent their use of the port or harbor. It was during this period, in 1863, that he courted and married Ida, who was 21 years younger than he.

After the Civil War ended, Henry and Ida settled in Los Angeles. But as life on their rancho was primitive and more difficult, they often spent time visiting San Francisco. It was there in 1875 when, on July 26, Ida gave birth to twin boys, George Allan and Harry. Unfortunately, Harry died in infancy. Two year later, a second son, Bertram, was born. tragically, he too had a short life, dying in 1893 at 16 of typhoid fever following a visit to the World's Fair in Chicago.

The Los Angeles Years

Tar and Oil

In late 1860, Henry, and his brother John, acquired Rancho La Brea, a 4,438-acre Mexican land grant, from the family of Jose Jorge Rocha, a prominent Portuguese immigrant. Henry would later establish wood-frame family home in a grove of eucalyptus and pepper trees on what would later be central Los Angeles. There were numerous natural deposits of asphaltum on land, a sticky, black tar that could either highly viscous liquid or semi-solid material. Many farmers and ranchers saw it as a smelly nuisance that fouled water sources. Major Hancock, however, saw it as a profitable substance. He had it dug out of his soil and sold it as paving material for sidewalks and roads. It was also useful in adobe roofing and ship hulls, as it was an excellent water-proof sealant. In a few years, employing about 25 Chinese laborers, Henry was shipping 5 tons of asphaltum daily to San Francisco by schooner.

Henry died in 1883 when he was 61 years old. He had carried a lot of debt on the rancho and when his estate was settled, not much money remained. He left his family land-rich but cash-poor. It would be left to his 30 year-old his widow and mother of two young boys to make the Hancock's notably wealthy.

Initially, Ida moved the family to San Francisco but found it impractical to try and run the rancho from afar. So she returned with the boys in tow. In 1885, she began oil drilling operations on La Brea by leasing out sections of land to oil speculators Lyman Stewart, Wallace Hardison, and Dan McFarland. They began exploration under the lease of Pacific Coast Oil Company. Ida was to receive "1/8 royalties" of the oil profits but there were none; the venture failed and in 1888 it was bankrupt.

Later, more land was leased to the Salt Lake Oil Company. This time things were different and the enterprise was a great success and both oil and money flowed for the family. In 1900, Allan, who went by his middle name, learned the business by working with Salt Lake as an oil rigger. The family story is that Allan drilled for oil in seventy-one locations on the property, striking oil every time. By 1909, the Hancocks had more than 250 wells and were producing 200–300 barrels a day, or more than 3.8 million gallons of oil a year. They also operated the Rancho La

Brea Oil Company which sold its own oil and natural gas. Their great wealth had arrived. Often they earned more $1,000 a day—at the time, this was equal to two year's income to millions of American workers. Ida had become one of the richest women in California with a personal fortune of nearly $4 million.

Ida was an active philanthropist. She had a fondness for her time in Paris and anonymously sent funds to help pay for the education of Parisian girls. In Los Angeles, she contributed significant sums of money to Catholic charities. She had a particular interest in helping organizations that cared for orphans. She was a prominent contributor to the city's fine art scene and took part in the campaign to place bells along the historic route of the El Camino Real.

Although oil production did not end, in 1916, Allan and Ida decided to donate ten acres of La Brea land to Los Angeles county, giving it the exclusive right to excavate the pits. From prehistoric times forward, the tar pits had trapped countless animals, many now long extinct, who had come to drink water in the mucky soil. It was the Hancock's hope that the pits would be preserved for scientific excavations. Since that time, over one million fossils have been recovered. Interestingly, only one was of a human. This person, who has come to be known as "La Brea Woman," lived over 9,000 years ago. There is bone evidence that she may, in fact, have been deliberately killed. If so, she may be California's oldest known murder victim.

In 1991, the Rancho La Brea Adobe was designated Los Angeles Cultural and Historic Landmark #534. The adobe stands on Gilmore Lane between 3rd Street and Fairfax Avenue and is the corporate offices for the Farmer's Market, which opened in 1934 and remains a popular local and tourist destination.

Real Estate, Banking, and USC

Determining the actual wealth of Allan Hancock or the Hancock family in general is difficult. The family oil holdings were privately held and Hancock was too discreet to divulge such intimate information. Perhaps the best way to get a sense of the prosperity he accrued is to examine the projects he undertook after 1920.

In 1921, Hancock used some his oil profits to subdivide and develop most of Rancho La Brea into what is now called Hancock Park. This affluent Los Angeles neighborhood, 1.5 square miles, is bounded by Melrose, La Brea, Wilshire, and Rossmore avenues. The site included a 105-acre Wilshire Country Club (which still exists today and charges a $20,000 membership fee.) For the housing development Hancock hired the renowned architects Paul Williams (at the time, one of the few African-American home designers), A.C. Chisholm (one of Boston's best-known builders), and John Austin (English-born, he would design many important Los Angeles buildings.) Styles of the lavish houses included Tudor, Beaux-Arts, Regency and Greek Revival. Hancock insisted the streets be made out of concrete (the first in the city) as he preferred the lighter color and smoother surface compared to asphalt. He had utility lines placed at the back of each house, so they would be out of sight. He paid the Los Angeles Railway to extend its track to provide service for the area. Many of the initial residents came from some of the city's most notable families: Chandler, Huntington, Crocker, Van de Kamp, Doheny, Van Nuys, and Newmark.

Close to Beverly Hills, Hancock Park has maintained its upper-class status as home to the well-heeled resident since its beginning. In 2018, the median price house of houses for sale was $3.5 million with the most expensive homes ranging upwards of $10 million. In 1976, the Windsor Square-Hancock Park Historical Society was founded to preserve the architectural landmarks, historical sites and the approximately 1,200 houses within the greater Rancho La Brea area. It is one of twenty-two historic preservation zones in Los Angeles and residents may not alter or demolish house exteriors without first gaining permission from their local board.

The Hancocks themselves did not live in Hancock Park. In 1909, Ida hired one of Los Angeles' most prominent architects, the English-born John C. Austin, to build her home on the corner of Wilshire Boulevard and Vermont. Patterned after Villa de Medici in Florence, Italy, the 23-room neoclassical mansion, named *Villa Madonna*, featured twin four-story towers, stained glass windows, an elevator, and a chapel. The interiors were an eclectic design in luxurious French, German, Italian, English, and Roman motifs.

The same year the *Villa* was completed Ida remarried, her new husband being Erskine Mayo Ross, a long-time judge for the U.S. Court of Appeals, Ninth Circuit. Ross had lost his first wife two years before. Unfortunately, the new marriage was short-lived. Ida died of a stomach ailment at the age of 70 on March 15, 1913. Allan moved into *Villa Madonna*, bring his first wife, Genevieve Deane Mullen, a native of Milwaukee. They had married in 1901 before 1,000 guests in the Cathedral of St. Vibiana in Los Angeles. The couple had two children, Bertram born in 1902, and Rosemary in 1904 According to the *Los Angeles Times*, Genevieve died of a heart ailment in 1936, following a two-year illness

Allan was rarely at the house after Genevieve's death and fully moved out in 1938. The next year the building was torn down. However, prior to demolition, the interiors of four of the rooms—the library, dining room, music salon, and reception hall—were preserved. They are now on display at the University of Southern California, in the Allan Hancock Foundation Building. Hancock had a long association with USC and, over the course of his life, it is estimated he donated $7 million to the school. He was particularly interested supporting the music and science programs.

Hancock made other imprints of the history of Los Angeles. He was an investor in the commercial development of a section of Wilshire Avenue that became known as the "Miracle Mile." Adjacent to Hancock Park, in 1921, the road passed through oil fields and agricultural land. It was the developer A.W. Ross who had the vision to turn it into the first major retail and business center in the city that was away from downtown Los Angeles. Today, it is nicknamed, "Museum Row" that includes the Los Angeles County Museum of Art (LACMA), the Peterson Automotive Museum, the Page Museum at the La Brea Tar Pits, and more.

Hancock held a number of executive positions and was a member of many exclusive southland clubs. He was a founder and officer of the California Bank, vice-president of Los Angeles branch of Hibernia Bank and treasurer of the Los Angeles Symphony. He was a member of the California Club, a private, member-only social club founded in 1888, whose unofficial adage is "*people who 'own' Los Angeles belong to The California Club.*" Another private organization, the Los Angeles Athletic Club, founded in 1880, counted Hancock as a member, as did the Gamut Club, another Los Angeles group, this one for the "*brotherhood, assistance to the musical fraternity, and the uplifting of the art.*" And being an avid sailor, it was logical that he was a long-time member of the South Coast Yacht Club.

He second president of the American Automobile Association, Southern California chapter in 1908–1909. Hancock was said to own one of the first private cars in Los Angeles, a Milwaukee Steamer. These early vehicles, built between 1899–1902, were more motorized carriages then automobiles. Photographs show Hancock driving a "*Stanhope*" model, holding a steering rudder (no steering wheel yet) while sitting the roofless, two passenger device. For a price tag of $700, the vehicle offered a 2-cylinder, chain-drive engine which generated all of 5 horse-power.

Santa Barbara Earthquake

At 6:45 a.m. on June 29, 1925, a 6.3 earthquake convulsed Santa Barbara. For nineteen seconds it violently shook the town. Allan Hancock had arrived the evening before. He had checked into the Grand Hotel where he was to meet up with his son, Bertram, once an aspiring actor who had agreed to give up the theater to take a prominent role in his father's business interests. There were no rooms close to his father's, so Bertram was put in a wing on the opposite side of the hotel. Early the next morning, as the two men slept, the hotel began to violently shake and then to crumble. A large water tank concealed in a roof-top tower broke loose and crashed into the suite below, crushing Bertram, killing him instantly. Allan was seriously injured and would hospitalized for over a week. Three days after the quake he described the ordeal to the *Santa Barbara News-Press*. He recounted the moments of the hotel collapse as "an indescribable inferno of sound." He told how he and a maid crawled out of the building but, as for Bertram: "My son probably never awakened from his sleep. His skull was fractured and his neck broken. It was best if he had to go that he go without suffering."

The Santa Maria Years

It was in the 1920s, that Hancock began to shift his interests and focus on Santa Maria. For nearly forty years he would make his home there and, in doing so, left a legacy that may allow him to be considered one of, if not the most, significant individual in influencing the history of the town.

In March, 1926, Hancock opened the first radio station in all of Santa Barbara County. The station's studio was located at the Santa Maria Valley Railway office building at the corner of Jones Street and McClelland Street. This was just six years after the first radio station in the entire country began operating in Pittsburgh, Pennsylvania.

Farming & Rail Road

In 1911, Hancock created G.A. Properties incorporated. Since 1925, it has been based in Santa Maria. It remains in Hancock family to the present. In 1925, Hancock purchased the Santa Maria Valley Railway for $75,000. A fifteen-mile "short-line" that served as a connection between the valley and the main rail line that ran through Guadalupe, it had been started in 1911. It primarily hauled sugar beets, asphalt, and oil. When Hancock took it over, rail traffic had been on the decline and the company was in bankruptcy. Hancock made a slight name change to Santa Maria Valley Railroad (SMVRR.) In 1927, he earned a license qualifying him as a railroad engineer. For the next thirty-five years he could be seen operating locomotives in and around the Santa Maria Valley. In 1962, the last of the steam locomotives were retired. Hancock made one final run with Walt Disney sitting as a guest in the locomotive cab alongside. (The steam engines now on display in Griffith Park in Los Angeles.)

Hancock spent considerable sums to build an infrastructure that would enable farm products to become the major items of transport. Hancock added new track and built a locomotive depot. He invested in packing sheds and the Santa Maria Ice & Cold Storage Plant so vegetables could be shipped. He bought his own 400-acre farm in Santa Maria and named it Rosemary, after his daughter. There he planted row crops, such as carrots, that were irrigated by water lines he had installed. The farm eventually expanded to more than 5,000 acres. There were cattle, a dairy, and egg production. By 1935, the railroad was making a profit, and hauling more than 20,000 train-car loads of goods a year. In 2006, the Hancock family sold the railroad to the Coast Belle Rail Corporation; it remains in operation to the present.

Flight College

In 1926, Hancock purchased an 80-acre plot of land in Santa Maria that had been the George Tunnell Ranch. The next year he founded The Hancock Foundation College of Aeronautics (commonly known as "Hancock Field"). The year after that, the field was dedicated by Hancock in honor of his son, Bertram. The ceremony was attended by representatives from the U.S. Army and Navy, along with thousands of spectators, some of whom, no doubt, were attracted by the sight of flying machines, still a novelty though it had been a quarter of century since the Wright Brothers historic first flight. In 1929, the first small class of aviation cadets enrolled in a ten-week program. There were five airplanes, unpaved runways, hangers, mechanical shops, and barracks. Hancock was the sole owner, operator, and president. While the enrollment grew in subsequent classes it was not enough to counter the effects of the economic calamity of the Great Depression. There was not enough demand for pilots and Hancock shut down the flight college in 1934.

For four years the flight school languished until 1938, when the demand for pilots had again increased. War clouds had settled across Europe (World War II began in 1939), and fighting was already happening in Asia where China and Manchuria had been invaded by Japan. Although the United States was officially neutral on both fronts until 1941, military preparedness took hold in the country.

On July 1, 1939, Hancock Field officially became one of eight civilian academies in the nation chosen by the U.S. War Department to provide training for the U.S. Army Air Corps (later the Air Force.) Hancock entered into contract with both Santa Maria High School and the Junior College to teach the cadets airplane mechanics and engineering, navigation and meteorology. The coursework was intensive and thorough. A school day was between 6:00 am and 10:00 pm. There were modeling classes in airplane design. A wind tunnel was installed to mimic weather conditions a pilot might face. Course standards were high; 32 percent of the initial class of forty-nine cadets failed to graduate.

As the Second World War progressed, so did the demand for pilots. Sixty-three acres were added to the original eighty. As the number of cadets increased so did the size of the barracks. Two additional hangers were built (eventually there would be eight), along with a new mess hall. By the war's conclusion in 1945, Hancock College had successfully trained 8,414 pilots through its programs. As Hancock told one graduating class during its commencement service:

"You men of the Class 44-H have established an enviable record here at Hancock Field. . . What you have learned of the fundamentals of good flying will always be with you. Don't forget any part of it. And remember that every flight you make from here on out will be another training flight. Each new flight is a new experience and you'll never cease learning."

Hancock's last contract with the federal government ended June 30, 1945, seven weeks after the surrender of Germany to the Allies. The fight with Japan would continue until August of that year but with a virtual dominance of the skies by U.S. aircraft at that point, there was a greatly diminished need for additional pilots.

With the war over, Hancock agreed to lease his College of Aeronautics to USC for $1 and the university began offering a degree in Aeronautical Engineering. (The College was used again during the Korean War, mostly to train aviation mechanics.) In recognition of his contributions to the military, Hancock was given the Air Force Exceptional Service Award, its highest honor accorded to a civilian. He was also awarded Hancock received a certificate of merit from President Harry S. Truman. This was given to civilians who "performed a meritorious act or service" in the waging of World War II.

Hancock's interest in aviation extended beyond Santa Maria. In 1928, he financed the flight of the *Southern Cross*, the first airplane to fly across the Pacific Ocean. Hancock had purchased the plane and had it outfitted for such a purpose. The feat was accomplished just one year after Charles Lindbergh's solo flight across the Atlantic Ocean. Piloted by Charles Kingsford Smith and crew, the plane took off from Oakland, California on May 31st. There were fuel stops in Hawaii and Fuji until June 9th, when the plane reached its final destination of Brisbane, Australia where a crowd of 25,000 greeted it. In 1930, the *Southern Cross* made a stop at Hancock Field in Santa Maria. Today the plane is displayed in an air museum in Brisbane.

Exploration

Hancock's title of "Captain" came by way of sailing. In 1933, he was licensed as a "Master Mariner," which enabled him to sail ships of nearly any size. Hancock's first ship was a ketch, a modest two-masted sailboat named the Cricket. In 1916, he began construction on *Velero* (Spanish for "smooth sailing.") It would be the first of four ships of the same name, but each successive one larger than the last. The *Velero* II (1922) was a 125 foot diesel-powered vessel. The *Velero* III (1931) was specially designed for marine science. When the *Velero* IV was launched in 1948, it was the largest privately owned scientific research vessel of its kind. It was outfitted for deep sea capabilities with echo-ranging technology, dredging gear, underwater cameras, and sub-sea microphones. Although it is unassociated with the Hancock family today, in 2018, the *Velero* IV remained in service, working with universities doing marine research and supporting salmon and herring fisheries.

Between 1932 and 1938 Hancock undertook ten ocean expeditions, the most extended and important ones to the Galapagos. The purpose was to study and document marine and wildlife life on and around the islands. The Hancock- Pacific Galapagos Expedition of 1934 was one of three major trips that he financed and led to the islands. Hancock put together a group of experts including Waldo Schmitt, of the Smithsonian Institution, a scientist who would later accompany Franklin D. Roosevelt during his fishing trip to Galapagos in 1938.

In 1941, USC dedicated the Allan Hancock Foundation for Scientific Research. Hancock, who funded the building, deeded it to the university, along with the *Velero* III. Today, the Hancock Natural History Collection consists of 78,000 rare books in the field of natural history, published between 1525 and 1944. Most of the works was acquired by Hancock with his 1944 purchase of the Boston Society of Natural History library. There are also thousands of papers, films, photographs, and sound recordings.

The College

In 1920, the population of Santa Maria was 3,943. That year, the board of trustees for the Santa Maria Joint Union High School District established the Santa Maria Junior College. Its first class had six students. In 1937, The citizens of Santa Maria voted to pass a bond measure to fund the construction of a college wing on the corner of the Santa Maria High School campus.

Hancock Field closed between 1957–59. Just a few years prior, Santa Maria Junior College had begun to lease classrooms at the facility to accommodate its growing enrollment. As he with done with USC, Hancock leased the site to the college for $1 a year. In 1958, Santa Maria voters approved a bond to purchase Hancock Field and construct a larger, modern campus. In 1960, groundbreaking was held for the 104-acre campus. Two years later the college fully relocated as its new buildings opened: student center, library, science complex, and gymnasium. A bronze bust of Hancock was dedicated in front of the library. In 1963, the college was renamed the Allan Hancock Joint Junior Community College District.

In Summary

Capt. G. Allan Hancock was

- sea captain
- oilman
- explorer
- land developer
- banker
- aviator
- marine scientist
- businessman
- farmer
- railroad engineer
- musician
- philanthropist

Allan Hancock died in Santa Maria, May 31, 1965, one month short of his 90th birthday.

A Statistical Profile of California with Trends and Comparisons to the United States

A statistical accounting of a land and a people cannot tell the whole story. On the other hand, the whole story cannot be told without an accounting of numbers. They can provide insights into the past and trends for the future. The demographics presented here offer information during specific points in time and allow comparisons of California to the United States as a whole. The details below are intended to help you gain a broad understanding of California and to use in conjunction with other readings and research.

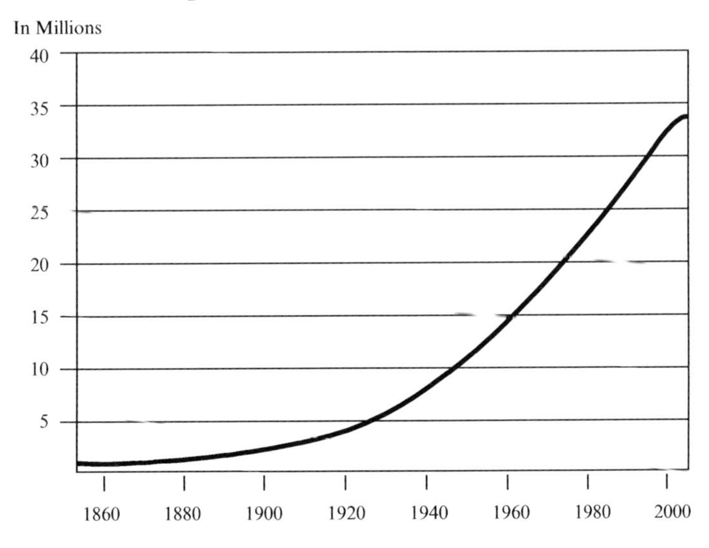

California:	31st State
Statehood:	September 9, 1850
Capital:	Sacramento
Number of Counties:	58
Number of Incorporated Cities:	482
First European Settlement:	San Diego, 1769 (Spain)
First Town Founded:	Monterey, 1770 (Spain)
First Incorporated City:	Sacramento, February 27, 1850 (United States)
Most Recent Incorporated City:	Jurupa Valley (Riverside County) July 1, 2011

(Unless otherwise noted, data is from U.S. Census)

Population

State Population: 39,776,830 (2018)

Population as a Percentage of the United States

1940:	5.2%,
1950:	7.0%,
1960:	8.8%,
1970:	9.8%,
1980:	10.5%,
1990:	11.2%,
2000:	12.1%,
2010:	12.0 %
2017:	12.1%
2018:	12.2%

Ten Largest Cities by Population (2018)

1. Los Angeles: 4,030,668
2. San Diego: 1,438,060
3. San Jose: 1,030,796
4. San Francisco: 888,653

5. Fresno: 529,153
6. Sacramento: 507,298
7. Long Beach: 467,512
8. Oakland: 424,275
9. Bakersfield: 384,188
10. Anaheim: 354,553

Note: Over half of California's population reside in five counties:

Orange, Riverside, Los Angeles, San Diego, and San Bernardino.

Five Largest Counties by Population (2016)

11. Los Angeles: 10,137,915
12. San Diego: 3,317,749
13. Orange: 3,172,532
14. Riverside: 2,387,741
15. San Bernardino: 2,140,096

Note: For the statistics below, "Latino" includes Cuban, Mexican, Puerto Rican, South or Central American, or other Spanish culture or origin, regardless of race.

In 2016, compared to other U.S. states, California had:

- largest population of White Americans (including Latino) (22,200,000)
- largest population of Asian Americans (4,400,000) (one third of national total)
- largest population of Native Americans (285,000)
- fifth largest population of Black Americans (2,250,000)

In 2016, 36% of all Asians and 28% of all Latinos living the United States resided in California. Asians (primarily from China, Indian, and the Philippines) and Latinos are the first and second-fasted growing populations both the United States and California.

Note, in 2016, California had the largest state population of Bulgarians, Hmong, Hungarians, Indian, Latinos, Mexicans, Native American, Romanians, Salvadorans, Thai, Vietnamese

Percentage of Population (2016)

White,

1990:	57.2%,
2000:	46.7 %
2010:	39.7%
2016:	37.7%

Latino,

1990:	25.8%,
2000:	32.4%
2010:	38.1%
2016:	38.9%

Asian,

1990:	9.1%,
2000:	10.8%
2010:	13.6%
2016:	14.8%

Black,

1990:	7.0%,
2000:	6.4%
2010:	6.6%
2016:	6.5%

Multi-Race,

1990:	n/a,
2000:	2.7%
2010:	3.6%
2016:	3.8%

American Indian and Alaska Native,

1990:	.6%,
2000:	.5 %
2010:	1.7%
2016:	1.7%

Hawaii or other Pacific Island,

1990:	.2%,
2000:	.3%
2010:	.5%
2016:	.5%

Selected Comparisons Between California and the United States

Persons Per Square Mile, (2017)

California:	251
United States:	92.2

Female Persons as Percent of Population, (2017)

California:	50.3%
United States:	50.8%

Life Expectancy,

California:	79.0 years	(Men: 76.6, Women: 81.3) (2000)
California:	80.3 years	(Men: 77.9, Women: 82.7) (2010)
California:	80.7 years	(Men: 78.3, Women: 83.1) (2014)
United States:	76.8 years	(Men: 74.1, Women: 79.3) (2000)
United States:	78.3 years	(Men: 75.7, Women: 80.8) (2010)
United States:	78.8 years	(Men: 76.3, Women: 81.3) (2014)

(source: World Life Expectancy.org)

Median Age,

California:	33.3 years (2000)
California:	35.0 years (2017)

United States:	35.3 years (2000)
United States:	37.9 years (2017)

Persons Under Age 5, (2016)

California:	6.3%
United States:	6.2%

Persons Under Age 18, (2016)

California:	23.2%
United States:	22.8%

Persons Over Age 65, (2016)

California:	13.6%
United States:	15.2%

White Persons as Percentage of Population, (2016)

California:	37.7%
United States:	61.3%

Hispanic or Latino Persons as Percentage of Population, (2016)

California:	38.9%
United States:	17.8%

Asian Persons as Percentage of Population, (2016)

California:	14.8%
United States:	5.7%

Black Persons as Percentage of Population, (2016)

California:	6.5%
United States:	13.3%

Persons of Two or More Races as Percentage of Population, (2016)

California:	3.8%
United States:	2.6%

American Indian and Alaska Natives Persons as Percentage of Population, (2016)

California:	1.7%
United States:	1.3%

Native Hawaiian and Other Pacific Islander Persons as Percentage of Population, (2016)

California:	.5%
United States:	.2%

Latino Population Increase between 2000-2016

California:	37% (to 15 million)
United States:	56% (to 55.4 million)

Latino Persons in the United States, Country of Origin

Mexico:	58% (2000)
Mexico:	63% (2010)
Puerto Rico:	10% (2000)
Puerto Rico:	9% (2010)
Cuba:	4% (2000)
Cuba:	4% (2010)

Latino Persons in California, Country of Origin

Mexico:	77% (2000)
Mexico:	84% (2014)
Central America:	5% (2000)
Puerto Rico, Cuba, or Dominican Republic:	2% (2000)

Latino Persons in the Majority of the County Population (2010)

California:	9 (of 58 counties)
United States:	82 (of 3,143 counties)

Foreign Born Persons as Percentage of the Population

California:	26.0% (2000)
California:	27.2% (2010)

California:	27.0% (2016)
United States:	11.0% (2000)
United States:	12.7% (2010)
United States:	13.2% (2016)

Language Other Than English Spoken at Home by People Over Age 5

California:	39.5% (2000)
California:	43.0% (2010)
California:	44.0% (2016)
United States:	18.0% (2000)
United States:	20.1% (2010)
United States:	21.1% (2016)

Note: There are 224 languages spoken in California. This does not include differing dialects. The Los Angeles Unified School District has identified 92 languages spoken among its students. (source: www.laalmanac.com)

Households (2016)

California:	12,807,387
United States:	117,716,237

Persons per Household (2016)

California:	2.95
United States:	2.64

Homeownership

California:	56.9% (2000)
California:	57.4% (2010)
California:	54.1% (2016)
United States:	66.2% (2000)
United States:	66.6% (2010)
United States:	63.6% (2016)

Multi-Unit Housing

California:	31.4% (2000)
California:	30.7% (2010)

United States: 26.4% (2000)
United States: 25.9% (2010)

House, Median Value

California: $548,000 (2005)
California: $458,500 (2010)
California: $522,400 (2018)
United States: $213,000 (2005)
United States: $188,400 (2010)
United States: $188,900 (2014)

Per Capita Income:

California: $35,019 (2004)
California: $43,104 (2011)
California: $66,232 (2017)
United States: $32,937 (2004)
United States: $40,584 (2011)
United States: $52,194 (2017)

Median Household Income

California: $48,440 (2003)
California: $60,883 (2010)
California: $63,763 (2016)
United States: $43,318 (2003)
United States: $51,914 (2010)
United States: $55,322 (2016)

Persons Below Poverty (single income under $11,139 or a family of four income under $22,113)

California: 13.8% (2003)
California: 16.3% (2011)
California: 14.3% (2017)
United States: 12.5% (2003)
United States: 15.1% (2011)

United States:	12.7% (2017)
Gross State Product:	$2,810,000,000 (2017)

This was 13% of the United States' Gross Domestic Product (GDP) for that year.

Schools and Education

High school graduates by age 25,

California:	76.8% (2000)
California:	80.7% (2010)
California:	82.1% (2016)
United States:	80.4% (2000)
United States:	85.0% (2010)
United States:	87.0% (2016)

Bachelor's degree or higher, by age 25,

California:	26.6% (2000)
California:	30.1 % (2010)
California:	32.0% (2016)
United States:	24.4% (2000)
United States:	27.9% (2010)
United States:	30.3% (2016)

Number of California Public Schools, K-12,

10,477 with enrollment 6,228,635 million (2017)
(source: Education Bug.org)

Number of California Community Colleges,

114 with approximate enrollment 2.1 million (2018)
In 2008, the approximate enrollment was 2.9 million
(source: California Community Colleges Chancellor's Office)

Number of California Four-Year Colleges and Universities,

Public:	32
Private:	135

with combined enrollment: 2,323,522 (2010)
(source: State of California, Postsecondary Education Commission)

Roads and Transportation

Maintained Public Roads,

169,835 miles (2004)
172,138 miles (2010)
180,740 miles (2015)
(source: State of California, Department of Transportation)

State and Federal Highways & Freeways,

29,759 miles (2004)
31,723 miles (2010)
51,685 miles (2015)
(source: State of California, Department of Transportation)

Note: Los Angeles may be considered the city of freeways, but actually it has the lowest number of freeway miles per capita of any American city or urbanized area. The city itself has 6,499 miles of streets, but just 181 miles of freeway. In 2007, the city had 2,499,764 registered vehicles. In L.A. county there are 527 miles of freeways and 6,675,888 registered vehicles. (source: City of Los Angeles, Department of Transportation)

Registered Motor Vehicles,

Automobiles: 21,699,936 (2004)
Automobiles: 22,083,049 (2011)
Automobiles: 25,244,537 (2017)

All registered vehicles: Automobiles, trucks, commercial, non-commercial & trailers, motorcycles: 35,310,566 (2017)
(source: State of California, Department of Motor Vehicles)

Total Number of Persons with a Driver License/ I.D. Card

23,484,646 (2017)
(source: State of California, Department of Motor Vehicles)

Note: In 2017, Californians drove in total 339 billion miles on all roads in the state.

Mean Travel Time to Work (in Minutes), Workers Over Age 16,

California:	27.7 (2000)
California:	26.9 (2010)
California:	28.4 (2016)
United States:	25.5 (2000)
United States:	25.2 (2010)
United States:	26.1 (2016)

Quotes and Unique Facts for California

Introduction

This mix of facts, opinions and unusual bits of information regarding California, some significant, some much less so, affirms the point the state cannot be defined by any single thing. It is, by its nature and the people who inhabit it, a mosaic of ideas, attitudes, interests and perceptions which, stitched together, form a unique and memorable whole. To once more quote Theodore Roosevelt, "It is just California."

State Flag

The official flag of California, was designed by William Todd, a nephew of Mary Todd Lincoln. The flag pictures a grizzly bear facing a red five-pointed star that was similar to the star used for the Texas Republic. It was first used on June 14, 1846 after a group of American settlers marched on the Mexican garrison at Sonoma and took the commandant prisoner. They issued a proclamation declaring California to be a Republic, a "free and sovereign state," independent of Mexico. The uprising, which only lasted one month, became known as the Bear Flag Revolt after Todd quickly designed his flag. The original "Todd flag" was destroyed in the 1906 San Francisco earthquake. Todd's design, with some modifications (the most notable was an enlarged and reshaped bear) was not officially adopted until 1911. It is believed that the bear on the flag was modeled after an actual one which had been caught and named Monarch. After Monarch's death in 1911, his remains were stuffed. He remains on display at the Academy of Sciences at Golden Gate Park in San Francisco. The symbolic meaning of flag is as follows: the bear represents strength and unyielding resistance; the color red reflects courage; the star indicates sovereignty; and the color white conveys purity.

California
The Golden State

State Seal

The official state seal was designed by Major Robert S. Garnett of the U.S. Army. Although Major Garnett was not commissioned to create the seal, his sketch was shown to delegates who were attending California's first Constitutional Convention of 1849. They adopted the seal before California had become a state. The central figure of the seal is Minerva, the Roman goddess of wisdom and war. In mythology, she was born fully grown out of the head of Jupiter, her father. This was quite appropriate as California, too, was "fully born," never being a territory but moving right into statehood. At Minerva's feet stands a grizzly bear, the official state animal and prominent feature on the state flag. A bundle of grain in the foreground represents the state's agricultural production. Near the upper edge of the seal are 31 stars, anticipating California's 1850 admission. California's motto, the only state motto in Greek, *Eureka* ("I have found it") appears under the stars. *Eureka* refers to the discovery of gold in California. A miner works near the Sacramento River as ships pass by. He is using the tools of his trade: a pick, a shovel, a pan, and a rocker for sifting dirt. The Sierra Nevada Mountains rise in the background.

Today in the state capital, a statue of Minerva sits high up on the wall overlooking the Senate Chamber.

In an irony, during the American Civil War, Garnett, a career soldier, joined the Confederate States of America, while California remained a part of the United States. He rose to the rank of brigadier general. On July 13, 1861, he was shot by Union soldiers in northern Virginia, and became the first general on either side to be killed in the conflict.

California's rush to statehood was remarkable. In comparison, New Mexico became a U.S. territory on September 9, 1850 (the very day California became a state), but it would not be granted its own statehood until 1912.

State Quarter

In 1999, the United States Mint began a 50 state quarters' program. Each state was allowed to submit their own commemorative design for their coin. The quarters were introduced according to each state's entry into the nation. Thus, California would have the 31st quarter in the series. Five final designs were sent by the Department of Treasury to then-Governor Arnold Schwarzenegger who made the final selection. The four runner-up finalists were titled "Waves and Sun," "Gold Miner," "Golden Gate Bridge," and the "Giant Sequoia." The winning entry was "John Muir/Yosemite Valley" was conceived by Garret Burke, an artist and member of the Sierra Club. It would be engraved by Don Everhart.

John Muir was the early leader of environmental conservation in California so it was particularly fitting that his image was placed on the copper and nickel quarter. Muir's relationship with Yosemite reminds people of the powerful connections humans have to nature and how natural beautiful can move and inspire us. The desire to preserve and partake of nature was essentially Muir's dream when he founded the Sierra Club in 1892. He is regarded as the "father" of the national parks. In addition to "*E Pluribus Unum*" that appears on all state quarters, the California coin bears the inscriptions "California," "John Muir," "Yosemite Valley" and "1850." The California condor, with a wingspan as wide as nine feet, is also featured in a tribute to the successful repopulation of the once nearly extinct bird. More than 520 million California quarters have been minted since it was first released in 2005.

Official "State" Designations

Nickname:	The Golden State (named for the abundance of both gold and the poppy flower)
Motto:	Eureka
Colors:	Blue (representing sky) and Gold (presenting the precious metal)
Flower:	Golden Poppy
Tree:	California Redwood (among the tallest living things on earth)
Animal:	Grizzly Bear (made official in 1953; it had been hunted to extinction in the state, 1922)
Bird:	California Valley Quail
Fish:	Golden Trout
Marine Fish:	Garibaldi
Marine Mammal:	California Gray Whale
Insect:	California Dogface Butterfly
Reptile:	Desert Tortoise
Fossil:	Saber-tooth Cat
Mineral:	Gold
Rock:	Serpentine
Gemstone:	Benitoite

State Flower

Eschscholtzia California is more commonly known as California or golden poppy. Also called the flame flower, *La Amapola* (Spanish "the poppy") and *Copa de Oro* ("cup of gold") it was named by the German botanist and world traveler, Adelbert Von Chamisso (1781-1838). In 1816, he sailed into the San Francisco Bay and found the hills covered with the golden flowers. Poppies grows wild throughout the west coast of North America, from southern Washington state to northern Baja, Mexico. An easy-to-grow drought resistant flower that blooms between February and September, Native Americans used its leaves in cooking, its oil as a medicine, and its pollen as a cosmetic. The Indians valued the poppy as a food source and for the oil that they extracted from it. Today, it continues to be used as a herbal sedative and mild pain reliever. In 1903, the California state legislature selected it as the state flower. Every April 6th is California poppy day. A common misconception associated with the plant is that it's illegal to pick a poppy because of its state flower status. There is no such law. The confusion likely stems from the California Penal Code (section 384a) that makes it a misdemeanor to cut or remove any type of plant growing on state or county highways or public lands, except by authorized government employees and contractors; it is also against the law to remove plants on private property without the permission of the owner.

State Song

Frances Bernard Silverwood (1863–1924), a clothing merchant living in Los Angeles penned the lines to "I Love You California." Abraham Franklin Frankenstein (1873–1934), the conductor of the Orpheum Theatre Orchestra set the words to music. The song was published in Los Angeles in 1913. It had its public debut later that year when it was sung by Mary Garden, a leading soloist with the Chicago Opera. It was an immediate popular success. The song was played on the first ship that passed through the Panama Canal in August 1914. The following year it was performed at the Panama-California Exposition in San Diego. In 1951, the California Legislature passed a resolution declaring it the state song. Over the years, periodic attempts were 'wide to replace it—"California, Here I Come" was the most notable contender. The matter was ended in 1988, when "I Love You California" was sanctioned by law as the official state song.

"I Love You California" Written by F. B. Silverwood. Composed by A. F. Frankenstein (Adopted by state legislature, 1951)

I love you California - you're the greatest state of all.

I love you in the winter, summer, spring, and in the fall.

I love your fertile valleys, your dear mountains I adore.
I love your grand old ocean and I love her rugged shore.
Chorus:
When the snow crowned Golden Sierras,
Keep their watch o'er the valleys bloom.
It is there I would be in our land by the sea,
Every breeze bearing rich perfume.
It is here nature gives of her rarest. It is Home Sweet Home to me.
And I know when I die I shall breathe my last sigh,
For my sunny California.
I love your redwood forests - love your fields of yellow grain.
I love your summer breezes, and I love your winter rain.
I love you, land of flowers; land of honey, fruit and wine.
I love you, California; you have won this heart of mine.
I love your old gray Missions - love your vineyards stretching far.
I love you, California, with your Golden Gate ajar.
I love your purple sunsets, love your skies of azure blue.
I love you, California; I just can't help loving you.
I love you, Catalina - you are very dear to me.
I love you, Tamalpais, and I love Yosemite.
I love you, Land of Sunshine. Half your beauties are untold.
I loved you in my childhood, and I'll love you when I'm old.

Quotes and Quips About California

It is said that something is funny because it is true. Quotes directed at California can entertain but may also offer insights into popular perceptions of the state and its residents. If you read all the selections you will also see great praise and sharp criticism for singular aspects of the state's culture and society.

> *Growing up in northern California has had a big influence on my love and respect for the outdoors. When I lived in Oakland, we would think nothing of driving to Half Moon Bay and Santa Cruz one day and then driving to the foothills of the Sierras the next day.*
>
> —Tom Hanks, actor

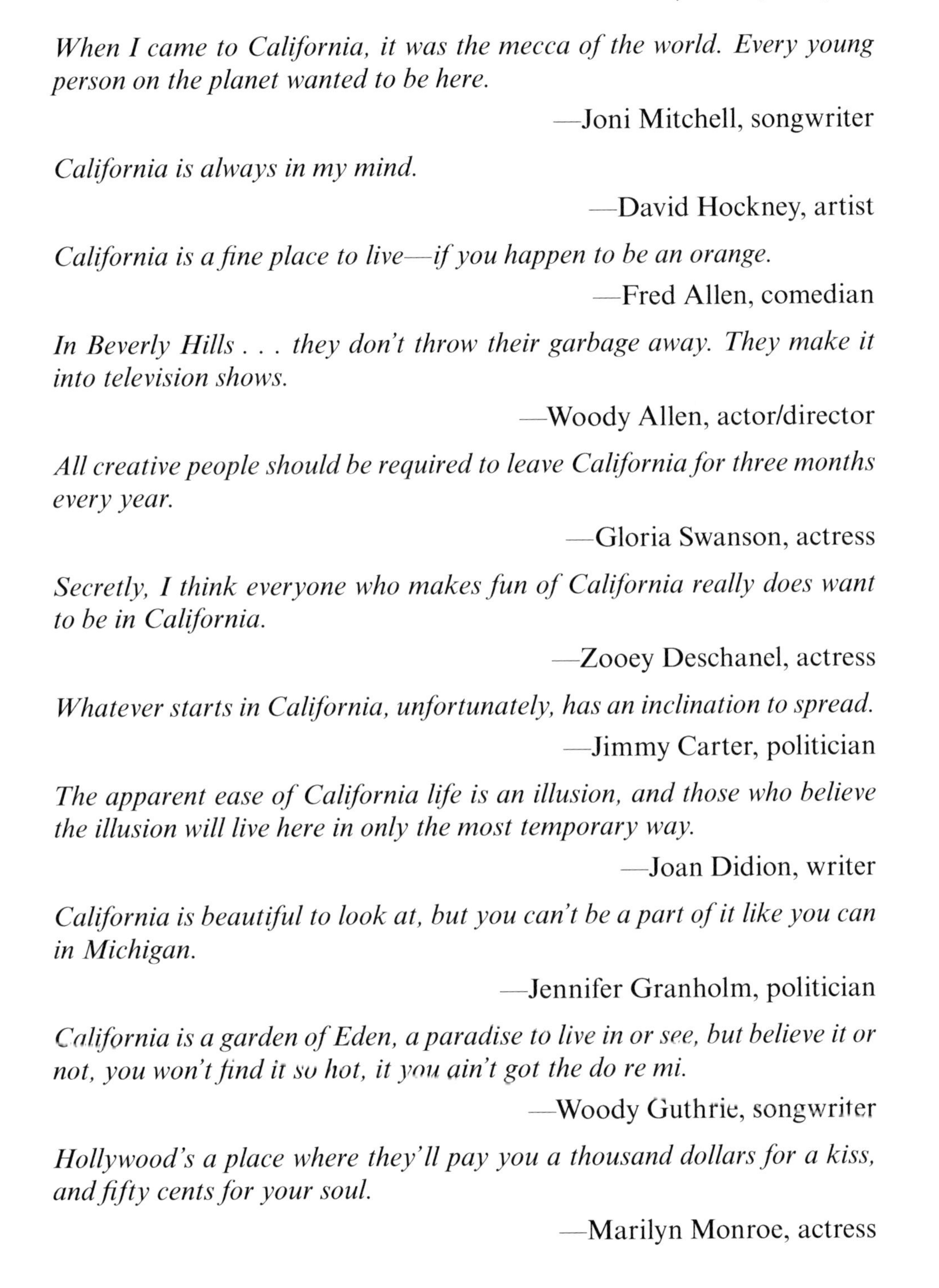

When I came to California, it was the mecca of the world. Every young person on the planet wanted to be here.

—Joni Mitchell, songwriter

California is always in my mind.

—David Hockney, artist

California is a fine place to live—if you happen to be an orange.

—Fred Allen, comedian

In Beverly Hills . . . they don't throw their garbage away. They make it into television shows.

—Woody Allen, actor/director

All creative people should be required to leave California for three months every year.

—Gloria Swanson, actress

Secretly, I think everyone who makes fun of California really does want to be in California.

—Zooey Deschanel, actress

Whatever starts in California, unfortunately, has an inclination to spread.

—Jimmy Carter, politician

The apparent ease of California life is an illusion, and those who believe the illusion will live here in only the most temporary way.

—Joan Didion, writer

California is beautiful to look at, but you can't be a part of it like you can in Michigan.

—Jennifer Granholm, politician

California is a garden of Eden, a paradise to live in or see, but believe it or not, you won't find it so hot, it you ain't got the do re mi.

—Woody Guthrie, songwriter

Hollywood's a place where they'll pay you a thousand dollars for a kiss, and fifty cents for your soul.

—Marilyn Monroe, actress

Hollywood is a place where a man can get stabbed in the back while climbing a ladder.

—William Faulkner, writer

You can take all the sincerity in Hollywood, place it in the navel of a firefly and still have room enough for three caraway seeds and a producer's heart.

—Fred Allen, comedian

If only those who dream about Hollywood knew how difficult it all is.

—Greta Garbo, actress

Hollywood is like Picasso's bathroom.

—Candice Bergen, actress

Hollywood is a place where the stars twinkle until they wrinkle

—Victor Mature, actor

Strip away the phony tinsel of Hollywood and you find the real tinsel underneath.

—Oscar Levant, musician

Los Angeles is mostly full of nonsense and delusion and egomania. They think they'll be young and beautiful forever, even though most of them aren't even young and beautiful now.

—Christopher Hitchens, writer

Southern California, where the American dream came too true.

—Lawrence Ferlinghetti, poet

The Mojave is a big desert and a frightening one. It's as though nature tested a man for endurance and constancy to prove whether he was good enough to get to California.

—John Steinbeck, writer

California is like a beautiful wild kid on heroin, high as a kite and thinking she's on top of the world, not knowing she's dying, not believing it even if you show her the marks.

—S.E Hinton, writer

In Los Angeles, all the loose objects in the country were collected as if America had been tilted and everything that wasn't tightly screwed down had slid into Southern California.

—Saul Bellow, writer

There are no real Californians. There are only people who live there and people who don't.

—Laura Kalpakian, writer

There is science, logic, reason; there is thought verified by experience. And then there is California.

—Edward Abbey, writer

If they can't do it in California, it can't be done anywhere.

—Taylor Caldwell, writer

California deserves whatever it gets. Californians invented the concept of life-style. This alone warrants their doom.

—Don DeLillo, writer

In California you can wear the same pair of shoes year-round.

—Owen Smith, state native

California, that advance post of our civilization, with its huge aircraft factories, TV and film studios, automobile way of life. . . its flavorless cosmopolitanism, its charlatan philosophies and religions, its lack of anything old and well tried rooted in tradition and character.

—J.B. Priestley, writer

In California everyone goes to a therapist, is a therapist, or is a therapist going to a therapist.

—Truman Capote, writer

There is a theory that almost anything that's fun is going to be ruined sooner or later by people from California. They tend to bring seriousness to subjects that don't deserve it, and they tend to get very good at things that weren't very important in the first place.

—Calvin Trillin, writer

California can and does furnish the best bad things that are obtainable in America.

—Hinton R. Helper, writer

California is a queer place—in a way, it has turned its back on the world, and looks into the void Pacific. It is absolutely selfish, very empty, but not false, and at least, not full of false effort...It's sort of crazy-sensible. Just the moment: hardly as far ahead as carpe diem.

—D.H. Lawrence, writer

California has become the first American state where there is no majority race, and we're doing just fine. If you look around the room, you can see a microcosm of what we can do in the world. . . You should be hopeful on balance about the future. But it's like any future since the beginning of time—you're going to have to make it.

—Bill Clinton, politician

The coldest winter I ever spent was a summer in San Francisco.

—Mark Twain, writer

Isn't it nice that people who prefer Los Angeles to San Francisco live there?

—Herb Caen, writer

The only cultural advantage LA has over NY is that you can make a right turn on a red light.

—Woody Allen, actor

In Los Angeles, it's like they jog for two hours a day and then they think they're morally right. That's when you want to choke people, you know?

—Liam Neeson, actor

When its 100 degrees in New York, it's 72 in Los Angeles. When its 30 degrees in New York, in Los Angeles it's still 72. However, there are 6 million interesting people in New York, and 72 in Los Angeles.

—Neil Simon, writer

I love Los Angeles. I love Hollywood. They're beautiful. Everybody's plastic, but I love plastic. I want to be plastic.

—Andy Warhol, artist

The final story, the final chapter of western man, I believe, lies in Los Angeles.

—Phil Ochs, songwriter

As one went to Europe to see the living past, so one must visit Southern California to observe the future.

—Alison Lurie, writer

California is the diamond on the diamond ring.

—John Aidan, musician

Los Angeles makes the rest of California seem authentic.

—anonymous

Adultery is not grounds for divorce in California. As a matter of fact, adultery in Southern California is grounds for marriage."

—Allan Sherman, comedian

When future archaeologists dig up the remains of California, they're going to find all of those gyms their scary-looking gym equipment, and they're going to assume that we were a culture obsessed with torture.

—Douglas Coupland, writer

California: By 30, Our Women Have More Plastic Than Your Honda

—Bumper sticker

You know you are in Southern California when. . .

- the fastest part of your commute is down your driveway.
- you were born somewhere else.
- your family tree includes 'significant others'.
- your child's third grade teacher has purple hair, a nose ring, and is named Breeze.
- you know how to eat an artichoke.
- your monthly house payment exceeds your annual income.
- you pack shorts and t-shirt for snow skiing, and a sweatshirt and wetsuit for the beach.
- you identify the four seasons as Fire, Flood, Mudslide, and Drought.
- you have a glass on reserve at your favorite winery.
- you can't schedule a meeting because you must 'do lunch'.
- you measure distance by numbers of cars, not miles.
- you dive under a desk whenever a large truck goes by.
- all highways into the state say 'no fruit'.
- you drive to your neighborhood block party.
- your cat has its own psychiatrist.
- you go to the tanning salon before going to the beach.
- a really great parking space can move you to tears.
- rain sprinkles is the lead story on the local news and is titled "Storm Watch."

"That's Odd:" Trivia

Pet Rocks

California's reputation for quirky, off-the-wall fads and attractions was enhanced by what was arguably the most ridiculous toy fluke of modern popular culture, the Pet Rock. The brainchild of Gary Dahl an advertising executive in Los Gatos (Santa Clara County), the "pets" were small smooth rocks imported from Rosarito Beach in Baja, Mexico. Each stone came in a small box with a bed of straw and punched with air holes. Included was an "owner's manual" with instructions on how to train, play, and house-break the rock. There were birth certificates and papers attesting to its "pure bred" lineage.

Pet Rocks were first introduced in the San Francisco area in mid-1975 and sold for $3.95, earning a $3 profit on each rock. In the next six months, over five million rocks were sold nationwide. By Christmas, 75 percent of all daily newspapers in the country had published stories about Pet Rocks. Imitators quickly flooded the market with their own rock pets and interest in the faddish toy soon faded. An attempt to repackage the rocks as a Valentine's Day gift flopped. Today, they serve as a reminder that California entrepreneurialism coupled with a sense of silly humor will always have a market.

Pink Donut Boxes

Donuts are a southern California favorite. In 2017, there were nearly 700 donut retailers in Los Angeles county, 1 shop for every 15,000 people. That is two hundred more shops than in all of New York City, and twice the number in Chicago. The majority of these businesses are local "mom-and-pop" establishments, many operated by immigrants from Southeast Asia. And nearly all of them, sell their products in bright pink boxes, a distinctly Los Angeles tradition.

In the 1970s, the biggest local distributor of boxes was Westco. According to company lore, a Cambodian donut shop owner, Ted Ngoy, asked if there were any boxes available that were less expensive than the standard white cardboard. So Westco pink cardboard stock boxes that cost a few cents less than the standard white (about $5 less for 200 boxes.) For shops that used hundreds, if not thousands, of boxes a week, that was appealing. Even better, in eastern Asian culture, pink is a lucky color (while white is the color of mourning.)

Soon, pink boxes appeared in donut shop after donut shop. While pink boxes were not new, they came into vogue in the 1970s simply because they were less expensive to buy. Today, the trend has reached other states. Pink donut boxes are increasingly common in Arizona and Texas. And in Portland, Oregon, at the hip and trendy, Voodoo Doughnut shop, the company's long-running slogan is, "Good things come in pink boxes."

Surfing Padre

In 2018, the Reverend Christian Mondor died at the age of 92. Mondor, who lived in Huntington Beach and worked at Saints Simon and Jude Catholic Church, had first taken up the sport of surfing in 1990, when in his mid-60s. He became locally known as the "Surfing Padre" and began to be asked by surfers to bless them before they paddled out into the waves. Eventually, Mondor started a yearly interfaith prayer service on the beach with other religious leaders. It became known as the Blessing of the Waves and drew thousands of people. Mondor wore a wetsuit under his clerical robe and after the service he took off his robe, picked up his board, and headed out with other surfers. In 2013, Mondor was honored with a star on Huntington Beach's Surfing Walk of Fame.

The California Dream

I was born in Africa. I came to California because it's really where new technologies can come to fruition, and I don't see a viable competitor.

—Elon Musk, businessman, investor

Of all the states in the union, only California has attached to its identity the concept of dream.

—Kevin Starr, author and professor of history

Dream: A Cherished Aspiration, Ambition, or Ideal

This final section is partly a summation of ideas that have been expressed within other readings in this book. The "California Dream," of course, may or may not have any basis in reality. Much of that depends on the particular circumstances of the individual. There is plenty of evidence that California has long attracted and accepted innovation and dynamic ideas. It has been the birthplace of countless inspirations that have spread far and wide. Still, California is like other states. It has poverty, crime, social turmoil, as well as periodic natural disasters. But the Dream is a powerful concept that has played a prominent role in the state's development. Perception plays a significant part in all manner of the human experience. Historical memory is thick with perceptions that may trump facts in the minds of many. Countless decisions in a person's life are made on the basis of what one believes is true, not necessarily on what is true. Although sometimes believing in something can make it a reality.

Origins of the Dream

Because dreams are imagined they mean many things to many people. California first came into the European conscious as a fantasy. It was the mythical paradise imagined by the Spanish novelist Garcia Ordonez de Montalvo; a land of gold and pearls ruled by the Amazon Queen *Calafia*. While it always was home to many native people, and Spain would eventually, with limited success, attempt to colonize it, California remained about as well known to most people as the country of Andorra is to us today. For centuries, this was due to two arbitrary geographic factors. One, its location was distant from most of the world's major population centers. Two, it was bounded by the Pacific Ocean on its west side and large mountains and deserts on its east side. After a long period of this nature enforced dormancy, in 1849, it suddenly and permanently became known the world over. Simultaneously, the first chapter of the California dream was created.

> *California is a place of invention, a place of courage, a place of vision, a place of the future. People who made California what it is were willing to take risks, think outside convention and build.*
>
> —Nicolas Berggruen, philanthropist, investor

In the United States' popular culture today, people are regularly enticed to engage in an activity, to buy into a program, to purchase a product, or to learn the secrets of a system, all of which are said will lead to effortless and rapid wealth. Given the preponderance of these appeals, it may be difficult to think of a time in which "getting rich quick" was not a common part of popular society. The California gold rush helped to create the current outlook. The incremental accumulation of money from a combination of persistent labor and prudent saving gave way to realizing great riches, quick and easy. Much of this seemed possible because no one owned the gold. Come to California and seize your share. California was, in this regard, freer, more open, more democratic, and more egalitarian. Realities aside, it was a powerful draw. Some forty-niners struck it rich; others went home, poor and broken. Failure was common. But most people, then and now, understand that dreams are not a guarantee, and the other side of great expectation is great disappointment. Just having the chance is part of the appeal.

The dream would persist beyond the rush and come to include other facets. After 1849, California was seen as a special place with a unique role in the United States. "Go to the west of the West and do what you could not do elsewhere." The state motto, "Eureka" — "I have found it!" succinctly captured that positive certainly of success. And what is found in California? Whatever one wants—one of greatest appeals. The question is, where the line between perception and reality?

Economics of the Dream

Transform and reinvent yourself just as California itself had done. In the span of less than two years, it went from "nothing" (as far as the United States was concerned) to being one of the wealthiest regions in the world. Fortunes would be made by men and women who, only months before would never have imagined that could be a possibility in their lives. Discover yourself or be discovered. It was in the rush that writers such as Bret Harte and Mark Twain found their first audience of readers, businessmen such as Henry Wells and William Fargo found their profession (banking), and many others such as John Studebaker (wagons, later automobiles), Philip Armour (canned meat), and Levi Strauss (dry goods, later clothing) made enough money to develop important new companies.

California had a population that was so diverse and fluid—it was, and remains, an exotic land ripe for entrepreneurism, innovation, and originality. The gold rush attracted four men who would never be successful miners but, in the 1860s, would risk their collection financial future to try and accomplish the greatest industrial enterprise of the century. And arriving along with Colis Huntington, Leland Stanford, Mark Hopkins, and Charles Crocker were thousands of Chinese men who, unbeknownst to them, would one day be the foce that would turn the dream of building a rail line across the United States into a reality.

The lure of swift and dramatic gain was sustained as explosive population growth became a fulcrum of California's economic success. Boosterism for the state was not simply a matter of enthusiasm and pride but also a financial necessity. The railroads needed customers, land developers needed homeowners, agriculture needed farmers and ranchers, business needed employees, and attractions needed tourists. The financial motivation to propagate the California dream was evident. The task was made easier by nature. The climate was moderate and the landscape was beautiful. And it worked for a long time.

Through much of the twentieth-century, particularly in the decades after World War II, California would come to epitomize the best of the United States: a prodigious economy that surpassed all states and most nations, excellence in public education, cutting-edge technology, artistic creativity, and agricultural abundance without peer. The state was a trendsetter in political innovation, progressive judicial reform, popular culture (and counter-culture), and social activism.

It therefore seems appropriate that California has long been the center of the entertainment industry and is home to major companies specializing in advanced aviation, electronics, and space technology. Thousands of high-technology companies are in "Silicon Valley," including Apple Computers, which produced the first personal home computer. Two of the largest Internet search engines, Google and Yahoo, were both created and are headquartered in the region as well. Google was founded by Larry Page and Sergey Brin, while Yahoo was begun by Jerry Yang and David Filo. All four men attended Stanford University in Palo Alto where they met each other as students and developed their companies.

The proliferation of major phone apps has been dominated by California companies and people. The messaging service Twitter was created in San Francisco in 2006 by Jack Dorsey, Noah Glass, Biz Stone, and Evan Williams. In 2017, it had 330 million daily users and was worth more than $5 billion. In 2010, the imaging service, Instagram, also had its start in San Francisco by Kevin Systrom and Mike Krieger. Within five years, more than 40 billion photos had been uploaded. Another messaging app, Snapchat, was begun in 2011 by former Stanford University students Evan Spiegel, Bobby Murphy, and Reggie Brown. In 2018 it had 187 million daily users.

Evidence of the wealth of the nation's largest state economy is abundant. California has 12 percent of the national population but produced 16 percent of all new jobs between 2012 and 2017. In the same span, federal data from the Department of Commerce showed that California's gross domestic product increased by $127 billion, bringing the total economic output to $2.7 trillion. This moved the state's economy ahead of Great Britain (a nation with 25 million people than California), and landing it as the world's fifth-largest. Only the United States, China, Japan, and Germany had larger economies. This is the highest position the state has had since 2002. As recently as 2012, it had declined to tenth-place. The three foundations of the state's wealth were technology (Silicone Valley), entertainment (Hollywood), and agriculture (Central Valley.) Despite relatively high taxes, considerable government regulations, the state has clearly recovered from the Great Recession, 2007–2010.

The wealth, however, is concentrated by region. Much of the economic growth is found along the coast in large urban centers such as San Diego, Los Angeles, San Jose, and San Francisco. Rural regions and the interior of the state are, by comparison, far less prosperous. The disparity of wealth is found by household too. In 2018, according to Forbes, there were 124 billionaires living in California, 21 percent of the nation's total. There were twenty each in Los Angeles and San Francisco. Not only are there more than in any other state, the only two nations in the world with more billionaires are the United States (585) and China (373.) That same year, there were 775,000 California households with assets exceeding one million dollars. Of course, these numbers are fluid owing to a wide variety of financial factors but the point would be clear; California attracts and retains a lion's share of individual wealth.

But it hasn't all been about business and making money. California is tied with Alaska for the most national parks (8), which are complemented by the 278 sites managed by the state park service. The appreciation of California's beauty created compassion for nature, and by the 1970s, the state had become one of the leaders in environmental protection. This has resulted in many conflicts over what and how are the best ways to preserve, regulate, and access the scenic parts of the "dream" while still accommodating a rising population coming in search of homes, jobs, and businesses.

Demographics and the Dream

Population growth has been a defining characteristic of California. Burgeoning populations have been both a spark of its powerful economy engine as well as a cause of a diminished quality of life. The numbers tell the story. In 2011, the state population was by far the largest of any other state and accounted for one out of every eight Americans. It contained four of the fifteen largest American cities: #2, Los Angeles, #8, San Diego, #10 San Jose, and #14 San Francisco. Los Angeles County was the most populated county in the nation, and seven other California counties were in the nation's most populous twenty-five. On the other hand, while the state's population is hardly diminishing, its heyday of growth may be in its past. In the 1950s and 1960s, the population of the state rose at three times the rate of the rest of the country. By contrast, in 2018, of the 25 fastest growing cities, eight were in Florida and five were in Texas, but not one was in California.

To some extent, California has been a victim of its own success. The appeal of the dream has attracted so many people for so long that it has come to threaten, overwhelm, and perhaps destroy the very features and opportunities that brought people to it. Population pressures helped raise the costs of living. In 2017, California was ranked as the 3rd most expensive state to live in, only trailing New York and Hawaii. Schools struggled to accommodate the sheer number of students. With the harmful impact on the environment and the stress on the infrastructure, some argue the dream has already ended and the state is living on its past reputation that is less and less a reality of the present.

Is the California dream colorblind? Unlikely. While it is clear that immigration has been one of California's strengths and challenges, the demographic diversity that comes with it has fed racism and intolerance. The state had the most diverse population in the world in 1850, and it still does today. For some people, social change is unsettling and California has experienced more than its share of dramatic change in the racial and ethnic make-up throughout its history. One example that is both literal and symbolic of this condition is Anaheim, the home of Disneyland. When the theme park opened in 1955, it projected a white California dream from a city with a large Anglo population. As late as the 1990 U.S. Census, 57 percent of the population was white. Yet, in 2017, Latinos, Asians, and African Americans comprised 70 percent of Anaheim's population, as the proportion of whites dropped to 27 percent.

The attraction of California has been worldwide, and a large segment of the population growth has come from immigration. It has been a key to the state's success in agriculture, small businesses, and the service sector. One out of every four immigrants to the United States comes to California, and one-third of the state's residents are foreign-born. The state has also been a magnet for illegal immigrants as well, again attracting about one out of every four persons who unlawfully enter and remain in the United States. It is estimated there are three million people living illegally in California.

The large number of immigrants has put pressure on public education and health care. One-quarter of public school students are English language learners. Two-thirds of immigrants from Mexico do not have a high school degree. Low-income immigrants are twice as likely to lack health insurance as compared to low-income citizens.

The Future of the Dream

"I have seen firsthand coming here with empty pockets but full of dreams, full of desire, full of will to succeed, but with the opportunities I had, I could make it. That is why we have to get back and bring California back to where it once was." This was said by Arnold Schwarzenegger, an Austrian who moved to California in 1968 at the age of twenty-one, where he parlayed a successful career as a body builder into major film stardom and, even more startling, became a two-term governor of the state.

"Southern California. Where the American dream came *too true*." The quote is from Lawrence Ferlinghetti, a poet and native of Yonkers, New York. In 1953, he moved to San Francisco and co-founded City Lights Bookstore, soon to become a center of the Beat writers, literary rebels who were precursors to the revolutionary counter-culture of the 1960s.

Two quotes from two men who question the future of the dream that they successfully experienced. Is it over? A 2009 survey by the Public Policy Institute of California, showed that 75 percent of the respondents said things in the state were going in the *wrong* direction. This answer was given by people who were in the midst of a severe recession, so their views were likely colored by their immediate concerns.

By contrast, in 2017, a poll from the UC Berkeley's Institute of Governmental Studies found that 54 percent of registered voters saw the state headed in the *right* direction. In assessing the status of the state, perhaps a consideration should be made that the California dream was by its nature a utopian notion. Utopia is an imagined place where everything is perfect. By it very definition, it is a place that does not exist. This begs the question, can something that is not real truly be lost?

Those who want the spirit of the dream to continue can take a measure of comfort in the fact that people have been issuing warnings to about the limits and short-coming of California for a long time. In 1849, after witnessing the massive influx of miners coming into San Francisco by land and by sea, Lt. Henry Wise of the U.S. Navy wrote, "Under no contingency does the natural face of Upper California appear susceptible of supporting a very large population." Wise's assessment was an early example of the shortsighted wrongness of those who predicted failure for the state and its people. The dream has endured against the odds before; why should it not continue? It is, after all, California.

Compilation of Assignments

This pool of assignments each refers to specific chapters and sections of the textbook. In some cases, you are instructed to search sources outside the textbook. The point values, which vary, are shown for each assignment. There are more assignments here than you will be asked to complete. Be sure to check your syllabus and the course assignment folder on Canvas to see which assignments are being required for your class. A few assignments, such as self-guided field trips and a final exam (if offered) are not included here.

Assignments each have an expected minimum length. While this is to help in the grading assessment, it is a good practice for you to not think in terms of always aiming toward a minimal response. You are not required to write beyond the minimum but do not short yourself either. If you have something that adds value, I suggest you include it. Concise writing is most effective when the details are precise. Remember, these are academic exercises and your work is being evaluated on how well you inform a reader.

Assignment #1: TR Quote & Origins of the State Name

What do the mythical origins of the state's name have as a common theme with Theodore Roosevelt's quote?
The expected minimum length for this response is one paragraph.
(Read quote in preface and Chapter 1) (10 points)

Assignment #2: State Comparison

1. Research any one of the other 49 U.S. states and create a check list that answer these 15 questions. Be sure your data is current:

   Year of statehood?

   Capital city?

   Current state population?

Largest city and its population?

Total square miles?

Number of counties?

Highest point of elevation (in feet) with name?

Average annual precipitation? (for the entire state)

Racial composition? (percentage of population by race, be precise)

Median family or household income?

Top three (3) industries?

What U.S. presidents, if any, were born there?

Political preferences? (percentage of registered voters who are Democrat, Republican, Independent, or No Preference)

Two famous inventors or writers? (include specific accomplishments)

Two examples of state trivia?

2. Write a parallel second check list for California that answers these same 15 questions.

3. In 1–2 paragraphs note what information most stands out which differentiates the two states? Also, did anything surprise you?

(Information can be found throughout textbook, also outside research) (20 points)

Assignment #3: California Place Names

There are 482 cities in California. They vary in innumerable ways, but they all have a name. How a place got its name is one thing, what the name means and represents to its inhabitants and the outside world is another. Sometimes a town name is changed to enhance its appeal or because of infamy associated with it. For example, Placerville was formerly called Hangtown because of the many executions by hanging held there. So names are much more than a label to locate on a map.

California place names often have Spanish or native influences. For example, Nipomo is named from the Chumash word *nipumu,* which means "a house place, village." Carpinteria is Spanish for "carpenter's shop," because explorers in 1769 saw natives building canoes there. And, many towns are named after people. Oxnard was named in 1900 for Henry Oxnard, who built a beet-sugar refinery at that location.

Names can also be a source for interesting stories such as Modesto, which was given the Spanish word for "modest" after the man for whom the town was intended to be named turned down the honor. Mad River was named for the leader of a group exploring the river after he became angry that his companions did not wait for him one morning. In 1849, a group of emigrants came west as part of the gold rush. They took a shortcut off the Spanish Trail into the valley, became trapped in the desert until they were rescued by two mountain men. As they were leaving, a woman in the party looked back over the land and said, "Goodbye, death valley." The irony was they had all survived. Nevertheless, the name stuck.

For this assignment, the task is to research the name of any town in California and describe how and why it was named, note if the name has changed, include dates, and to explain the meaning of the name. Make sure you write a history of the *name*, not the town.

On on-line search of the specific location will often provide the results. There are printed collections of place names books that help in this assignment. One such excellent book is *1500 California Place Names: Their Origin and Meaning,* by William Bright.

The expected minimum length for this response is two paragraphs.
(Outside research) (20 points)

Assignment #4: New Timeline Entry

The timeline in this book cites more than 250 entries. Select any year, including the long period prior to statehood, and research it looking for California history. The goal is to discover a single noteworthy historical event, action, or law that is *not yet included* in this timeline but that you argue should be.

Thus, your task is to explain its significance to the history of California, just as has been done in the existing timeline. In essence, you would be adding one item to it. The assessment of your work will be based on how well you argue the significance of the item you present.

The expected minimum length for this assignment is 1–2 paragraphs.
(Outside research) (20 points)

Assignment #5: The Diversity of Land & Geography

What are the natural geographic and climate features of California which set it apart from other states and regions in the country? Your response should be thorough, specific and include many details and factual evidence to prove the point.

The expected minimum length for this assignment is 3–4 paragraphs.
(Read Chapter 3) (20 points)

Assignment #6: California's Icons

California has thousands of official landmarks and historic sites. Some things have come to represent certain characteristics, traits, or perceptions of the state that could be are used to complete the sentence, "*When I think of California, I think of . . .*"

The assignment is to **pick one of the items from the lists below** and explain how and why it has attained iconic status. Be sure to explain what makes something an icon. While this will require you to research its history and or development, that should not be the focus of your writing. That is why, for instance, "Spanish missions" are listed, but not individual missions. For that choice, the goal would be to describe what the missions as a group symbolize about the state in general. You should explain the enduring popularity, aesthetic quality, or widespread awareness of your selection.

The expected minimum length for this assignment is three paragraphs.
(Information can be found throughout textbook and outside research. 20 points)

Natural Landmarks and Icons

Alabama Hills
Alcatraz Island
Channel Islands
Coronado Island
Fan Palm trees
Gaviota Pass
Grizzly Bear
Half-Dome, Yosemite
Morro Rock
Mount Whitney
Mount Shasta
Pacific Ocean and beaches
Poppy flowers
Redwood trees
San Andreas Fault
San Francisco Bay
Sequoia trees
Emigrant Gap, Sierra Nevada

Human Landmarks and Icons

Ahwahnee Hotel, Yosemite
Bixby Bridge, Big Sur
Buena Vista Winery
Cabrillo National Monument, San Diego
California cuisine
Cannery Row, Monterey
Chinatown, San Francisco
Disneyland
Freeway system, Los Angeles
Golden Gate Bridge
Haight-Ashbury district, San Francisco
Hearst Castle
Highway 1
Hollywood sign
Hotel Del Coronado
Marshall Monument, Coloma
McDonalds Restaurants
Overland Emigrant Trail
Panning gold miner
Presidio, San Francisco
Rose Bowl, Pasadena
San Quentin Prison
Santa Monica Pier
Silicon Valley
Spanish Missions
Surfboards
Sutter's Fort
Tournament of Roses Parade
Trans-Continental Railroad
U.S. Mint, San Francisco

Assignment #7: Native Americans & Europeans

1. In the colonial era, what were the European and Native American attitudes toward the natural world and why did they differ so much? How did these differences affect their respective behaviors towards nature? Why did it lead to conflict between Europeans and natives?

2. How did the Spanish missions in California specifically impact the life, culture, and society of the Chumash people?

The expected minimum length for this assignment is 4-5 paragraphs.
(Read Chapter 4) (25 points)

Assignment #8: The United States Takes California

Think about the events and circumstances between 1800-1850 that resulted in California becoming a part of the United States.

Consider these two claims:
A. The U.S. accomplished this because its people made good decisions and actions.

B. The U.S. was simply lucky, the benefactor of the misfortunes of Spain and Mexico.

Write a response that clearly states which claim was the more significant factor in the United States' acquiring of California and why.

The expected minimum length for this assignment is four paragraphs.
(Read Chapter 5) (25 points)

Assignment #9: Gold Rush: Beginnings & El *Dorado*

1. What were Bayard Taylor's own impressions and descriptions of the early years of the gold rush? Was he excited or dismayed by what he saw in California? Include specific information from his writings to support your position.

2. How does Taylor's perception compare with the fates of the five key figures who were central in the start of the rush? Make sure to provide information on the fate of each of the five discovers.

The expected minimum length for this assignment is four paragraphs.
(Read Chapter 6) (25 points)

Assignment #10: Gold Rush: The Impact on Nature

Assess the impact of the Gold Rush on California's environment and society. What were its most significant and profound effects, both short- and long-term? Be specific and detailed.

The expected minimum length for this assignment is four paragraphs.
(Read Chapter 6) (25 points)

Assignment #11: Gold Rush: The Bernard Reid Example

In many ways Bernard Reid was representative of the typical gold rush miner.

Create a checklist with as many examples as you can that would "prove" Reid was a typical miner. Support items on the list with evidence or arguments. Look at his personal background, his journey west, and, most important, his time spent in California. Be thorough and complete. Here is one example of an entry one could make showing he was a typical miner: "He was male, young (in his 20s), single, and looking to make a quick fortune in California."

Make a good-sized descriptive list (15 examples would be the expected minimum but there could be many more then that)
(Read Chapter 6) (20 points)

Assignment #12: Gold Rush: The Experiences of Women

Accurately describe the experiences of women in the gold rush, offering both positive and negative features. Would you have wanted to be a woman in the rush? Overall, were their experiences more positive or more negative? Take a clear position on this and explain why.

The expected minimum length for this assignment is three paragraphs.
(Read Chapter 6) (20 points)

Assignment #13: Gold Rush: Assessing Its Legacy

Read the arguments both for and against the gold rush. Write a brief summary of each. Taking all of the information offered throughout Chapter 6, make a detailed and logical stand for the position you believe makes the stronger case and state why. In essence, was California made better or worse by the gold rush?

The expected minimum length for this assignment is three paragraphs.
(Read Chapter 6) (20 points)

Assignment #14: Slavery and Race in 19th Century California

Accurately characterize the impact that slaves and slavery had on the social and political conditions in California in the 1800s. Notably, how was the issue of statehood effected. Be sure to include timeline information in your response.

The expected minimum length for this response is four paragraphs.
(Read Chapter 7, plus timeline entries for 1850, 1854, 1862, 1865, 1875 & 1882) (25 points)

Assignment #15: California's Nuts & Fruits

Agriculture has been big business in California for more than a century. Explain how both nature and people made it so. Note its marketing techniques. Note obstacles that had to be overcome, both natural and human. Include in your explanation an overview of the size and scale and what is unique about the state's agriculture.

The expected minimum length for this assignment is 4–5 paragraphs.
(Read Chapter 8) (25 points)

Assignment #16: John Muir & the Sierras

Why did John Muir enjoy the Sierra Nevada Mountains? What benefits did he see in them? What did Muir believe would be lost to later generations if they were unable to experience the Sierras as he did? Specifically, how did he go about trying to prevent this loss from happening and assess how successful he was?

The expected minimum length for this assignment is three paragraphs.
(Read Chapter 9 and timeline entries for 1890, 1892 & 1907) (20 points)

Assignment #17: Water & Southern California

1. Why and for how long has Southern California faced a particular challenge in having enough water?

2. How did the city of Los Angeles meet its water needs between the 1870s and 1940s?

3. What obstacles (both natural and human) did the city face in meeting those needs and how were they overcome?

4. What was the importance of William Mulholland in the water history of Los Angeles?

The expected minimum length for this assignment is 4–5 paragraphs.
(Read Chapter 10) (25 points)

Assignment #18: The Battle Over Mono Lake

1. What is the value of Mono Lake to California?

2. Why was the lake considered to be "dying " in the 1970s?

3. Who "saved" Mono and how was this done?

The expected minimum length for this assignment is three paragraphs.
(Read Chapter 11) (20 points)

Assignment #19: Mark Twain's "*Roughing It*" reading on Mono Lake

How does Mark Twain's descriptions of Mono Lake compare with a factual assessment of the lake? What is your reaction to this reading?

The expected minimum length for this assignment is 2–3 paragraphs.
(Read Chapter 12) (15 points)

Assignment #20: The Unlikely Campaign of Upton Sinclair

1. What were the economic, social & political conditions in California in 1934 which inspired Sinclair to run for governor?

2. What specific plans did Sinclair propose to help California's workers?

3. Who opposed Sinclair's candidacy, why, and how did they go about defeating him?

4. What were the important long-term results of 1934 election?

The expected minimum length for this response is 4–5 paragraphs.
(Read Chapter 13) (25 points)

Assignment #21: Internment of the Japanese

Assume is it February 942. The attack on Pearl Harbor has occurred and the United States is at war with Japan.

1. Create a list of all the possible reasons to support the internment of all persons of Japanese ancestry in California. Support items on the list with evidence or arguments. Keep in mind what you could and could not know at this time.

2. Create a list of all possible reasons against internment. Again, support items on the list with evidence or arguments.

3. Decide which position made the best case in 1942, for or against, and explain.

Make two good-sized descriptive lists (6 examples would be the expected minimum but there could be many more then that) AND two paragraphs of analysis. *(Read Chapter 14) (25 points)*

Assignment #22: Fast Living in California

After World War II, several major changes occurred that, while national in scope, significantly affected the lives of Californians. Offer a good overall description of the following developments since 1945—California's population boom, the creation of mass-produced suburban housing, the rise of the fast food industry, and the building of the interstate freeway system. Within your answer state whether these changes have been more positive or negative.

The expected minimum length for this assignment is 3–4 paragraphs. *(Read Chapter 15) (20 points)*

Assignment #23: The Chinese in California: Perseverance in the Face of Prejudice

Describe the social conditions and various discriminatory legal actions faced by the Chinese in California since 1850 (this may include national-level actions). Be specific in the names and purpose(s) of the laws, ordinances, and court rulings you cite. Note the methods in which the Chinese challenged these obstacles and the degree to which they were successful.

The expected minimum length for this assignment is 4-5 paragraphs. *(Read Chapter 16) (25 points)*

Assignment #24: G. Allan Hancock: Man on the Go

Make four (4) lists of the major accomplishments and major setbacks or tragedies of G. Allan Hancock and his family (grandfather, mother, father). Detail the items on the list with sufficient information. Considering the lists, answer the question, "Would you like to have lived life just as G. Allan Hancock had?

Make four (4) good-sized descriptive lists (the number of examples will vary by person) AND two paragraphs of analysis regarding the question on G. Allan Hancock. *(Read Chapter 17) (25 points)*

Assignment #25: California by the Numbers

The information to answer the questions for this assignment needs to be drawn from *"A Statistical Profile of California with Trends and Comparisons to the United States."*

1. Where are the current large population centers of California and in what regions of the state is the population growing the fastest?

2. Compared to the United States, are Californians younger/older, educated better/worse, wealthier/poorer, and do they live longer/shorter?

3. What notable statistical trends do you see regarding the racial demographics of the state since 1990? How do you think these trends will affect the future of the state?

4. What does the data on education reveal? What are the trends in education?

The expected minimum length for this assignment is 4-5 paragraphs with a lot of supporting numerical data.
(Read Chapter 18) (25 points)

Assignment #26: Commenting on Current Events in California

This assignment will involve a current reading (usually a newspaper article or other short piece) to be selected at the start of the course. You will be asked to write an intelligent response in reaction to questions specific to the reading.

The expected minimum length for this assignment is two paragraphs.
(Reading will be made available online on Canvas) (15 points)

Assignment #27: Essay: A "Theme" of California

In tracing the history of California, one can identify major historical themes that emerge in the development of the region that are both notable and recurring. Using information from this book, instructor-provided content, and additional research, you are asked to construct an essay that examines with detail and informative explanations, one of these themes. You will want to cover a significantly broad time period of California's history. Consider and **select one** of the six topics below to be your paper's theme:

- Rapid Change
- Growth
- Diversity
- Youth

- "California Dream"
- Unique

You should "prove" your theme's validity by presenting relevant examples of facts, events, actions, statistics, attitudes, perceptions, quotes—in short anything that you believe supports it.

Notes:

There may be overlap between two or more themes. That is fine but maintain as much focus as you can on a single theme.

Keep in mind the essential rules of putting together a meaningful research essay. You should:

—find, read, and select valid information
—assess and evaluate that information
—organize, edit, and present that information

Essays will be assessed by the following criteria:

Breadth

Does it adequately develop the topic over a meaningful period of time? Do not limit your examination to a single event or narrow time period.

Clarity

Is the information accurate and understandable? Is it relevant to the theme?

Specificity

Are there specific facts/examples to support your subject?

Accuracy

Are your facts and contentions truthful and correct?

Length

Is the essay the appropriate length with reasonable type size, spacing, and margins?

Presentation

Is the essay edited for grammar and spelling? Is it neat, and easy to read?

Directions

Did you follow all instructions correctly, including academic integrity?

Important: Assume the reader of your essay knows nothing about California history. It is your responsibility to provide sufficient detail to make your paper meaningful to the reader. You should include names, dates, definition of terms where needed, and explanation of the larger points. There should be an introduction that identifies the theme and notes something of its significance.

The expected minimum length for this assignment is 1,500 words (7–8 paragraphs.) *(Read throughout the textbook) (50 points)*

Suggested Readings and Films

Books

Barron, Stephanie, et al. *Made in California: Art, Image, and Identity, 1900–2000,* Berkeley, University of California Press, 2000. The book was produced in conjunction with an exhibition of the same name by the Los Angeles County Museum of Art. It offers an array of professional and pop art, photographs, paintings, and graphics with extensive related essays depicting California's twentieth century. Divided by decades, it examines mostly the social and cultural history of the state through art.

Belden, L. Rarr and DeDecker, Mary. *Death Valley to Yosemite: Frontier Mining Camps and Ghost Towns, the Men, the Women, their Mines and Stories,* Bishop. California, Spotted Dog Press, 2000. An entertaining and insightful collection of short histories of the people, places and events, mostly from the era of the California gold rush. The book has a large number of useful maps and photographs.

Carle, David. *Introduction to Water in California*, Berkeley, University of California Press, 2004. A comprehensive overview of water issues in California, the book is part nature and part history as it describes where exactly the state's water comes from and where it ends up being put to human use—the specific sources for most the state's cities are noted. There is considerable statistical data and maps throughout.

Clappe, Louise Amelia Knapp Smith. *The Shirley Letters: From the California Mines, 1851–1852,* Berkeley, Heyday Books, 1998. The twenty-three letters Clappe wrote to her sister while living in mining camps on the north fork of the Feather River offer an engaging first-hand account of the life during the early years of the gold rush from the rarely heard viewpoint of a woman. There is a very useful biography of Clappe included by Marlene Smith-Baranzini, who edited the volume.

Clough, Charles W. et al. *Fresno County in the 20th Century, 1900 to the 1980s, vol. II,* Fresno, California, Panorama West Books, 19862This twenty-two author anthology offers an encyclopedic written and visual history of California's sixth-largest county. It includes considerable information on the development of its agricultural industry and how it came to be the leading farm county in the nation.

Dana, Richard Henry, Jr. *Two Years Before the Mast,* New York, Signet Classics, 2000. This book, originally published in 1846, is Dana's recount of his life between 1834–1836, when, as a common sailor, he served aboard a ship that sailed from Boston to California by traveling around Cape Horn at the tip of South America. His vivid descriptions of the California coastline, its peoples, and some of its nascent towns such as San Francisco, were among the very first writings on the region by an American.

Forbes, Jack. *Native Americans of California and Nevada,* Happy Camp, California, Naturegraph Publishers, 1982. This comprehensive history of the Native Americans of the Far West provides an overview of the heritage and evolution of natives from their ancient beginnings through their contact and troubles with Europeans to a contemporary appraisal of native society.

Gibson, Robert 0. *The Chumash,* New York, Chelsea House Publishers, 1991. A short but detailed history of these people who once inhabited much of the central coast and Channel Islands of California. The book focuses on the early history and culture of the Chumash with a brief summary of their contemporary status. Included are a number of illustrations, maps, and photographs.

Gordon, Mary McDougall, ed. *Overland to California with the Pioneer Line: The Gold Rush Diary of Bernard J. Reid,* Palo Alto, California, Stanford University Press, 1983. This first-hand account by Reid of his participation in the gold rush begins with his 1850 journey on the Oregon and California trail through his return to Pennsylvania in 1852. McDougall includes biographical material of Reid before and after his time as a gold miner. Reid's story is a richly detailed and engaging example of the trials and tribulations faced by most miners.

Haraszthy, Argoston *Grape Culture: Wines, and Wine-making, with Notes Upon Agriculture and Horticulture*, New York: Harper 1862. This publication by one of the founders of California's wine industry (and grandfather of G. Allan Hancock) became an essential handbook for many California vintners.

Hartman, David *N. California and Man,* Santa Ana, California, Pierce Publishing, 1981. This reference book offers extensive information on the state's environmental conditions. While some sections regarding human development are dated, its descriptions of the land and climate remain quite relevant. It also includes an informative chapter on water resources.

Holliday, J.S. *The Rush for Riches: Gold Fever and the Making of California,* Berkeley, University of California Press, 1999. This book is both a companion and an extension to Holliday's 1981 seminal history of the gold rush, *The World Rushed In: The California Gold Rush Experience.* The writing is both thoughtful and accessible. The book includes a lavish visual pictorial of the miners, their methods and tools, and the consequences, both positive and negative, of their being part of the rush.

Houston, Jeanne Wakatsuki and James D. Houston. *Farewell to Manzanar,* New York, Bantam Books, 1973. This recollection by Ms. Wakatsuki Houston of her time living in the Japanese relocation camp during World War II offers not only an eyewitness account of a young girl who experienced the event, but the book also played a key role in bringing public and academic attention to what had been a widely-ignored part of the war on the home front.

Limerick, Patricia Nelson. *The Legacy of Conquest: The Unbroken Past of the American West,* New York, Norton Publishers, 1987. A groundbreaking revisionist history of the settling of the American West, this work focuses on race conditions and factors have shaped the human narrative of American history. One valuable contribution is the examination of how different generations have perceived and interacted with the natural world. In addition to the section on California agriculture, there is a short but well-researched part on the impact of the gold rush on the land.

McGinty, Brian. *Haraszthy at the Mint (Famous California trials),* Dawsons Pub. 1975. McGinty is the lawyer, historian and great-great-grandson of Agoston Haraszthy. This book is an account of Agoston's time (and troubles) working at the U.S. Mint in San Francisco in the middle of the gold rush.

Reisner, Marc. *Cadillac Desert: The American West and Its Disappearing Water,* New York, Penguin Books, 1993. A highly critical examination of the water policies and practices in the western United States from its earliest period to the present day. The Bureau of Reclamation and the Army Corps of Engineers come under particular criticism for, according to the author, mismanaging the regions precious and limited water supplies and bringing the west to the verge of a water crisis with no clear solutions.

Stephanson, Anders. *Manifest Destiny: American Expansion and the Empire of the Right,* New York, Hill and Wang Publishing, 1995. This compact book offers a smart analysis of the beliefs and rationalizations that justified American expansionism along with the political policies that helped make these concepts a reality. While only a short section on the Mexican War directly addresses California, it offers a valuable contribution to understanding the ideas that brought the region under the control of the United States.

Taylor, Bayard. *Eldorado: Adventures in the Path of Empire,* Berkeley, Heyday Books, 2000. This first-person narrative is a compilation of Taylor's chronicling of the first years of the California gold rush as he saw it, 1849–1850. Taylor travelled from New York to San Francisco and then to the gold fields by way of Panama. His writings offer the first widely read, and highly influential, professional reporting of the gold rush.

Wyatt, David. *Five Fires: Race, Catastrophe, and the Shaping of California,* New York, Addison-Wesley Publishing, 1997. Using fire as a metaphor, the author examines five key periods and events, including the gold rush, the San Francisco earthquake, and the internment of the Japanese to offer a sweeping cultural history of California from the time of the Spanish missions to its contemporary period.

Films

California Missions, Produced by Huell Howser, 2000. DVD. KCET, California Gold, 2000.This film is a collection of all ten episodes produced by Howser for the California Gold series on the Spanish missions in the state. All 21 missions are toured by Howser who looks at some of the unique features of each. Also, there are two additional episodes, one focusing on mission gardens (at La Purisima) and one looking at mission art, now kept at the Huntington library.

Divided Highways. Produced by Lawrence Hott and Tom Lewis. DVD. PBS Video. 1997.Films for the Humanities and Science, 2004. This 85-minute documentary examines the reasons for, and impact of, the creation of the national highway system in the United States in the mid-twentieth-century It includes several sections related to California and looks at why some cities, notably San Francisco, began to consider the highway system to be detrimental to the region.

The Gold Rush. Produced by Boettcher/Trinklein. 1996. Videocassette, Films for the Humanities and Science, 1996. This one-hour documentary is a useful overview of the origins, events, and legacy of the gold rush. It offers a balanced interpretation of race relations, the status of women, and the environmental and cultural effects mining had on California through its use of historic photos and commentary by professional historians.

The Grapes of Wrath. Director John Ford. 1940. DVD. Twentieth Century Fox Home Entertainment. 2004. The feature film version of the classic novel by John Steinbeck tells the story of the Joad family, poor Midwestern farmers who come to California as a result of the Dust Bowl during the Great Depression. Although fiction, like the novel, many elements of the film were based in the realities of the period.

The Great Depression. Director Jon Else. 1994. Videocassette. PBS Home Video 1994. This seven-part documentary of the United States' worst economic crisis, 1929–1941, includes numerous in-depth sections on California history including migrant labor, Upton Sinclair and the 1934 governor's race, and the effect of New Deal programs on the West. The concluding volume covers the nation's entry into World War II and the internment of the Japanese in California.

Land of the Eagle. Produced by BBC Atlas of the Natural World. 1990. DVD. BBC Video 2006. This one-hour documentary is part of a six-hour, six-volume set that looks at people and their relationship with the natural world. Included in this part is an extensive look at the California Chumash, their interaction with nature, and the impact of the arrival of Spanish missionaries on both the natives and the ecosystem of the region.

Remembering Manzanar. Produced by Signature Communicatiqns, 2004. DVD. National Park Service 2004. This 22-minute documentary was created for the park service in conjunction with its Interpretative Center at the Manzanar National Historic Site. Using historic photos, films, and eye-witness recollections, it tells the history of the Japanese in California up to, and during, their forced relocation to this and other remote facilities during World War II.

Transcontinental Railroad. Director Mark Zwonitzer, 2002. DVD. PBS Home Video 2008. This two-hour documentary is a densely packed narrative of every major aspect of the motives, planning, construction, and historical significance of the creation of the transcontinental railroad between Omaha, Nebraska and Sacramento, California, 1862-1869. It has an array of photographs and stories that would entertain and educate both the casual armchair historian as well as the academic professional.

The West. By Ken Burns. Director Stephen Ives. 1996. DVD. PBS Home Video 1996. This twelve-hour documentary of the western third of the United States includes many sections on California history including the Spanish missions, the Overland Trail, the gold rush, the construction of the transcontinental railroad, and the rise of Los Angeles and the building of the Owens Aqueduct.

About the Author

Roger Hall missed being a California native by three years. Born in Springfield, Massachusetts, in 1965, his family drove across the country in a Volkswagen bus to Fresno, where he lived in the heat (dry) through the end of high school. He began his college education with a vague shakiness at Howard Community College in Columbia, Maryland. Only partially righted, he earned his B.A. in history from California State University, Fresno (1985). Finding his groove and passion for teaching college history, he earned a M.A. (1989), and Ph.D. in history (1993) from Bowling Green State University in Ohio. He has been happily employed at Allan Hancock College since 1996, and California Polytechnic State University since 2013. He teaches United States and California history. As long as his knees hold out he will continue to hike, bike, and otherwise explore the west of the west.